THE OTHER SPANISH CHRIST

THE MACMILLAN COMPANY
NEW YORK · BOSTON · CHICAGO · DALLAS
ATLANTA · SAN FRANCISCO

THE
OTHER SPANISH CHRIST

A STUDY IN
THE SPIRITUAL HISTORY OF SPAIN
AND SOUTH AMERICA

by

JOHN A. MACKAY, D.Litt.

NEW YORK
THE MACMILLAN COMPANY
1933

PRINTED IN THE UNITED STATES OF AMERICA
BY THE POLYGRAPHIC COMPANY OF AMERICA, N.Y.

A LA COMPAÑERA DE MI VIDA

PREFACE

WHILE South America is the main subject of this book, whoever would understand the spiritual history and problems of South American countries must first turn his thoughts to the Iberian birth-land of their conquerors. A true appreciation of this Continent's spiritual pilgrimage depends on a knowledge of the psychic forces emanating from Spain and Portugal which have moulded all life and history in the countries which compose it from the time of the Conquest until now.

The fall of the Spanish Monarchy, and the subsequent transformation of a country to which belongs the honour of having given to history the first great modern state, have awakened fresh interest in Spain and things Spanish. The Revolution of April 1931, while strengthening the spiritual bonds that unite the peninsular motherland to her former colonies in the Americas, gave Spain a genuine title to form part of the new Hispanic world which may, without exaggeration or unkind reflection, be described as " a rosary of craters in activity." Part of this volcanic action grows out of inherited sociological conditions which make it inevitable ; part, however, an increasing part, is an expression of that conflict of ideas by which modern opinion is so tragically divided in respect of the form which a true social order should take. In the world of to-morrow, which lies beyond the dust and din of the present crisis of society, the countries forming the Hispanic group of nations will, for many reasons, occupy a unique place in the international arena.   Their situation at the moment recalls the early vision of the Prophet of Anathoth, when he saw in the Judæan wilderness an almond spray in bloom and in the immediate neighbourhood a seething cauldron.   A new Springtime is clearly coming, but who will venture to predict what God's spring breezes will first blow over pampa and sierra, whether the aroma of almond blossom or the froth of the storm-brewing pot ?

This book treats but a single aspect of the life and thought of the countries with which it deals, namely, the religious aspect ; but this it endeavours to do in the most comprehensive way possible.   Its purpose is to provide a general introduction to the study of what is admittedly the major problem of the Hispanic world.   Yet not the whole Hispanic world is specifically dealt with.   Ten daughter-lands of Spain north of the Panamenian Isthmus do not enter into the picture. Their exclusion, however, does not essentially alter the representative character of the study here undertaken, for the reason that these lands reproduce in general the same spiritual features and tendencies as sister-countries to the south of them.   Their inclusion, on the other hand, would introduce Mexico, and Mexico, because of the religious struggle which goes on within her borders, giving rise to numerous original features, some of which will probably never become representative of most Hispanic countries, could be dealt with adequately only by a special study.

It will further be observed that Spain and the South American lands colonized by Spain receive more attention than Portugal and her great offspring, the

modern Republic of Brazil. The reason why the
Iberian soul has been treated as being fundamentally
the Spanish soul is that in the golden days of peninsular
history Portugal was but a " variant " of Spain, as
spiritually akin to the larger country as are Cataluna
and the Basque provinces to-day. As for Brazil, that
extraordinary country territorially and spiritually, the
author hopes that someone thoroughly imbued with
her spirit, life and literature will shortly make her
vocal on the religious issues which confront her in a
way in which he has not felt capable of doing, because
of the limitation imposed by his almost exclusive
connection with the Spanish-speaking republics of the
Continent.

What is here offered to the reader is a pioneer
attempt to deal with the religious problem of these
lands in its wholeness. The interpreting voices to
which he will listen in these pages are almost entirely
those of representative figures in their respective
countries, not a few being of international repute
where the Spanish tongue is spoken. One spokesman, Miguel de Unamuno, ranks among the few
prophetic voices of our time. He is being increasingly read in the English-speaking world, but most
of the others referred to are still unknown to Anglo-
Saxondom.

The conception embodied in the title very readily
raises the question whether there is not also another
British-American Christ who awaits rediscovery. For
if Spain received a religious vision in the sixteenth
century which it refused or was not allowed to follow,
British-American religion has tended in recent times
to lose the spiritual vision which the sixteenth
century bequeathed to evangelical Christianity. A

number of romantic figures, each bearing the name of Christ and incarnating the ideals of their several groups of admirers, have taken the place of *the* Christ. In reality a common need presses upon the Spanish and Anglo-Saxon worlds : to " know " Christ, to " know " Him for life and thought, to " know " Him in God and God in Him. Paul the Tarsan, history's greatest " Christopher " and " Christologue," that is to say, the supreme bearer and interpreter of Christ in the Christian ages, occupies the common ground where they and we must stand together. To that spot a line of guides extending from Unamuno, Barth, Kierkegaard and John Wesley, through Luis de León, Martin Luther and Augustine, the Bishop of Hippo, will help them and us. The salvation of both depends on the recognition of the fact that Christianity is something quite different from what commonly goes by that name.

JOHN A MACKAY

MEXICO, D.F.
14th April 1932, *first anniversary
of the Spanish Republic*

CONTENTS

PART ONE

IBERIA AND THE CATHOLIC EPIC
IN SOUTH AMERICA

xiii

PART TWO
A PHILOSOPHY OF SPANISH CHRISTIANITY

PART THREE
NEW SPIRITUAL CURRENTS IN SOUTH AMERICA

CONTENTS

CHAP.   PAGE

XI. The Advent of Protestantism   .   .   .   231
    (*a*) Precursors.
    (*b*) Foundations of the Modern Missionary Movement.
    (*c*) Landmarks.
    (*d*) Some Indigenous Movements.
    (*e*) An Ecumenical Expression of the Protestant Spirit.

XII. A Critique of Protestantism in South America   257
    (*a*) The Validity Question.
    (*b*) The Evangelical Task.
    (*c*) As Regards Religious Ecumenism.

INDEX   277

PART ONE
IBERIA AND THE CATHOLIC EPIC IN SOUTH AMERICA

CHAPTER I

THE IBERIAN SOUL

" AFRICA begins at the Pyrenees." This dictum of a famous French writer has never been seriously challenged by France's southern neighbour. There are distinguished living Spaniards who even exult in its implications. South of the mountain barrier that shuts off the Iberian Peninsula from Europe the characteristic landscapes are African. The people also who inhabit this region, especially that larger and more important part of it called Spain, belong ethnically and spiritually to the African rather than to the European continent, in much the same way as Russia belongs to Asia. According to many anthropologists the Spaniard is " the first-born of the ancient North African, now widely regarded as the parent of the chief and largest element in the population of Europe." [1] In the texture of his soul, the most perfect expression in history of the humanly primitive and unsophisticated, the basic strands are not Celtic or Phœnician, Roman or Goth, but Iberian, and therefore African. That most Spanish of Spaniards, Don Miguel de Unamuno, glories in the kinship of his Basque forbears with the Berbers or the Khabyles of Mount Atlas.

The Moorish invasion, followed by eight hundred years of a defensive struggle, in the course of which the Islamic soul of the invader passed into the Christian defender, made Spain more African still. It thus became doubly true that the maritime belt of North Africa gave Spain to Europe. This was the same

[1] *The Spirit of Spain*, G. Havelock Ellis, p. 29.

3

coastal strip which in the early centuries of the Christian
era gave to Europe the great Augustine and Tertullian.
Let us beware of despising Africa as a racial mother.
" The Black Continent," says Count Keyserling,
" possesses the greatest creative power of any in the
world. Whatever has its origin in Africa, remains
African forever in mind and spirit." [1] The Spaniard
has been called an eternal African, and through him
the indelible stamp of Africa has been imprinted forever on the pampas and sierras of Spanish America.

What were the characteristics of the great people
who turned South America into a projection of
Iberia ?

(a) *Intense Individuality*

Unique, naked, primitive individuality has been the
chief characteristic of the Iberian race. The true
Iberian is the quintessence of the natural man, the
man who loves life first and foremost. He is a
humanist, but his humanism is *sui generis*. " I am of
flesh, I am of flesh, not a painted thing," [2] Unamuno
once heard a boy of his humming, as he drew human
figures on a table-cloth. [3] The words express a favourite
sentiment of a Spanish thinker who himself claims to
be the genuine incarnation of his race. They symbol-
ize the truth that Spain is primarily and tenaciously of
the flesh and of the earth. Her deepest self aspires
to be flesh, and to live a full, concrete, fleshy existence
rather than a sublimated life of the spirit.

So strong is the individuality of a genuine Spaniard
that he feels himself to be the born equal of any
and every man. The ancient form of government
in Spain was a kind of " democratic Cæsarism." A
number of classic phrases descended from the remote
past admirably express that overweening pride and

---

[1] *Diary of a Philosopher*, Vol. I., p. 23.
[2] " *Soy de carne, soy de carne, no pintado.*"
[3] *El niño se creía sin testigos.*

that innate sense of equality which are so genuinely characteristic of the Iberian race. " Each one of us is worth as much as you, and together we are worth more than you," said a group of early Spanish nobles to their monarch. " We are knights as the king is, only with less money," is equally illuminating as an expression of the primitive Spanish sense of equality. "Every Catalonian has a king within him," is a traditional saying of the region which has insistently claimed autonomy from Spain. In the bottom of his soul each true son of Iberia feels himself to be a monarch, a man apart, a being divinely chosen for some task. It is for this reason that the humblest peasant in the Peninsula treats his social superiors with the most unceremonious naturalness. There is nothing servile or cringing about him.[1]

We are not surprised to find, therefore, that historically Spain has been a mother, not of ideas, which belong to the spirit, but of men, of proud, full-blooded men. Many of the masterpieces of Velazquez, her greatest painter, are portraits of men, each one of which fills a whole enormous canvas. The arts of sculpture and architecture in which Spain has most excelled are essentially masculine arts. Even the seraphic Santa Teresa wrote in one of her letters that she wished the nuns of her order to be, not women, but " strong men," and so virile as to " startle men." [2]

One of the earliest of Spain's great men was Seneca the Stoic. He was a genuinely Castilian soul. His message, as summed up by Angel Ganivet, a penetrating student of the peculiar genius of his race, paints most admirably the traditional Spanish spirit. " Do not allow yourself," Ganivet makes Seneca say, " to be overcome by anything alien to your spirit.

[1] Keyserling relates a most illuminating experience with Spanish peasantry in the chapter on Spain in his book entitled *Europe*.
[2] " *Espantar a los hombres.*"

Reflect amid the accidents of life that you have within you a primitive force, something strong and indestructible, like an adamant axle around which circle the mean events that form the web of daily life. Whatever happenings may become your lot, whether they be favourable or unfavourable, or such as seem to debase us by their contact, keep yourself so firm and erect that it can at least be said of you that you are a man." [1]

The beau ideal of manhood in the golden age of Spanish history was the soldier. Even the priests, monks and nuns of that period had the hearts and ways of men-at-arms. The great Spanish mystics have been well named " divine knights." [2] This military ideal, which is the most natural way of expressing strong primitive individuality, served as the medium of Spain's proud will and became the jealous guardian of her honour. The country, as George Borrow remarks, [3] is not naturally fanatical. She is, however, terribly and fatally proud, and has ever been more concerned about her honour than her life. It was no native fanaticism, Borrow maintains, but her proud sense of honour, that turned Spain for a time into a religious butcher and made her waste her precious blood and treasure in the Low Country wars. As the elect and privileged daughter of Papal Rome, she must needs prove herself worthy of so great a distinction. "Let me die, but let my honour live," is a significant Spanish motto.

The intense individuality of the Spanish character forms a kind of a primitive universal. It is unity without difference. In it, as in the great literature it produced, there are no intermediate tones. It is one extreme or another. All is sunshine or starless night, with no twilight glimmer. The Spaniard is incapable of irony, that delicate nuance in which the Frenchman

[1] *Idearium Español*, p. 276. [2] " *Caballeros a lo divino*."
[3] *The Bible in Spain*, Preface.

excels. He makes demigods by praise and devils by blame. By the same law of polarity Don Quixote and Sancho Panza are ever found side by side on the road of life, and not infrequently a Spanish wayfarer becomes both by turns.

The striking personages who are idealized in the literature and art of Spain are Spanish to the core. Compare, for example, the characters of Shakespeare with those of Calderón de la Barca, the most genuinely Spanish of Peninsular dramatists, or the Madonna of Raphael with the Virgin of Murillo. The English Shakespeare creates universal human figures; the Spanish Calderón figures which embody purely national traits. The Italian Raphael paints a Madonna so ideally human that traces of race and nationality have entirely faded away; the Spanish Murillo paints a Virgin whose face is that of a beautiful Andalusian maid.

Such naïve and constant self-assertion leads inevitably to individualism, and the Spanish character is historically the sublimation of this quality. It appears, to begin with, in an insatiable acquisitiveness and in the lack of a social instinct. The self must possess. The lust for booty played no small part in the campaigns of the Cid and the Duke of Alva, and, of course, as we shall see later, in the conquest of the New World. But wealth and possessions were craved not to be miserly hoarded, but to be lavishly expended; not as instruments of work but as a release from the necessity of work, and so as a means to freedom, to anarchic, knightly freedom. For a Spanish gentleman to work was a shame, to beg was not. " To be born poor is a crime," says one of the characters of Tirso de Molina. " The ideal of every Spaniard is to become pensioned after a few years' work, and, if possible, before he has worked," is a statement of the world-famous Spanish scientist Ramón y Cajal. Moreover, if personal independence can be secured through the bounty of the

State or by a lucky draw in the National Lottery, why should one seek it through work alone ?

The Spaniard's lack of a social instinct is another of the fateful derivations of his extreme individualism. If social instinct meant no more than gregariousness, the love of meeting in a home or café for free and friendly intercourse and to talk through the problems of the universe, the Spaniard would have to be regarded as the most socially-minded being on earth. But the moment the warm spontaneous glow of sociability passes into the cold and rigid limitations imposed by union in a common enterprise, Spanish individualism makes its presence felt immediately. The innate dislike to be bound together by obligation or mutual consent underlies the problem of Spanish regionalism, and has militated against the success of corporate enterprises carried on by Spaniards.

No rational principle of self-interest has ever succeeded in transcending the innate individualism of the Spanish nature. Only a great passion has been able to do that, a passion for the State or a passion for the Church. But in both cases the manifestation of this self-transcending passion has had a peculiarly Spanish quality in which the old individualism reappears. Speaking of the patriotism of Spaniards, Madariaga makes the following acute observation : " The Spaniard feels patriotism as he feels love, in the form of a passion where he absorbs the object of his love and assimilates it, that is to say, makes it his own. He does not belong to his country so much as his country belongs to him." [1] The passion of Spaniards for the Roman Church reveals the same characteristic. The Church was absorbed and its destinies made that of the Spanish nation. Honour demanded conformity to its rites and dogmas and the propagation of these throughout the world. But not even the Church was permitted to conserve its

[1] *Spain*, p. 37.

personal identity in the depths of the Spanish soul, nor did Christianity ever succeed in modifying the fundamental Spanish attitude towards life. In point of fact the Church belonged to Spain much more than Spain belonged to the Church. The historic consequence has been, as will appear later, the dechristianization of Christianity in the Spanish world.

It is in the great mystics, however, that the distinguishing features of Spanish individualism are most perfectly exemplified. In these, as in no other representatives of the race, do we discover the soul of Spain. Spanish mysticism is not, like Neoplatonic and German mysticism, of an intellectual and metaphysical mould. It is a spontaneous and indigenous spring, naturalistic in character, whose source is an ethical passion for inward liberty. So narrow is the environment, both social and religious, of the mystic's soul and so measureless his aspiration, that a high tension is set up within him in which he empties himself of every desire, thought and feeling. Passing through a " dark night " he ascends to the summit of the spiritual Carmel. On this sublime height he contemplates or rather possesses God. The passion of the Spanish mystic as it appears, for example, in St John of the Cross, its most classic type, is not to become lost in God but to draw God into himself, to possess Him in the fullest and most absolute sense. His individuality is so strong that it would absorb even Deity. As might be supposed, this most unique type of mysticism formed no school. The Spanish mystics are great individual, solitary souls, each of whom feels he " has a king within him," whom he has obliged to descend into his heart.

" This divine union of love in which I live makes God my captive and my heart free," says Santa Teresa in one of her most famous verses. " But," she adds, " it causes me such suffering to see God my prisoner that I die of longing to die." [1] Death would be the affirmation of supreme liberty for God and for her.

The primitive individualism of the Iberian race has been a determining factor in the history and life of South America. In the course of time Spanish arrogance became transformed into " creole arrogance," an extreme form of egotism—egolatry we might call it—which the eminent Argentine sociologist, Carlos Octavio Bunge, regards as one of the three principal traits of South American psychology.[2] Two of the minor illustrations given by Bunge of this quality are extremely suggestive. One is from the heraldry, the other from the literature of South America. The motto of the Chilean republic is " *Por la razón o por la fuerza.*" " Where reason fails let force prevail." When the poet José Hernández, the author of *Martín Fierro*, the classic epic of the Pampas, had finished his poem, he broke his guitar in pieces so that no other fingers might strike its chords and continue the narrative of the Gaucho's exploits.[3] The passage is an obvious echo of a similar action of Cervantes. On finishing the life of *Don Quixote* Cide Hamete Benengeli hung up his quill where it should remain long ages, for he alone had been born to write the life of the great Manchegan.

This arrogance has appeared, however, in much more serious ways in South American life. It has shown itself in an inordinate desire to have power over others. A Mexican writer, referring to the

---

[1] " *Aquesta divina unión*
  del amor con que yo vivo
  hace a Dios ser mi cautivo,
  y libre mi corazón :
  mas causa en mí tal pasión
  ver a Dios mi prisionero
  que muero porque no muero."

[2] Vide *Nuestra América.*

[3] *En este punto el cantor*
  Buscó un porrón pa consuelo,
  Echó un trago como un cielo,

  Dando fin a su argumento ;
  Y de un golpe el instrumento
  Lo hizo astillas contra el suelo.

  " *Ruempo,*" dijo, " *la guitarra,*
  Pa no volverme a tentar,
  Ninguno la ha de tocar
  Por siguro tenganló ;
  Pues naides ha de cantar
  Cuando este gaucho cantó."

passion for administrative positions in the government service, coined the colourful phrase "bureaucratic cannibalism." It has reduced the capacity for admiration to a minimum and engendered a levelling spirit of envy. "Our America," says the Argentine Manuel Ugarte, "has lacked the sacred faculty of being able to admire. Instead of levelling upon the peaks it has wanted to level on the plains by throwing down every individual superiority." In an article entitled "The Cruelty of South America," [1] the brilliant young Peruvian writer and politician, Haya de la Torre, draws attention to a sombre consequence of the same trait. He points out that the moment a man achieves eminence in any sphere he is cruelly set-upon by jealous rivals itching to annihilate him. Later, when he is safely dead, all join in his apotheosis. The truth of this, he adds, was brought forcibly to his attention by a German sociologist, well acquainted with South America, whom he met in Berlin. Said the scientist: "You South Americans don't respect anything in others; only the dead are safe in Latin America." On this principle he explained the exaggerated cult of the dead in the Southern Continent, the beauty of the cemeteries, the lack of critical capacity to appraise the work of a man who has passed away. "While they are alive they are cruelly torn to pieces, when they die they are superstitiously respected."

The tendency never to acknowledge a mistake is a further expression of this quality. Honour and self-respect seem to demand that when once a position has been adopted it must be adhered to, even if one has become convinced that it was wrong. Herein lie the roots of many unhappy divisions within the Latin-American family. Herein also is one of the factors which make co-operation difficult between sister nations and between different groups within the same nation. This peculiar sense of knightly

[1] In *Universal Gráfico*, Mexico City, April 6, 1931.

honour [1] is hidden in the most primitive recesses of the Iberian soul. Says Guillén de Castro in *Las Mocedades del Cid*: "Let the honoured chief always try to hit on the right thing to do, but should he make a wrong move let him defend and not change his attitude." [2]

(b) *Predominance of Passion*

Beside this strong, primitive, almost savage self-assertiveness of the Iberian character which we have just analysed into its various facets and fruits, there appears the predominance of passion over reason and will. Every conquest of the Iberian race, as every disaster it suffered, have not been the outcome of a calm reasoning process, in which the adequacy of means to ends were carefully calculated, nor yet the consequence of dogged persistence in a plan of action agreed on beforehand as the best. It has always been the result of a volcanic impulse produced by the sudden explosion of a dominant sentiment. For the Spaniard Don Quixote is very far from being a comic personage. In the deeds of the Manchegan knight he sees his own inmost being and his people's. The greatness of both has ever consisted in *quijotadas*, in blind, reckless, unstudied loyalties to ideas which momentarily possessed them.

The presence of passion in a most human and romantic form occurs in the influence exercised on the great Spanish saints by the ideals of mediæval chivalry. Raymond Lull was a soldier and a lover before he became a saint and "the knight-errant of philosophy."

Reading romances of knight errantry and not the lives of saints was the chief pastime of Santa Teresa in her girlhood days, and to the end of life she never ceased to be a lover. Teresa's love for Christ, her

[1] *Honor caballeresco.*
[2] "*Procure siempre acertarla el honrado y principal*   *pero si la acierta mal defenderla y no enmendarla.*"

Divine Husband, became increasingly passionate and romantic as she advanced in years.

Ignatius of Loyola also began life as a soldier and a lover. Severely wounded at the battle of Pamplona, he wished to regale his weariness during the early days of convalescence by reading his favourite romances. As it happened that there were none at hand they brought him a Life of Christ and *Flos Sanctorum*, a collection of lives of saints. Before his recovery was complete Loyola became converted. Soon afterwards the ex-soldier, now a cripple, limped his way to a shrine of the Virgin in Monserrat. When night came down he went secretly to the house of a poor man, to whom he handed over the clothes he was wearing, putting on in their place a coarse habit he had bought for the purpose. Arrayed in his new garb he presented himself before the altar of the Virgin. The object of this visit and what took place in the shrine are described by Loyola's earliest biographer, Rivadeneyra : " As he had read in the books of knight errantry that the new knights were accustomed to mount guard over their arms, he, as a new knight of Christ, in order to imitate in a spiritual manner that knightly practice, kept vigil the whole night before the image of Our Lady. He there watched his new arms, so apparently poor and weak, but in reality most rich and strong, with which he had equipped himself in opposition to the enemy of our nature. Commending himself with all his heart to the Virgin he wept bitterly for his sins, and promised to live a changed life in the future." [1]

A people in whom passion predominates tends inevitably to give a personalized expression to its ideals. The cult of the Virgin in Spanish Christianity is evidence of this principle. Nowhere so much as in Spain and her old colonies has the Virgin occupied so central a religious position nor the doctrine of the

---

[1] Rivadeneyra, *Vida de Ignacio de Loyola*, p. 33.

Immaculate Conception been so insistently proclaimed and so strenuously defended. The Virgin is the symbol of Spain's innate sense of youthfulness and purity. This is one of the truest insights of Angel Ganivet into the soul of his people. " The dogma of the Immaculate Conception," says Ganivet, " has seemed to me to be the symbol, the admirable symbol, of our own life, a life in which, after a long and painful process of maternity, we come to find ourselves in old age with our spirit virgin. The dogma of the Immaculate Conception refers of course to original sin ; but this sin being blotted out, the dogma sets forth the highest purity and sanctity. . . . Let us ask all Spaniards one by one and we shall find that the *Purísima* is always the ideal Virgin whose symbol in art is the Conception of Murillo. The Spanish people see in that mystery, not only that of the Conception and that of the Virgin Birth, but the mystery of a whole life. There is a written dogma which is immutable, there is also a living dogma which has been created by the popular genius." [1]

It should be added at the same time that the passionate idealization of the Virgin and of Spain in the figure of the Virgin was possible for the Spanish people, in the last analysis, because of their essentially unethical view of sin. There is nothing in Spanish literature corresponding to that agony of conscience which is so common a feature in Russian and Anglo-Saxon authors. The Spaniard fears death, not sin. It is his inherent lack of a sense of sin which opened the way for the creation of a female sinless figure to whom the Spanish religious consciousness later returned for personal security here and hereafter.

In the secular realm the passionate affirmation of virginity has appeared in recent years in connection with the youth movements in Spain and South America. The youth of former generations, says a

[1] *Idearium Español*, pp. 266-267.

Spanish student—José López Rey—were associated simply and solely with what was colourful, ephemeral and anecdotic.   It was reserved for the new generation of youth to affirm youth's essentially creative impulse. " The youth of to-day," he goes on to say, referring to the youth of Spain, " are far removed from the many-coloured and irresponsible human medley which constituted youth in former times.   For the note of colour by means of which the latter expressed themselves we have substituted the essential purity of the sculptured figure.   We have replaced anecdote by purpose.   Instead of feeling ourselves to be excursionists through the realm of youth, we affirm ourselves to be its citizens.   We do not feel youth to be a light which illuminates a single movement of our lives, but a force which shapes life in its wholeness." [1] The new generation in Spain would be passionately and eternally young.

One of the most interesting and significant documents in the history of South American culture is the *Manifiesto* of the students of the old Argentine University of Cordoba, which they addressed in 1918 " to the free men of South America," [2] as the signal of revolt against the traditional university regime.   The document is a genuine ultimatum of the Iberian soul, tinged by the sadness, the measureless aspiration and romanticism, and the human passion characteristic of one of the great peoples in whom that soul became incarnate in the New World.   " Members of a free republic," the document reads, " we have just broken the last chain which, still in the Twentieth Century, bound us to the ancient monarchic and monastic control. . . . Cordoba is being redeemed. . . . Voices in our hearts advise us that we are treading a revolutionary way, that we are living an hour of transcendental importance for the whole American

[1] *Juventud :* Conferencia de Luis Jiménez de Asúa y *Réplica* de José López Rey, pp. 122-124.
[2] "*A los Hombres Libres de Sud-America.*"

Continent. . . . The universities have come to be the faithful reflection of these decadent societies which are bent on offering the painful spectacle of senile immobility. . . . Youth always lives heroically. It is disinterested ; it is pure. It has not had time to become contaminated. It never makes a mistake in the election of its own teachers. In dealing with youth none can secure himself merits by flattery or gold. Youth must be given liberty to elect its own teachers and directors in the certainty that its decisions will be happily made. From now onwards they alone shall be allowed to be masters in the future university republic who are true builders of souls, creators of truth, beauty and goodness." [1]

On account of the predominance of passion in all their efforts Spaniards have been gloriously indifferent to many of the comforts and amenities of so-called civilization. They were born to express incandescent passion, and the moment another ideal sufficiently great burns in their souls they will again be found in their bygone potency and splendour on all the highways of the world. For this race is everlastingly virgin. It possesses qualities which, if inadapted in many respects to the soulless civilization of to-day, may secure it a leading place in the more spiritual civilization of to-morrow. On the other hand, it is equally true that where passion is not stirred by a noble ideal, the Spaniard becomes the plaything of base appetites and excitement. He becomes equally indifferent to the passage of time and the claims of duty. He lives solely for the low impulses of the passing hour. The Spanish attitude towards life, at its most sordid level, has been crystallized by Unamuno in the following words : " Bread and the bull-fight, and to-morrow will be another day. When we can, let's get the best out of a bad year. After that—well, it doesn't matter."

[1] *La Reforma Universitaria*, Vol. VI., pp. 9-12.

(c) *An Abstract Sense of Justice and a Concrete Sense of Man*

A special and peculiar sense of justice is a third characteristic of the Iberian soul. It is no accident that some of the greatest jurists of the sixteenth century were Spaniards, and that some of the greatest jurists of to-day are Ibero-Americans. Throughout Iberian history a sense of justice and right has predominated over the feeling of tenderness and pity. Humanitarian action has been determined by the claims of justice rather than by the welling-up of sympathy. No consideration of mere expediency must be allowed to interfere with the course of justice. No matter what upheaval may prove necessary justice must have its course. Of this order of justice was that which inspired the actions of Don Quixote. His was anarchic justice, carried out at the point of the lance. He liberated galley-slaves, although they afterwards stoned him. He saw wrongs where there were none, but he put them right just the same. " Alms for the love of God," says a Spanish beggar. If he receives something he adds, " May God repay you." [1]

Paradoxically enough, however, once the principle of justice has been established the door is left open for the manifestation of clemency. Yet it is never mercy that triumphs over justice ; friendship alone can achieve that victory. It thus comes about that what could never be obtained in the name of right, or even through a plea for mercy, can generally be obtained on the ground of friendship or through the good offices of a friend. Whatever law or justice may do, a friend can undo. And he does it not by modifying law but by transcending it. The law stands and is enforced, but some people are not under law, but under the grace of personal privilege.

[1] " *Dios se lo pague.*"

B

Personal-mindedness, or a sense of man, is one of the glories, as it is also one of the perils of Spanish and South American psychology. There is nothing that is not laid at the feet of one who is *simpático*, who possesses the qualities which evoke an instinctive sympathetic response in the breasts of others. The abstract principles of Liberty, Equality and Fraternity are conceived and applied in personalized terms. A personal criterion also determines the functions and relations of the three chief departments of state, the Legislative, the Executive and the Judiciary. In the course of South American history it has not been principles but *caudillos*, bold personalities, who, incarnating popular aspirations, have succeeded in producing political loyalty. When some *caudillo* has caught the popular imagination by crushing out opposition and giving rise to expectations of national prosperity, he is tacitly allowed to incarnate the constitution and exercise dictatorial powers. It was some of the perilous fruits of this same personal-mindedness which gave rise to the phrase in the Argentine: " Perfect laws and rotten customs." [1]

In recent years inter-American relationships have provided a notable example of how the Latin-American sense of man can lead to results of the highest international significance when it finds a noble and friendly object. Relations between the United States and Mexico were steadily growing worse. The United States Ambassador was unfortunately a man of a purely legalistic case of mind. Lacking absolutely in personal-mindedness, and considering that his mission consisted solely in keeping the claims of his government and countrymen before the government of Mexico, he made himself profoundly *antipático*, and his country with him. Happily he was withdrawn before the break came. His successor, Mr Dwight Morrow, followed a diametrically opposite policy.

[1] " *Leyes perfectas y costumbres pésimas.*"

With a great capacity for friendship he resolved, as he expressed it to the writer, to like the Mexican people and to do his utmost to understand them. He gave himself accordingly to the business of friendship and appreciation. The Mexican government and people responded. Ere long Mr Morrow and his family were venerated figures in the country, and relations between Mexico and the United States entered upon a new era of mutual understanding and goodwill.

(d) *Catholicity*

Paradoxical though it may appear, catholicity is also an attribute of the Iberian soul, a quality no less native to it than the individualism which is its basic trait. Spanish catholicity is a concrete instance of the inherent tendency towards polarization to be found in the Spanish nature. The Spaniard has as true a sense of the universal as he has of the individual. His interest tends to oscillate between man and the cosmos, terms which for him do not constitute a mutually exclusive either-or. He absorbs the universe, individualizing it, remaking it after his own image, imposing upon it his conception of abstract, undiversified unity. In the historic drama of Spain, the individual, as we have seen, tended to absorb the nation; the nation then proceeded to absorb the world. In its passion for universality Spain absorbed the Church, the most universal reality in existence. The result was the conversion of the state itself into a church.

The instinct for catholicity has produced many interesting phenomena in the history and life of Spain, and has projected itself into the soul of South America. Charles the Fifth's great preoccupation at the Council of Trent was that there should be no disruption in the ecumenical unity of Christendom. Father Vitoria was the founder of International Law and the natural precursor of the League of Nations. The first polyglot Bible in existence was compiled by the eminent Cardinal Cisneros, against the will of Rome.

At the dawn of South American independence the liberator, Simon Bolivar, advocated the idea of a Federation of American nations. His words breathe the catholic spirit of his race. " The old ideal of Christianity," said the most ecumenical figure who has appeared in the world of Columbus, " must become once again our inspiration and our object-lesson, in order that the political frontiers of the Americas may not become barriers that separate, but buttresses that lend greater solidity to the social structure." Having in mind the dictum of a North American president, " America for the Americans," an Argentine president formulated the South American doctrine : " America for humanity."

There is doubtless a strain of phantasy in the phrase " cosmic race," coined by the Mexican Vasconcelos to designate Latin-Americans, a race destined, according to him, to become a fifth member of the cosmic family by transcending the traditional four. At the same time, it is profoundly true that in South America race hatred as such does not exist. The most catholic of nations in the racial sense is undoubtedly Brazil. This republic has the greatest absorptive power of any existing country. For some decades it has deliberately embarked upon the ethnic adventure of absorbing all races which knock at its doors, and with the most remarkable results. The Brazilian people of the future will more nearly approach a cosmic race than any other in the world. Indians, negroes and Japanese will be woven into the same web with Syrians and Portuguese, Germans and Italians, in the great Brazil of the future.

The tendency towards catholicity which the Iberian peoples have conserved as a precious legacy from the past, gives them a uniquely important place in the modern world. " The post-war period will exalt afresh the spiritual conception of Spain," is a remark of the French philosopher Bergson, the truth of which is being borne out by the passage of time. Catholicity is the greatest need of our modern world, a form of catholicity, however, which shall succeed in winning the spontaneous and enthusiastic adhesion of individuals who love and cherish liberty. How can the fatal exaggeration of individualism in nations, churches and races be transcended? How can that kind of unity be achieved which is the fruit of common loyalty to great principles and the indispensable condition of a true and stable culture?

The type of catholicity represented by Spain failed, because it was an attempt to impose upon reality a narrow abstract unity of forms and dogmas, in which no provision was made for difference. " Spain," said Nietzsche in the last moments of his life, " Spain is a people that wanted too much." The old problem remains, however, and becomes more and more acute. At the present moment Russia, converted also into a church, is following the historic course of Spain, propagating and imposing the same ideal of catholicity. But among the creative forces which the Russian ideal confronts in the modern world are a new Spain and new Iberian lands in which the old ecumenical spirit burns, but in a totally transfigured form. The catholicity of Russian Communism can only be met by a catholicity capable of transcending the disruption of the Christian consciousness which took place in the sixteenth century, and for which Spain, by her intransigent championship of an abstract unity must share no small part of the blame.

(e) *A Soul Iberian by Nature*

Were we to name a figure of history who has incarnated more perfectly than any other all the greatness and weakness of the Iberian race during its

greatest age, we would say Ignatius Loyola. Loyola
the Basque, son of the most primitive stock on the
Peninsula, who imbibed after his conversion the
religious spirit of Old Castile, has been well described
as " a soul Iberian by nature." [1] Having donned his
new armour as a knight of " Our Lady," Ignatius
retired for a period from the world. But he became
a hermit in the cavern of Manresa not to spend his
days there or elsewhere in solitude and renunciation
of self and the world. He went to Manresa in search of
a new principle capable of transcending both renunciation and solitude. This principle he found in blind
obedience to the Roman See. He solemnly vowed to
submit himself to Rome in the most absolute sense,
and to lead others into the same submission. In the
grotto of Manresa the Jesuit order was born, that
most terribly genuine creation of the Iberian spirit.
It was in very truth the formulation of the iron will
of Spain, the incarnation of her ideal of abstract unity.

Two things in Loyola are prophetic of Spain's
future, both as a political and religious power. One
was said about him, " He had the delirium of greatness." The other was said by him, as a reference to
the kind of reformation which he felt was needed,
" Let us be like a dead body, which of itself is incapable of movement, or like a blind man's staff."

A delirious thirst for power and blind unstudied
loyalty : these are the keynotes of Spanish history,
especially of Spanish religious history, both in the old
world and in the new.

---

[1] " *Anima naturaliter iberica.*"

CHAPTER II

THE RELIGIOUS EPIC OF THE IBERIAN CONQUEST

(a) *The Mystic Motive of the Conquest*

WHEN in 1492 the standards of León and Aragón floated on the turrets of the Moorish Alhambra in Granada, eight hundred years of constant struggle between Christian and Moslem came to an end, and Spain achieved her unity. The Cross had vanquished the Crescent, but ere the latter disappeared for ever from Iberian shores, the fanaticism of the Moslem had been injected into the followers of Christ. The unifying process must not stop. Ferdinand and Isabel, the conquerors of Granada, willed that the united Spain should be only for Christ and Christians. That same year the Jews were expelled from the Peninsula.

Before this historic year was out another event took place in peninsular history not less dramatic than the conquest of Granada and the expulsion of the Jew. A Genovese sailor, Christopher Columbus, had sailed westward early in the year under the Spanish flag, in search of a new route to Asia. His particular goal was the kingdom of the Great Khan in the China sea, whose wonders and riches had been described by Marco Polo and his successors, the Venetian, Acosta, and the Englishman, John Mandeville. Returning to Spain in the fall of the same year Columbus announced that he had discovered the eastern extremities of the Asiatic continent.

No matter that the famous admiral died in the belief that it was new lands in Asia that he had found and not a wholly new continent, the psychological

effect of the discoveries upon the Spanish people was
the same.   It seemed as if God had given to Spain the
gift of virgin lands because she had gifted her virgin
self to Him, and, as a pledge of her loyalty, had
expelled Moslem and Jew from her borders.   The
coincidence was so great that it was small wonder
that the mystic glow in Spanish Christianity should
be fanned by it into a fiercer flame.   The virgin unity
of Spain must now be projected beyond her own
frontiers, the virgin lands across the Western Ocean
made virgins of Christ.

The mystic fervour of the Catholic Kings, as
Ferdinand and Isabel are known in history, became
universal throughout the Peninsula.   The great
Iberian admirals caught it.   They felt they were men
of destiny.   Columbus himself was a mystic in no
small degree.   " I travel," he writes in one of his
letters, " in the name of the Holy Trinity from whom
I hope for victory."   He would dwell with pleasure
on the significance of his name Christopher : *Christo-
phorus*, " a bearer of Christ."   His great discovery he
regarded as a miracle which had been achieved in
fulfilment of an Old Testament prophecy.   " In
carrying out the enterprise of the Indies," he says,
" it was not reason nor mathematics nor charts that
helped me ; the discovery was simply a fulfilment of
what Isaiah had said."   By this he meant that " The
ships of Tharshish " had been divinely guided to the
distant isles to bring León's new-born sons from far,
" their silver and their gold with them unto the name
of the Lord." [1]   Columbus even wrote a book on
prophecy which has unfortunately been lost.   The great
sailor's ambition was to bring from the newly-
discovered lands the amount of money necessary to
equip an army of 10,000 cavalry and 100,000 infantry,
and with these organize an expedition to the Holy
Land to rescue Jerusalem from the Turk.

[1] Isaiah lx. 9.

The famous Portuguese mariner, Vasco da Gama, felt no less strongly that God was his pilot over unknown seas. On one occasion when his sailors and pilots mutinied, " the noble captain called a council of the pilots of the fleet on board his own ship. They all went. On one side of the deck he had his charts and nautical instruments, on the other a heap of fetters. Taking hold of the former and throwing them into the sea, he said as he pointed with his finger in the direction of India : ʻ That is the route, the pilot is God.' " [1]

It is always an impressive spectacle to see a man at work who believes that God has given him a task to do. Such a man is a power to be reckoned with. It is infinitely more impressive to see a whole nation in which every one, from crowned head and minister of religion to soldier, sailor and beggar, is convinced that his country has been elected by God for a high destiny. Such a nation becomes for the time being invincible. This is the spectacle that begins to be staged in Spain at the end of the fifteenth century, and continues to be enacted throughout the whole of the sixteenth. Let us look into the soul of Spain as the land gets ready for its great religious epic.

Spain received a sense of mission. Like her own Don Quixote, she could now say, " I know who I am and what I can be." She felt herself to be a " chosen vessel," the " arm of the Lord," to establish His righteousness upon earth. Her conception of God was virile. He was no cold remote divinity, nor any mere good-natured, easy-going, celestial grandfather. " He was a God," a writer of that heroic epoch said of Him, " whose attention and care extend from the last ant, taken individually, to the greatest and most splendid of the suns." Saint-worship had not yet ousted the sense of Deity from the popular consciousness.

<hr/>

[1] Oliveira Martins, *Historia de la Civilización Ibérica*, p. 314.

Christianity during Spain's greatest age had a decided Old Testament flavour. God was above all else a God of battles. The favourite New Testament text seems to have been the words of Jesus : " I came not to send peace but a sword." The sword and the cross entered into partnership. It was this partnership, formed in the name of evangelism, in which the sword opened the way for the cross, and the cross sanctified the work of the sword, that constituted the originality of Spanish Christianity. In the Crusades, some centuries before, the sword had put itself at the service of the cross to redeem the birthplace of the latter ; the sword has been employed on many occasions to defend religious rights and liberties, and even to persecute heretics within national frontiers. But for the first and last time in the history of Christendom did the sword and the cross form an offensive alliance to carry Christianity, or what was considered to be Christianity, to other lands.

This most original and sinister *entente* was a natural consequence of the peculiar conditions in which Spanish religious life had been nurtured during eight previous centuries. " Spain," says the brilliant and lamented Angel Ganivet,[1] " was the nation which created the form of Christianity most personal and original, in so far as originality is possible within Christianity. The most original and fruitful creation of our religious spirit dates from the Moorish invasion. While in the schools of Europe Christian philosophy was being beaten out into sterile and often ridiculous discussions, in our land it was being transformed into unending warfare. And as the truth was not born among pens and ink-wells, but amid the clang of arms and boiling blood, it is not to be found in library volumes but in our popular war poetry. Our theological and philosophical Summa is in our *Romancero*." [2]

Spain became religiously intoxicated. The state

---

[1] *Idearium*, p. 279. [2] Book of Ancient Ballads.

was conceived not as an end in itself, as democratic states have wrongly conceived themselves to be, but as a means to a higher end. It received a religious finality, and at the same time a precise dogmatic content. The Roman Church was nationalized in the country, and became fused with the state in such a way that the juridical distinction between church and state disappeared. The throne and the altar, patriotism and religion became identified. As a logical consequence no minorities nor heretics could be tolerated within the borders of the state. The Spanish monarchs became priest-kings as the Egyptian Pharaohs had been. Ferdinand sought and was given the title of *Patriarch of the Indies*. Some time later when the Christian Church of the time became broken up as a result of the Protestant Reformation, Spain championed the cause of Rome, standing for what she conceived to be the ecumenical position. The appearance of heresy added fresh fuel to her fanatical religious passion. And so, at a time when all Europe was getting ready for a new period of activity, Spain did the same, only she set before herself the conquest of souls as her supreme objective, souls who must yield to be converted by the cross or be disembodied by the sword. This idea—the complete identification of church and state—" is the controlling idea of the church-state of Spain in the sixteenth century," says the distinguished Spanish writer, Fernando de los Rios. " It throws light upon her attitude both in Europe and America, and as a result of this union the Spanish state of the sixteenth century is the historic instrument of the Catholic epic." [1]

Thus the great epic began. The reality of Isabel's desire that the new world should be converted to the Catholic faith appears in royal decrees and in the instructions to expeditionary leaders. Every galleon was required to have its chaplain and every expedition

[1] *Religión y Estado en la España del Siglo XVI.*

its confessor. As time went on and Spanish power became consolidated in the Indies, priests and monks were embarked in great numbers for the task of evangelization. And certainly in the golden age of Spain there was no lack of these. The clergy formed the fourth part of the adult population of the country. In the reign of Philip II. there were 312,000 priests, 200,000 clergy belonging to the minor orders, and 400,000 monks.

The Pope gave Spain absolute spiritual power over the inhabitants of the New World whom the Catholic Monarchs were eager to convert to the Holy Catholic faith. " Thus, after the manner of Segismundo,—a personage in *Life is a Dream*, the greatest and most symbolic of all Spanish dramas,—was Spain dragged violently from her obscure cavern of combats with Africans, launched into the focus of European life, and converted into owner and mistress of peoples whom she did not even know." [1]

(b) *The Last of the Crusades*

When the crusades of the Middle Ages had become a distant memory, Spain emerged from her cavern and added yet another to their number, perchance the greatest and most far-reaching in importance of them all. From her age-long obscurity she set out, in the wake of Columbus, to imprint upon the new world he discovered the image and likeness of her own unity and that of her faith. Her dream was not to rescue for the present something belonging to the past, but to project both past and present into the future.

The new crusaders were enlisted from knights and monks who thronged the Peninsula. The souls of those classic personages had so intermingled in the long wars against the Moor, and Castile had so

[1] Angel Ganivet, *Idearium*, p. 18.

breathed into both her mystic warrior spirit, that the
typical resultant was an ascetic paladin and a martial
monk. There was a monk in every helmet and a
knight in every cowl. It could not be otherwise in
a land which possessed an Avila and a Salamanca.
The former gloried in the double name of " Avila of
the knights " and " Avila of the saints," while in the
learned and mystic Salamanca the mediæval synthesis
was reborn, leading to a fresh fusion of the symbols of
church and state. Pizarro and Cortez were almost
contemporaries, almost neighbours of St John of the
Cross and Fray Luis de León. In the Castile of Spain's
golden age the mystic and the *picaro* [1] rubbed shoulders
every day. The spiritual Don Quixote and the
materialistic Sancho Panza both embarked for the
Indies. This, however, must be said : the relatives
and progeny of the latter who found their way to the
New World were infinitely more numerous than those
of the former.

What were the guiding principles of the men who
crossed the Western Ocean with Columbus, or followed
in the wake of the great mariner ? Don Gonzalo de
Raparaz, editor of the famous *History of the Indies* of
Fray Bartolomé de las Casas, thus describes the fellow-
adventurers of the Genovese : [2] " The Spaniards who
shared Columbus' adventure across the ocean were in
truth adventurers and nothing more, men whom the
eight centuries in which the Re-conquest lasted had
educated in the following three principles : first, that
it is pleasing to God to kill and rob unbelievers ;
second, that warriors and priests form the noblest
social classes (as in India) ; third, that work is
debasing, and that the land belongs to the crown and
the nobility who conquer it, and to the church which
sanctions and shares its possession. Sentiments such

[1] The *picaro* was the classic rogue of Spanish life and literature in the
sixteenth and seventeenth centuries. The name gave rise to a special form
of literature called the " picaresque."
[2] Prologue to *Historia de las Indias*, Vol. I., pp. ix and xiii.

as these, purely Aryan in origin, with an admixture
of Old Testament or Semitic ideas, but in nowise
Christian, were destined nevertheless to form the
guiding principle in the colonization and Christianization of the new lands. The official Gospel was
that of Christ, but the popular Gospel was that of
Lazarillo de Tormes." [1]

There is abundant evidence to prove that the
Catholic Kings, and after them the Emperor Charles V.,
were perfectly sincere in their desire that the natives
of America should be converted to the Christian faith,
and that upon their conversion they should be treated
in accordance with Christian principles. But in addition to his official commission each crusading captain
was the possessor of a secret commission conferred
upon him by the unbroken traditions of his caste from
the days of the Cid. Ganivet has thus formulated the
traditional law of Spanish knight errantry. " The
knight's judicial code," he says, " reduced itself to
this : to carry in his pocket a legal letter containing
one single article : ' This Spaniard is authorized to do
whatever he takes into his head.' " [2]   In the history
of the Iberian occupation of the New World those in
authority followed their unhallowed caprice, with the
utmost disregard of legal ordinances and the terms of
their official commission.

Let us watch the crusaders in action. What magnificent *quijotadas* marked the course of the Conquest !
North of the equator Hernan Cortez burned his ten
ships behind him, and, with a handful of daredevil
Castilians, conquered the Aztec kingdom of Moctezuma. Francisco Pizarro, the ex-swineherd of Extre-
madura, marooned on a barren isle of the Pacific,
drew a line on the sand with his sword, and invited
every true Castilian to signify by crossing it that he
would follow him thereafter to the conquest of Peru.

---

[1] Lazarillo de Tormes was the hero of the first and most famous of the
Picaresque novels.   [2] " *Lo que le de la gana.*"

With the two hundred odd warriors who crossed the line, Pizarro scaled the Andean Cordillera and conquered the great Inca empire with its millions of subjects, taking captive the august Inca himself.

From the beginning of the enterprise they discovered an absorbing interest in the prospect of booty. The cross, if it were a motive in the thoughts of the successive Catholic monarchs who ordered the enterprise, became no more than a pretext in the minds of men who carried it out.

> " It is not Christianity that leads them on,
> But gold and covetousness," [1]

are the words which the dramatist, Lope de Vega, puts into the mouth of the Devil, regarding the crusaders. In this case the Devil was right. Worse still, there was no popular sentiment in the Spain of the time against satisfying the innate lust of gold in the most unscrupulous way. The " picaresque " literature abounds with examples. The popular attitude towards theft we find crystallized in a saying of one of Tirso's characters. " Son, this matter of being a thief is not a mechanical but a liberal art."

It was the lust for gold that lured the crusaders. One of the first things that struck the mariners of Columbus when they put foot on the shores of the New World was the bracelets and rings of the Indians. And while we find no trace of covetousness in the great captain himself, yet, owing to the greed of the Spanish Court, and the many enemies he had on account of his being a foreigner, he had to devote himself very largely, if his work of discovery were to go on, to amassing bullion for Castile.[2]

Ever on the trail of *El Dorado*, two crusading captains, Pizarro and Almagro, reached the Panaman isthmus. Here they made a pact with a certain friar

---

[1] " *No los lleva Cristiandad*
sino el oro y la codicia."
[2] *Historia de las Indias*, Vol. I., p. 208.

Luque, who offered to finance the enterprise of discovering the Golden Land. The monkish financier celebrated mass, and the three men partook of the same Host as a pledge that the spoils would be equally divided. The words of Pizarro as he drew his famous line on the sand are symbolic of the spirit of the Conquest. " Pass to this side and go to Peru to be rich, pass to that side and go to Panama to be poor." Later on, when the Inca monarch fell a captive to the Spaniards, and his vassals had brought from the capital of his empire the fabulous quantity of gold stipulated for his ransom, his treacherous captors broke their promise. Instead of liberating Atahualpa they executed him, while their spiritual father, the friar Valverde, absolved the murderers, lifting on high the cross. Those men were engaged in a crusading cause under the protection of the cross. Their official mission was to make the heathen submit to the sacred symbol. They therefore felt in their heart of hearts that they could do no wrong.

The religiosity of the *conquistadores* is no less striking than their lust for gold and their unscrupulous behaviour. They took themselves seriously as apostles of Christianity, though their personal religion was merely words and form. Listen to a proclamation of one of the most famous of their caste : " I, Alfonso de Ojeda, servant of the most high and powerful kings of León, conquerors of barbarian nations, notify you (Indians of the Antilles in 1509) as their emissary and general, and declare in the most categorical way that God our Lord is the only and eternal Lord, who created the heaven and earth and one man and one woman from whom you, I and all men who have been and will be in the world, descend." [1]

Cortez, the conqueror of Mexico, in spite of his

---

[1] Oliveira Martins : *Historia de la Civilización Ibérica*, p. 184. A graphic description of this famous knight occurs in Blasco Ibáñez's posthumous novel, *El Caballero de la Virgen*.

implacable ferocity never spoke to a priest without uncovering and bowing his head. It is related of him that when the messengers of Moctezuma arrived in the Spanish camp with the news of the Aztec monarch's wealth, Cortez figured out in his mind the immense booty that awaited him and exclaimed : " Moctezuma must be a great and very wealthy gentleman." But, adds the chronicler Bernal Díaz, "as it happened at the moment to be the hour of Angelus all went down on their knees and prayed." [1]

The Spanish *conquistadores*, like the Spanish Don Juans, were by no means irreligious men. Beneath the brutality of the former and the licentiousness of the latter, religion lived a hooded life of magic formulas and ritual practice. Compare the Don Juan of Tirso de Molina in his *Burlador de Sevilla* or the Don Juan Tenorio of Zorrilla with the Don Juan of Molière, and we discover immediately the innate irreligiosity, of the French compeer. The latter is completely incredulous, the former never denies a future life, but because of the remoteness of future justice he lives with the idea of divine sanctions banished from his mind.

(c) *Cross and Sword in Action*

The methods adopted by the *conquistadores* to propagate Christianity were in keeping with the unethical character of their religion. The course of the conquest of Peru from the arrival of the Spaniards to the death of Atahualpa, the Incan monarch, affords a perfect example of bellicose evangelism. When a representative of the Inca visited the Spaniards in Tumbes, the point at which the invaders landed on the Peruvian coast, Pizarro, in order to learn their intentions and communicate them to his sovereign, harangued him as follows : " We come from Castile, where reigns a most powerful king whose vassals we

[1] J. B. Terán, *El Nacimiento de la América Española*, p. 184.

C

are. We set out with the intention of bringing into subjection to our king the lands which we find. It is our chief desire to make you realize that you worship false gods, and that you need to adore the only God, who is in heaven. Those who do not adore Him nor keep His commands will go to be burned in the eternal fire of hell, and those who accept Him as the Creator of the world will enjoy everlasting bliss in heaven."

On the march through the Andean passes to Cajamarca, where the Indian sovereign happened at that time to have his court, Pizarro thus encouraged his troops : " Let not the fact of the multitude of our enemies and the smallness of our number make you afraid. Although we were fewer and they were more numerous, greater is the help of God who never abandons His own in time of need. He will help us to bring down the pride of the Gentiles, and bring them to the knowledge of our Holy Catholic Faith." [1]

The night before the perfidious attack on Cajamarca and the capture of the Inca, " The priests of the expedition, having invoked divine aid by long prayers and bloody acts of self-laceration, celebrated the sacrifice of the mass and promised victory in the name of God and His most Holy Mother. The Christian warriors sang with fervour the psalm 'Arise, O Lord, and judge Thine own cause.' " [2]

On the following morning, when all was ready for the attack, it was necessary before it commenced to fulfil a formula universally employed by the *conquistadores*. A summary of the Christian faith must be announced to Atahualpa, and his submission to the emperor and the Catholic Faith demanded. If he refused, as it was fully anticipated he would, the use of force became justified. The Dominican friar Valverde accordingly approached the monarch with the cross in his right hand and the Bible in his left. Having made the sign of the cross on the royal captive, he

[1] Lorente, *Historia del Peru*, Vol. II., pp. 62, 63, 124.   [2] *Id.*, p. 143.

delivered a homily adapted from a model composed by the theologians and jurisconsults of that age, saying in substance as follows : " I am a priest of God and I teach divine things to the Christians. I have come likewise to teach them to you. God who is one in essence and a Trinity of persons, created heaven and earth and all that they contain. He formed of clay Adam the first man and from one of his ribs Eve from whom we all descend. Our first parents having disobeyed their Creator, we have been born in sin, and no one would obtain divine grace nor go to heaven if Jesus Christ, who is the Son of God, had not become incarnate in the womb of the Virgin Mary and if He had not redeemed us by dying on a cross. Jesus Christ arose from the dead and ascended to heaven leaving the apostle St Peter as his vicar on earth, having put the whole world under his jurisdiction. The Popes, who are the successors of St Peter, govern the human race, and all nations, in whatever part they live and whatever their religion, should obey them. A Pope has given all these lands to the kings of Spain that they may pacify the unbelievers and bring them within the pale of the Catholic Church, outside of which no one can be saved. Governor Pizarro has come on this mission. You should, therefore, Sir, consider yourself tributary to the Emperor, abandon the worship of the sun and all idolatries which would lead you to hell, and accept the true religion. If you do so God will reward you and the Spaniards will protect you against your enemies." [1]

The Inca proudly replied that he would be vassal to no king. He denied the Pope's right to distribute lands that were not his. He refused to change his own sun-god for a God who had been put to death by the creatures he made, and wanted to know where Valverde had learned such doctrines. When the Dominican handed him the Bible the Inca took it

[1] *Id.*, pp. 149-150.

and threw it wrathfully to the ground. He swore he
would have satisfaction for all the outrages committed
by the Spaniards on their route from the coast.   " The
Gospel on the ground ! " shouted the monk, " Christians, vengeance !   Don't you see what is happening ?
Why dispute further with this arrogant dog?   The fields
are filling with Indians.   At him, and I absolve you." [1]

After Atahualpa had been nine and a half months a
captive, the Spaniards broke faith with him regarding
his release ; and after a farcical trial he was condemned
to be burned.   Valverde, who was chiefly responsible
for the sentence, now approached the condemned man
promising him that if he became a Christian, death by
burning would be commuted for the speedier one of
the garrotte.   The Inca consented and was baptized,
being given the name of John in honour of the
Evangelist, whose day it was.   After baptism he was
strangled on the terrible garrotte while the Spaniards
stood around and chanted the creed.[2]

A very similar scene is described by Don Alonsó
de Ercilla y Zuñiga in his famous poem La Araucana.
The great Araucanian chief, Caupolican, had fallen
into the hands of the Spaniards and was condemned
to death.   Before the sentence was carried out he
expressed his desire to be baptized and become a
Christian.   " This," says the poet, who himself took
part in the conquest of Chile, " caused pity and
great contentment among the Castilians who stood
around."   Caupolican was thereupon baptized " with
great solemnity, and instructed in the true faith as
well as possible in the short time available."   This
gave him the " hope of a better life."   After that
the Christian people, who were much elated by his
conversion, made him sit on a sharp stake and shot
him through with arrows.   A magnificent example of
" theological charity," evangelization by force to save
souls from hell!   As a precaution against backsliding

[1] Id., pp. 149-150.   [2] Id., p. 198.

on the part of " Christians " whose perseverance was open to doubt, their souls were dispatched to take possession of their celestial home before the baptismal water had time to dry on their bodies.

What reflecting Indians thought of this kind of religion stands out in the words of the proud Cuban cacique Hatuay. This dauntless chief, on being condemned to be burnt alive, was exhorted by his confessor to become converted and go to heaven. " Are there Christians in heaven ? " asked the cacique. " Why, of course," was the reply. " Well, I don't want to go to any place where I shall have any chance of meeting them." [1]

" But while their religious message was entirely devoid of ethical content and their own lives of Christian attractiveness and consistency, the *conquistadores* had a passion for the external rites of Catholicism," says a South American writer who has made a deep study of this period. " A church, a chapel, even an oratory of mud and straw was raised beside the shed which an exploring outpost improvised in the first place it made a halt. The religious ceremony was held sometimes under the shade of trees in the midst of the wilderness, with no ritual act save prostration before the cross which was held aloft by the monk of the band. The names of saints marked the stages of the march. There were liturgic formulæ for the slightest event connected with warfare : the setting out, the arrival at a great river, the sight of a mountain, the moment of attack, the erection of the tree of justice in the place where the adventurers proposed forming a settlement." [1]

(d) *The Fruits of the Crusade*

Accompanying the adventurers, or following their trail, went the missionary monks. These also opened

[1] J. B. Terán, *El Nacimiento de la América Española*, p. 194.

trails of their own through the jungle on their way to
the remote hinterland. All honour to these men.
Many of them were heroic Christian souls. The
names of the greatest will never be known. They
found unknown warrior graves in the forest. Some,
however, history has enshrined in its annals. Among
the very greatest must be classed the Jesuits Anchieta
and Nóbrega. When rich and beautiful regions of
Brazil were being desolated by incessant warfare
between Portuguese soldiers of fortune and savage
tribes of the interior, those missionaries penetrated
into the heart of savagedom and won the hearts of the
Indians by their Christlike spirit. They even offered
to leave themselves as hostages in the hands of the
savages as a pledge that no outrage would be committed by the distrusted adventurers. Of that great
and noble missionary Fray Bartolomé de las Casas we
will speak later. This, too, must be said in honour of
the crusading monks and their immediate successors :
they alone represented culture and humanity. They
were the teachers of many arts and crafts. Along with
their dogmas and rites they imported seeds, sprouts,
domestic animals and tools. They also studied the
customs of the aboriginal peoples, collected their
traditions and brought together data regarding their
early history.

Their religious labours, however, in spite of the
goodwill and self-sacrifice which they put into them,
were fatally defective, judged by any Christian standard.
Let us take the typical case of the evangelization of
Peru. The crusaders found a religion which was
bound up indissolubly with the reigning family and
the state. Inca religion was based on a moral code
rather than on a metaphysical conception, being thus
more nearly related to the religion of China than to
that of ancient India, with which it has sometimes been
compared. Religion and politics had their source in
the same principles and the same authorities. On

account of its identification with the social and political
regime, Inca religion could not survive the Inca state,
for its ends were temporal rather than spiritual. It
was more preoccupied about the kingdom of earth
than the kingdom of heaven. It constituted a social
rather than an individual discipline. The same blow,
therefore, was fatal to theocracy and theogony, while
the new religion of the conquerors was passively
accepted as a matter of course. For a people unable
to distinguish the spiritual from the temporal, political
domination involved ecclesiastical domination.

How was the latter brought about and consolidated ?
The gorgeous ritual and emotional cultus of Catholicism were uniquely adapted to captivate a population
which could not raise itself suddenly to a spiritual
religion. The Indians were baptized *en masse*. Their
ancient fetiches were given Christian names : Incan
gods were substituted by the effigies of Catholic
saints, while Catholic ritual made possible the emotional
experiences of the old faith which were now injected
into the new observances. " This," says a Peruvian
historian, Emilio Romero, " explains the pagan mad-
ness with which a throng of Cuzco Indians trembled
in the presence of the *Señor de los Temblores*,[1] in whom
they saw the tangible image of their recollections of
ancient worship. Needless to say the content and
spirit of the Indians' 'devotion' was entirely foreign to
the thought of the monks." This instance is symbolic
of a process whereby the Catholic religion was super-
imposed upon indigenous rites without transforming
their content. Such a policy had obviously great
psychological value where the whole aim of evangelization was no more than that converts should
learn correctly certain religious formulas correctly and
go through the mechanism of the established rites
of Catholicism. The transition to the new religion
became thus almost imperceptible. A state of things

[1] The Lord of Earthquakes.

was produced analogous to that which obtained among the Samaritan colonists in the Bible who "feared the Lord and served their own gods."[1] "I was informed for certain," says Castro, one of the early viceroys of Peru writing in 1565, "that of more than 300,000 baptized converts not more than forty were Christians. The rest were as much idolaters as ever."

The captivation of the Indian mind by a cultus and liturgy adapted to their aboriginal customs made the task of catechization easy. But, as a matter of fact, the lack of resistance offered to the work of the catechist made the work of the latter entirely sterile and ineffective. The very passivity with which the Indians allowed themselves to be catechized without understanding the catechism, spiritually weakened Catholicism in Peru. The missionary did not have to watch for dogmatic purity ; his mission was reduced to that of a moral guide, an ecclesiastical shepherd of a people utterly lacking in spiritual unrest. The cemetery ideal was abundantly fulfilled.[2]

A delightful story told by the chronicler Fray Reginald de Lizarraga throws a sidelight on the cate-chetical zeal and success of the missionaries. On his return from Spain, the prior of one of the religious orders received a visit from some of the principal Indians whom he had instructed in the Faith before his departure. When one of them, in the course of being catechized, was unable to answer the questions put to him, the prior said : "Did I not teach you doctrine, so that you knew it well ?" "Yes, Father," replied the Indian, "but as I taught it to my son I have forgotten it."[3]

The lay crusaders of the early period ended their days in internecine strife, creating an atmosphere of

[1] 2 Kings xvii. 33.
[2] The preceding section owes a great deal to an admirable study of religion in Peru by José Carlos Mariátegui contained in his book, *Siete Ensayos de Interpretación de la Realidad Peruana.*
[3] J. B. Terán, *El Nacimiento de la América Española,* p. 195.

intransigent political rivalry which has not been sweetened to this day. The hostility and hate between such groups as those of Pizarro and Almagro were as bitter as ever existed between Christian and Moslem. Meanwhile the royal coffers of Spain brimmed over with gold, and that became her ruin. She had emerged from her "cavern" to conquer and catholicize the New World. She conquered it, and in its catholicization de-Christianized herself, and returned not to a cavern but to a grave. With the gold of the Indies Philip II. built himself a tomb. Escorial, the pyramid of this Spanish Pharaoh, is the sepulchre of a great illusion.

CHAPTER III

COLONIAL THEOCRACY

FOR Spain the real end of the crusade was Escorial,
for America it was the beginning of a colonial theocracy which continued and consolidated the work of
the crusaders. Let us consider the condition and
progress of religion in South America during the so-
called Colonial period, that is, from the beginning of
the Viceroyalty to the War of Independence at the
beginning of the nineteenth century.

In 1493, the year after the New World was discovered, Pope Alexander VI. delegated to the Spanish
kings, by a special Bull, both temporal and spiritual
power over the Church in their dominions. This
action of the Pope is explained by the fact that the
Papal See was not in a position to propagate the faith
directly in America.

It thus came about that each successive Spanish
king regarded himself as an apostolic vicar. Ferdinand I., Charles V. and Philip II. all petitioned
the Pope for the right to use the hierarchic title of
Patriarch of the Indies. In each case the title was
granted. The king nominated bishops and settled
all questions arising between them ; while he or his
representatives determined the bounds of each diocese,
parish and curacy. Pope Calisto III. had already, in
1456, granted identical rights to the King of Portugal
for all the new Portuguese dominions. By another
Bull in 1501 the tithes of the Indies were ceded to the
Spanish kings in perpetual right, out of consideration
for the expenses incurred by the temporal and spiritual
conquest. The kings in their turn bound themselves

to erect and equip churches for the inhabitants of every new region occupied.

The consequence of this arrangement was that the patronage exercised by the Spanish and Portuguese States over the Church in America was much more absolute than that obtaining in the Peninsula. While in the mother lands the Church was independent of the civil power in economic matters, in the Indies it was subordinate to the state in this respect. The Iberian conquest and colonization of the New World thus took place under the auspices of a perfect theocracy. The propagation and care of religion was a function of the state. Until the birth of independent nations, the Pope occupied a secondary mission in the religious affairs of Ibero-America. A Christian Cæsar was supreme, whose title was his " Royal, Sacred, Catholic and Cæsarean Majesty." In an important religious document written by the Archbishop of La Plata in 1788, little more than twenty years before the revolutionary movement broke out, and recently published in Argentina, the King receives a much more central place than the Pope, who is mentioned only incidentally. He is called the " Great, above all the Great, the Catholic King of the Spains." [1]

(a) *Landlord Evangelists*

In order that the spiritual conquest of the new dominions might be more expeditiously and efficiently carried out, and effect given to the original motive of the crusade as well as to obligations entered into with the Roman See, there came into being the most original form of evangelistic organization known to Christian history. The crown charged the colonists with the conversion of the Indians to the Holy Catholic Faith. With a view to facilitating their work and vesting with greater authority their evangelistic

[1] *Carta a los Indios Infieles Chiriguanos.*

efforts, it granted them at the same time the most
absolute power over the indigenous race.   This was
an extension of the theocratic idea, whereby the
crown, for the fulfilment of religious ends, delegated
its spiritual and temporal authority.   The men who
accepted this responsibility were called *encomenderos*.
In return for their Christianizing zeal the *encomenderos*
had the right to employ the services of the Indians
and to exact tribute from them.   The latter thus
became the virtual slaves of their " evangelists."
Slavery was born as an economic expedient in order
to fulfil a religious task.   But what had been permitted as a spiritual instrument very quickly became
a commercial end.   The indigenous race fell under
the yoke of serfdom, from which in some South
American lands it has not yet emerged.

The cruelties exercised by the *encomenderos* on their
enslaved catechumens beggar description.   " No
Christian ear could listen to their crimes," writes a
certain Bachiller Sánchez to the President of the Council
of the Indies.   Terrible is the language in which
they are indicted by the noble Las Casas, the Indian's
friend and protector.   " They go about clothed in
silk, not only themselves but their mules, and, methinks, if the silk were well wrung, blood of Indians
would ooze out of it." [1]   In sixteenth-century Spanish
America, as has been well said, the work of the Indian
slaves had the same economic importance as the
public land in Republican Rome, or as coal in England
or cattle in Argentina.   But the painful thing was
that behind and underneath the serfdom in which
Indians lived from Mexico to Chile lay an evangelistic
motive and a theological ground.

To the former we have already referred.   As
regards the latter, the question whether it was right
to make slaves of Indians gave rise to endless discussions among Spanish theologians · of the time.

[1] 442 *Documentos del Bachiller Eucero.* ·

The following is a typical set of reasons used to justify the appropriation of the Indian's land and the enslaving of their persons: "First, because they do not know God! Second, because they kill one another! Third, because they eat human flesh! Fourth, because they sin against nature!" Sepúlveda, another Spanish theologian, maintained that as the Indians were not mentioned in the Holy Scriptures they did not belong to the human race, and for that reason could be legitimately used by Christians for their private ends. The official point of view is stated in one of the Royal Letters: "Slavery is justified only in case the Indians offer resistance to the Faith or refuse obedience by force of arms." How naïve is all this! Yet to the credit of the crown and the Council of the Indies be it said that they repeatedly expressed great concern for the Indian race, and enjoined on all governors and *encomenderos* the utmost consideration in dealing with them. But from the very beginning of the Conquest official intervention in the interests of humanity was wrecked on two formidable reefs. One was the theory that the kind of people employed on a religious errand was a very secondary importance, the only thing that mattered being the end. The other was the fact that every functionary in Ibero-America from that time to this has considered himself the living embodiment of the law. He has never given up possession of the famous letter of one article referred to by Angel Ganivet, and in terms of this letter he interprets and applies every code. Little wonder that "perfect laws and shocking customs" have been able to co-exist!

(b) *Las Casas, the Anticonquistador*

The Indians found a friend and protector in Fray Bartolomé de las Casas. This noble Christian soul, who has been justly described as the greatest philanthropist the Iberian race has produced, is known in Ibero-American history as the *Anticonquistador*. Because of his zeal for the welfare of the autochthonous race and his burning denunciations of the indignities it suffered, Las Casas was officially appointed " Protector General of the Indies." " There was an historic movement in America," says a distinguished South American writer,[1] " in which his was the only voice to remind us that there existed a new truth, more recent than the times of Nebuchadnezzar or Alexander, and unknown to Tamerlane, a truth which was instilled into the human conscience twenty centuries ago." In Las Casas' famous *Treatise of Thirty Propositions* occur the following sentiments : " The Kings of Castile are obliged to see to it that the Faith of Christ is preached in the form laid down by the Son of God : that is to say, peaceably, lovingly, sweetly and charitably, by weakness and humility and good example, caring for the unbelievers, and especially for the Indians who are by nature exceedingly meek and humble, giving them gifts rather than taking gifts from them. In this way they will esteem the Christians' God to be just and good, and so will want to belong to Him and to receive his faith and doctrine."

This Dominican monk, who became Bishop of Chiapas in Mexico, was theologian, sociologist, historian and man of action all in one. As a sociologist he anticipated the famous dictum of the Argentine statesman Alberdi: "To govern is to populate." He proposed that agriculturists should be introduced from Spain. His colonization schemes are still one of the unrealized dreams of some South American lands. Las Casas had the soul of a constructive revolutionary. He would have all confessors become active instruments of a social revolution. From whatever angle he is viewed, the Bishop of Chiapas

[1] Juan B. Terán.

stands out as the true hero of Ibero-America, the man in whom the moral consciousness of the latter found its highest embodiment, and to whose personality, ideas and work the thought of future generations must increasingly return for guidance and inspiration.

In his zeal for the Indians, however, the good Las Casas allowed himself, with the best and most humanitarian of intentions, to commit a grave ethical slip. Learning that the experiment carried out by the Portuguese of importing negroes into their territory had become successful, and that the children of Africa seemed to be much better adapted than the Indians to the labour conditions obtaining in South American mines, he advocated their introduction into the Spanish dominions. This was the beginning of negro slavery in Spanish America. The social problem became complicated, and another blot was formed on the Christian escutcheon. Las Casas later recognized his error, and abjured what he had once advocated. " I have bought Christ," he said bitterly, " and they did not give Him to me for nothing ! I had to pay for Him ! "

" I have bought Christ ! " These words of the greatest soul who ever breathed in Ibero-America are symbolic of the whole history of Christianity in the Western lands conquered by Spain and Portugal. The process of evangelization was carried on at a terrible ethical cost. The methods employed to bring Christ to those lands, and to make Him known to the people, cut His religion loose from morality while reducing Himself to a fetich, one among many.

We are prepared to believe that the evangelistic results of such a system were void. The heart was not changed, the mind was not enlightened, worship was offered to rebaptized idols. In a letter written in 1555 Las Casas refers to the lack of psychology shown in the religious teaching given to the Indians. " What doctrine," he says, " for those who do not

know if *Ave Maria* is a stick or a stone, or something
to eat or drink ! "

The Peruvian historian, Sebastian Lorente, lays
bare the musings of the Indian soul in view of the
Christian zeal of his feudal lords. " Evangelical
purity seemed incomprehensible and even contra-
dictory to a rude people who saw nothing but great
scandals in the Christians of their acquaintance-
ship. When an Indian was rebuked for living in con-
cubinage, he asked with some surprise, if it was a sin
to have a mistress. On receiving the reply that it
was, he retorted with warmth, ' Well, I thought it was
not, for the governor has a mistress, the priest has
a mistress, the *encomendero* has a mistress.' On the
other hand, the idolatry inherited through links of
blood and custom had a very powerful ally in in-
ebriety, its inseparable companion. It was buttressed
also by the fact that some of the chief objects of
worship were always in sight. On one occasion
when the missionary wanted to take away his idols
from an obstinate idolater, the latter said to him :
' Why, take away that hill, that is the god I adore ! ' " [1]

If it is true that the Indian race was never really
Christianized—unless to adopt the external rites of the
" Holy Catholic Faith " be considered Christianization
—it is equally true that the Christian colonists became
completely paganized in so far as religious living was
concerned. Let it be remembered that those men
were not true colonists. They did not leave their
motherlands to work, but to make others work for
their profit. They came, moreover, unaccompanied
by their wives ; and from the time of their arrival in
America they did everything in their power to keep
their legitimate partners from following them. The
colonial Ulysses never thought of Ithaca nor of
Penelope who pined for him in distant Spain or
Portugal. Instead he formed alliances with Indian

[1] *Historia del Peru*, Vol. IV., p. 137.

women in the Syren's Isle of America. The children
of these unions were brought up by their untutored
mothers. Home life was lacking. The absence of
the sacred and uplifting influence of religious homes,
where children could grow up under the care of parents
who were true companions to each other and genuine
examples to their offspring, formed one of the gravest
problems of colonial life in Ibero-America. The lack of
such homes was another cause of the failure of the Crown
and the Church to produce a truly Christian society in
colonial days. Here also lie the roots of what South
American writers of to-day describe as the fundamental
irreligiosity of life on the Southern Continent.

(c) *Safeguarding Theocratic Purity*

The initial passion to proselytize had begun to
wane ; immorality of all sorts was fast gnawing, like
cancer, the vitals of colonial life ; but the theocracy
abated not an ace of its zeal to maintain the unity and
purity of life and religion within its wide dominions.

To prevent pernicious intrusions from the outside,
especially the introduction of new religious forms and
ideas, the strictest censorship was established by the
colonial theocrats. From the very beginning of the
Conquest no foreign priests were admitted into South
America. A ban was likewise placed upon the
immigration of Moors, Jews, heretics and proselytes.
For the publication of all books relating to the colonial
possessions the consent of the Council of the Indies in
Madrid was required. In Chile, even as late as 1878,
the Church exercised a censorship over foreign books.
Every possible precaution was taken to ensure the
perpetual purity of the Holy Catholic Faith in the
virgin lands of America.

The founding of the Inquisition in the new Spanish
dominions in 1569 was, however, the chief and most
notorious means adopted by theocratic Spain to ensure

D

Catholic orthodoxy in faith and morals in her American colonies. Into the general characters and functions of the " Holy Crusade," this " state within a state " as an Italian writer has called it, a state with its " own dread army, an army anonymous, invisible and impalpable but with eyes and ears open in every direction," it is not our purpose to enter here. Let it suffice to say that, with headquarters in Lima, the Inquisition functioned at intervals from 1569 to 1813, when it was abolished. Re-established the following year, it dragged out a moribund existence, occupying itself chiefly with the readers of forbidden books, until the liberating forces of San Martín entered the Peruvian capital in 1821.

Don Ricardo Palma, probably the most eminent man of letters that South America has produced, devotes the last part of his famous *Tradiciones Peruanas* to the " Annals of the Inquisition in Lima." These brilliant pages form sad and fascinating reading. According to the royal decree by which the Inquisition was founded, it was considered necessary to establish the " Holy Office " in the overseas provinces, " in the interests of the increase and conservation of our Holy Catholic Faith and Christian religion." The first upon whom the extreme sentence of burning was carried out was a Frenchman, Matthew Salade, who was condemned for being a " stubborn heretic." This was in 1573. Looking through the records of the " Holy Office " from that year onwards to its abolition, we find a long list of unfortunate men and women who suffered its rigours. In the great majority of cases they were condemned for something they believed or had said. For being " followers of Luther," or " Jews," or " blasphemers," or " possessing forbidden books," or " dealing in witchcraft with the devil," or " celebrating mass without a priest," or perchance for some moral delinquency or childish freak, the very mention of which provokes hilarity, people went to the stake or the rack or suffered some indignity to their persons. The following annotations of Palma have special interest for a Briton. " John Drake, cousin of the English pirate, Sir Francis Drake, and his country-man Richard Ferrel, condemned for being Lutherans. They recanted to save themselves from burning. . . ." " Three pirates of Cavendish's fleet, Walter Tillet, his brother Edward and Henry Oxley, were burned for being Lutherans."

The Inquisition functioned in what is now the Senate building in Lima. When the decree announcing its abolition was published the populace stormed and sacked the eerie chamber. They found among other things a crucifix of natural size, the head of which could be manipulated by cords by a man secretly stationed behind the dais of the Tribunal. When the head of the Crucified moved it meant the accused was guilty and should be condemned. This crucifix occupied a place between two large green candlesticks on the table at which were seated the two Inquisitors and the Fiscal. The characteristic grouping gave rise to a famous description of the chamber by the Spanish writer Jovellanos : " One crucifix, two candlesticks and three darn fools." [1]

Majaderos the Inquisitors were, and much worse. They were themselves guilty of many of the things they tortured others for doing. On one occasion a special representative of the Supreme Court of Spain was sent to Peru to investigate charges against two inquisitors, Don Diego de Unda and Don Cristobal Calderón. It was proved that they had been living publicly with mistresses and had defrauded the crown of an immense sum of money.[2]

(d) *Religious Cameos*

And yet, so far from waning, the outward pomp of religion rather increased. The colonial township was

---

[1] " Un santo Cristo, dos candeleros y tres majaderos."
[2] Ricardo Palma, *Apéndice a mis últimas Tradiciones Peruanas*, p. 477.

a prolongation of a church or monastery, as were the cathedral towns of old Castile. There is a symbolic scene of colonial times, says the Argentine writer Juan B. Terán, which awaits the brush of the painter, and the pen of the novelist. " During the earthquakes which desolated Panama from May to August of 1621 the priests, seated on the stones that had been brought together for the construction of the cathedral, heard confession from the people of the district, who ran half-naked from their houses, as the roofs were falling and a hurricane was raging." [1]

Whoever has passed through the country districts of Mexico will never forget the number of church towers visible to the eye on some sparsely populated plain. There was a time when 17,000 churches covered the surface of this land alone, churches erected by rival religious orders with the hard-earned cents of the Indian population. Palatial sanctuaries amid unrelieved misery ! " The majestic towers of churches, with conventual doors and windows covered with thick copper gratings, from which silent prayers ascended to heaven," says a Chilean writer, describing eighteenth-century conditions in his country, " were the only beautiful objects to be seen in a dull and depressing country-side where everything was built of mud and straw." [2]

As in Spain, the religious festivals were the most popular, although by no means the most conducive to religious ends. They tended to accentuate in the people their original superstitions. The description given of a Spanish religious festival in the reign of Charles the Bewitched suits admirably the typical festivals of colonial South America, some of which exist, if in diminished splendour, to this day. " The most solemn, uproarious and merry days of the year

---

[1] Narrative of Juan Requejo Salcedo, quoted in *El Nacimiento de la América Española*, p. 217.
[2] Cabero, *Chile y los Chilenos*, p. 354.

were those in which the great mysteries of the faith were commemorated. And even apart from any such celebration, the fields, the winds, the rivers and the waters were blessed. The images of the saints were taken out in procession, both in time of drought and in times of difficulty, and even the Host served to quell popular tumults. Religion was disrespectfully mingled with the things most foreign to its sacred mysteries, and appeal was made to the most sacred means to attain the most prosaic and detestable results."[1] Anyone who has seen popular religious festivals in Peru such as those of " The Lord of Thunder," the " Lord of the Sea " or the " Lord of Miracles," will recognize some of the details of this description.

From being a tremendous crusading power imposing its rites and tenets upon indigenous races by fair means or foul, religion sank by swift degrees into a magical means of obtaining what could not be secured in ordinary ways. Christ and the Virgin became regionalized, and were given significant titles according to some special grace or benefit associated with their numberless images. The saints began to take first place in the popular religious consciousness, becoming patrons of individual as well as of collective desires. In Buenos Aires, towards the end of the eighteenth century, it was customary to offer prayers to San Martín that he might make it rain when the ground was all cracked after a long drought, to the Virgin of Lujan as liberator of captives and defender from epidemics, and to the saints Sabinus and Bonifacio because they were " so famous as patrons against the plague of ants and rats of this city." [2]

The Peruvian poet and essayist, José Galvez, gives some delightful sketches of the religious life of Lima in his book, *Una Lima que se va*.[3] These may be

[1] Juderías, *España en tiempos de Carlos II. el Hechizado*, p. 176.
[2] *Acuerdo del Cabildo de Buenos Aires*, 1776, Libro 40. Quoted by Julio Noé in *La Religión en la Sociedad Argentina*.
[3] *A Lima which is passing*.

regarded as relics of popular religion in colonial times,
which have come down to the near present.   Speaking
of the different kinds of *beatas* or " pious women " in
their classic *mantas* whom he had known in his life-
time, Galvez gives the following description of the
kind he calls *Las interesadas*.[1]   " The hope that all
good things come down from heaven and the certainty
that in heaven dwells the Giver of all these, inspires
the sordid interest which some *beatitas* put into their
prayers.   They pray that they may have good luck
in the lottery and that so and so may obtain a job, that
Margarita may have a good confinement.   And so
seriously do they take themselves as praying *beatas*
that they have saints for everything.   When the saints
do not listen to them they become angry and punish
them by making their images stand on their heads ;
or they thrust them into a shoe or something worse,
and even say bad words to them.   Full of primitive
ingenuity, they make a list of the specialities of their
saints.   Said a *beata* once, ' I asked Santa Rita to give
me luck in the lottery.   She did not, and so to punish
her I made her image face the wall.   A week later she
granted me two *soles*, just to let me know that she was
able to work the miracle, but that it was not good
for me to have more money.'   This is delightfully
picturesque in its childish paganism," is the author's
comment.

(e) *The Jesuit Empire*

In the century before republican life began, the epic
would have given place entirely to the melodramatic
in the religious life of South America, were it not for
its renewal in that famous episode known to history
as the founding of the Jesuit Empire in Paraguay.   If
it can be said that Ignatius Loyola is the most genuinely
Iberian soul in history, and the Jesuit Order the most
genuine organized product of the Spanish religious

[1] The interested ones.

spirit, it can be affirmed with equal truth that the
Jesuit Empire of Paraguay is a symbol and a micro-
cosm of the whole course of religious history in South
America during colonial times.

Before following the sons of Loyola to Paraguay,
let us consider their previous missionary efforts in other
parts of the continent. According to the Brazilian
writer, Manuel Oliveira Lima,[1] the Jesuits exercised
a much greater social influence in Portuguese America
than in Spanish America, the reason being that in the
latter other powerful organizations had preceded them.
During the sixteenth and seventeenth centuries they
were the principal agents of Brazilian national culture.
To José de Anchieta we have already referred. This
truly great soul, worthy of being classed with Francisco
Xavier, is known as the " apostle of Brazil." For
forty years he laboured for the conversion and protection of the Indians, defending them from the famous
bandeirantes, as the adventurous settlers of the State of
San Paulo were called.

In Argentina the Jesuits became a very influential
order, both among the lower and upper classes of
society. They influenced the former chiefly through
the confessional and the latter through the schools and
universities which they founded. " They knew the
secret ambition of each family," says the Argentine
writer, Julio Noé, " the intimate purpose of every
young woman, and the feverish passion of every young
man. They would thus further the desires of the maid
and help impatient women to find husbands, while
they would pass by with some easy penance the latest
escapade of every religious and adventurous youth.
In this way they won the adhesion of both." [2]

As we follow the Jesuits to Paraguay, let us recall
those tremendous words of Loyola : " Let us be like

[1] *The Evolution of Brazil compared with that of Spanish and Anglo-Saxon America.* Translation by P. S. Martin.
[2] *La Religión en la Sociedad Argentina a fines del Siglo XVIII.*

a dead body which of itself is incapable of movement, or like a blind man's staff." His ideal, as stated by himself, was to "rule in a cemetery."[1] When the world became transformed into a moral graveyard the Kingdom of God would have arrived. Towards that sepulchral goal the whole policy of the Jesuit Order was directed. Its aim was to win the world for God, by which was meant to universalize the passivity and peace of the cemetery. And this the Jesuit fathers proposed to achieve by whatever means were necessary, by the weapons of heaven when they could, by the weapons of earth when they could not.

The first Jesuits arrived in Paraguay in 1588. For a time they devoted themselves entirely to the evangelization of the Guaraní Indians. It is true they endeavoured to make Christianity attractive to the savages by very utilitarian considerations, by showing them, for example, what immense advantages in the way of food, entertainments and general good treatment became the lot of those who accepted baptism. Nevertheless, it cannot be gainsaid that at the beginning they aspired to nothing more than the spiritual good of their catechumens. Little by little, however, as their success and prosperity increased, they began to dream of the spiritual and temporal domination of the Indians, by forming a Christian oligarchy which should be independent of the tutelage of the Catholic Kings.

In the course of time a model theocracy was founded. The Jesuit kingdom grew in extent until it had a diameter of three hundred leagues. The territory was divided into thirty provinces, with thirty-three townships and over one hundred thousand inhabitants. Each township was surrounded by a moat and a palisade, with sentinels and a patrol on guard at night. No one could enter at any time without special permission.

[1] Oliveira Martins, *Historia de la Civilización Ibérica*, p. 381.

The form of social organization imposed by the fathers was a marvel of mechanical soulless perfection. To begin with, everything belonged to the padres ; the people owned nothing. Every man, woman and child had a specific task to do and was obliged to do it. There were rules and regulations for every aspect and detail of life. Not only was the religious and social life of the people standardized ; their economic and domestic life was equally so, even to the most trivial and ridiculous details. Men were obliged to marry at seventeen and women at fifteen. There was nothing to stimulate individual initiative, nor was such initiative rewarded in case it appeared. Work, obedience, equality and sameness were the rule. Jesuit townships were as much alike as drops of water.

To obtain posts as *doctrineros*, that is, as priests in charge of groups of Indians lately converted, became the chief ambition of the students of the Jesuit seminaries in the three provinces of Paraguay, Rio de la Plata, and Tucumán. The type of priest now wanted in the Empire was the good administrator. What had happened in lay life in the case of the *encomenderos* now took place among the Jesuit fathers in Paraguay. Business and not salvation became the chief motive of evangelistic endeavour. The classic " delirium of greatness " in its most mundane form took hold of the sons of Loyola. They became a commercial power and gravely damaged Spanish commerce in South America. Owning their own fleet of ships, they exported Paraguayan tea (*mate*), flax, hides and fruit to Chile, Peru and Brazil. According to the distinguished Paraguayan writer, Blas Garay, to whose valuable book, *The Communism of the Missions*,[1] we are indebted for most of these data, the annual income of the Jesuit fathers reached 1,000,000 Spanish silver *pesos*, while their expenses were 100,000. Nine hundred per cent. dividends !

[1] *El Comunismo de las Misiones.*

The extraordinary success of the Jesuit kingdom of Paraguay as a commercial enterprise was grounded on two basic factors : the Jesuits' weak moral sense of the rights of human beings and their supreme psychological sense of the power of gorgeous ritual over the primitive mind. As to the former, history possesses a catalogue of painful facts. We know, for example, that the Indians who transported *yerba de mate* from the plantation to the river ports suffered indescribable hardships. Often, we are told, when the carrier arrived at the river port his burden weighed more than himself. As to the latter, the Jesuits erected gorgeous temples, in which their Indian serfs were dazzled into awe and obedience by ritual splendour. The ideal of the cemetery was realized, the grandeur of art above the immobility of death.

The Empire flourished until 1767. About this time the intrigues of the Jesuits against the Spanish Crown became so evident, especially in connection with the cession by Spain to Portugal of part of the territory in which they worked, that, like a bolt from the blue, and in the year above mentioned, the order of Loyola was expelled from the Spanish dominions.

With the expulsion of the Jesuits all that is epic in a religious sense in the Iberian occupation of America comes to an end. Less than fifty years later all South America had cut itself free from the yoke of Spain and Portugal. From the War of Independence dates a new page in the religious history of the continent. Traditional influences continued, but the conditions under which they operated were greatly modified, while, at the same time, through doors that opened, one by one, around the continent, new spiritual forces poured in.

CHAPTER IV

THE PASSING OF THE KING AND THE COMING
OF THE POPE

TWELVE years at the beginning of last century deprived Spain and Portugal of their colonial possessions in South America. Between 1810 and 1822 the colonies shook off the yoke of the motherlands. In Brazil an independent monarchy was founded in 1822 which lasted till 1889, when the republican form of government was adopted. The Spanish colonies became republics at the time of the Revolution, and have continued ever since to enjoy democratic freedom save for frequent and prolonged periods during which they have been governed by dictators. Such dictatorships have been evidence of the fact that most South American lands were not ready for democracy when they became politically free.

Those fateful years meant much more for Spain than the loss of her richest colonies ; they involved besides the dissolution of the Spanish theocracy in the New World. The right of ecclesiastical patronage and government of the Church, which the Papal Bulls of Alexander VI. and Julius II. had vested in the Spanish Crown, became a dead letter. That new and most original form of canon law, which had governed the relations between church and state in South America for over three hundred years, was annulled by the work of the Liberators. The mystic column of Spain's colonial empire, her immemorial privilege of being a Vicar of Christ to do both the work of Cæsar and of God, crumbled with the rest of the edifice. The collapse of that column was the sorest stroke the Spanish monarchy had to endure.

For ten whole years after the last South American colony had proclaimed itself an independent state King Ferdinand VII. of Spain dreamed of the restoration of his lost dominions. He felt certain that if only the Pope would continue to grant him the privilege of nominating bishops to ecclesiastical sees in South America, it would be but a matter of time till the political breach in his empire had become healed. But when the diplomacy of South American republics succeeded in securing for themselves the right of patronage which had formerly belonged to the Spanish kings, Ferdinand's hopes were blasted for ever. At the same time a new era was inaugurated in the history of Catholicism in South America.

Leaving until later an account of the renaissance of papal influence in South American affairs, let us consider the course of events in their bearing upon religion from the year 1810, when the standard of rebellion was unfurled in Venezuela and Argentina, till 1831, the year in which the Pope recognized the new republics.

(a) *The Revolution and Religion*

The South American Revolution was the combined work of clergy and laity. While it is true that the hierarchy everywhere, and probably the majority of the minor clergy in the northern and west-coast countries of the continent were royalists, a very large and distinguished group of priests championed the revolutionary cause. These were, almost without exception, men of liberal sentiments and wide vision. This was particularly true of the eminent Brazilian and Argentinian priests who played a prominent part in the War of Independence and in the subsequent reorganization of their respective countries.

The revolution of 1817 in Brazil was to a very large extent a " revolution of priests." During the minority of the second Emperor it was a priest, the famous Feijo, who acted as regent from 1834 to 1837. Feijo was an ardent advocate of the abolition of clerical celibacy, which has been the source of some of the gravest evils in the history of South American Catholicism.

It is one of the legitimate glories of Argentina that the country possessed at the time of the Revolution a group of liberal clergy who were the soul of the movement. By their preaching, their gifts, and their influence in the army, they helped the cause of independence. And later, when the time came for constructive action, these men played a prominent part in drafting the new constitution. Sixteen priests took part in the Congress of Tucumán in 1816, at which the complete independence of the country was proclaimed, the total number of members being twenty-nine. The definite constitution of the new Argentine Republic, which was promulgated in 1818, bears the signatures of nine clergymen out of a total of twenty-four national deputies. The chairman of this group of congressmen was an eminent and patriotic churchman, Dean Gregorio Funes, Archdeacon of the Cathedral of Salta.

In the western and northern countries, on the other hand, the clergy, with some glorious exceptions, tended to be reactionary. One reason for this was that the Spanish tradition was much stronger in those parts than in the River Plate region, while there was much more Spanish blood in the priesthood. At the same time, we find a group of churchmen in the revolutionary period of Peruvian history who were quite as liberal as their Argentine confrères. Chief among these was the Arequipan, Luna Iglesias, Rector of the College of San Fernando of Lima, a man who returned to his country after a period in Europe, imbued with the ideas of the French Revolution. Iglesias, as a member of the National Assembly of 1822, which drafted a constitution for the new

Peruvian Republic, was in favour of complete liberty of worship. His proposal was that the article relating to religion should read as follows : " The religion of Peru is the Roman Catholic Apostolic religion." A layman, Doctor Justo Figuerola, proposed that the phrase should be added, " to the exclusion of the exercise of any other." The amended article became the finding of the Assembly, and the country entered upon a long period of religious obscurantism. It was not until 1856 that the modification of the fatal phrase into " the Nation . . . will not permit the *public* exercise of any other (religion) " gave a hint that henceforth the adherents of other faiths would be allowed to celebrate worship in private. " In private," meant in homes or in special places of worship the façades of which should not have the appearance of religious buildings nor suggest anything regarding their identity. This modification continued in the national constitution until 1915, when it was struck out. Since then Protestant congregations have been allowed to place notice boards on the outside of their chapels or preaching halls, and, theoretically at least, there has been religious toleration in the country.

Between the lay leaders of the Revolution in the northern and southern countries of South America there existed as great a difference as between the clergy of these regions. The generals who liberated Argentina and pressed on victoriously towards the west and north had no quarrel with religion or the Church, for the simple reason that in the south the clergy in general were with the Revolution. General Belgrano named the *Virgen de las Mercedes*[1] Commander and Chief of his army, while San Martín made the *Virgin del Carmen* patroness of the army which he led across the Andes into Chile. Both generals held impressive dedication ceremonies, in

---

[1] Virgin of Mercies.

the course of which each placed his baton in the hands of the image of Our Lady.   Incidentally, this action of the Argentine generals affords us additional evidence of the fact that in the history of religion in South America, Christ became identified less and less with anything that was virile and progressive.   He was the Lord of death.   Full-blooded men with a passion for life and liberty found their religious inspiration in the figure of the Virgin who had never died.

The reactionary and obscurantist character of the northern clergy produced a very radical type of military leader.   The great Venezuelan, Simon Bolivar, if not positively hostile to religion, considered that the state should be religiously neutral.   Religious toleration was proclaimed in Caracas in 1811.   In the following year, when a terrible earthquake threatened the fortunes of the Revolution in the north, the clergy interpreted the catastrophe as a divine judgment upon the godless revolutionaries.   The Archbishop of Caracas was asked by the government to issue a pastoral letter instructing the people that an earthquake is a natural phenomenon as common as rain, lightning and snow, and not a chastisement of heaven. On the prelate's refusal to do so he was expelled from the country.   It was about that time and in this connection that the indomitable Bolivar uttered the famous words : " If nature fights against us, we will fight against nature until we overcome her."   He was no less irreverent in his attitude towards apostolic succession.   During the period of his dictatorship in Peru he nominated an archbishop and two bishops, who immediately took up office, without receiving an investiture from Rome.

(b) *An Ecumenical Christian*

There lived in Argentina at this time a very remarkable priest called Juan Ignacio Gorriti.   He had been a national deputy and a leader of the Revolution. When an old man of seventy, living in voluntary exile in Bolivia on account of his opposition to the course of events in his country during the period following the Revolution, Gorriti published, in the year 1830, a striking book entitled *Reflections*. This book contains a series of thoughts "upon the moral causes of the internal convulsions in the new American states, and an examination into the means of remedying them." According to Ricardo Rojas, in the prologue to the new edition of *Reflections* of which he is editor, the book may be regarded as the "Manifesto of the Argentine Church, inasmuch as the latter took up, during that period, a position of independence of the Vatican, that is to say, an attitude which was nationalistic rather than Roman." [1]

Reflections is the work of a great Christian soul who, on the brink of eternity, set down his thoughts on South American problems and their solution. The book contains a section on religious education. In discussing the problem of ethical instruction, Gorriti mentions the difficulty of finding a suitable text-book. He immediately goes on to say that he has heard great eulogies of the *Course on Morals* of a certain Protestant Frenchman, M. Néker. Personally he has not seen the book, but he is sure that "it will not contain anti-social teaching, because the author was a pious, not a materialistic Protestant." He accordingly recommends that the book be adopted as a school text. The teacher would be able to call attention to and correct whatever Calvinistic errors it might contain, but "errors of that kind," says he, "cannot form the basis of his system inasmuch as there is no conflict between Catholics and Protestants in the matter of moral virtues and vices." [2]

Gorriti not only puts Christian charity and the interests of public morals above all narrow sectarian-

---

[1] *Reflexiones*, p. 34.   [2] *Id.*, pp. 207-208.

ism, he goes so far as to criticize very severely some of the customs and tendencies in his own Church.   He would suppress most of the feast days.   He deprecates the sinister influence on religion and morals of the Papal Bull of the *Holy Crusade*, in which were granted " pernicious dispensations " ! [1]   The scholastic method of religious teaching he would gladly see abolished, as " its sole value consists in teaching one to waste time methodically." [2]   Dogma he likes, but the subtilties of scholasticism disgust him.[3]   The habit of reading the Gospels and meditation upon the maxims they contain is his solution for the moral education of youth.[4]

This venerable priest and patriot holds up the time-honoured Protestant practices of family worship and Sabbath observance as an example to be imitated in his native land.   " We must frankly confess, to our own confusion," he writes, " that in this matter the Protestants have a form of morality more in accordance with reason and the Gospel.   Protestant parents devote a set period to the instruction of their children. On Sundays, the only feast day which they observe, no amusements of any kind are allowed.   After public worship is over they employ the whole time in the study of the Scriptures, which they explain to the members of their household, instructing them in regard to their duties as men, citizens and Christians. Heaven grant that practices so exemplary as these may become general in the whole of Spanish America, the religion of which is the Holy Roman Catholic Apostolic faith.   How much would be gained by education and morals." [5]

The figure and ideas of Gorriti awaken a series of reflections.   To begin with, no Roman Catholic priest or prelate in South America ever expresses himself to-day in this friendly and sympathetic way regarding

---

[1] *Reflexiones*, p. 138.   [2] *Id.*, p. 215.
[3] *Id.*, p. 220.   [4] *Id.*, p. 208.   [5] *Id.*, p. 99.

E

Protestants. If he did so publicly he would not escape ecclesiastical censure, and were he to prove recalcitrant in his utterances, he would probably be excommunicated. It is not uncommon nowadays to hear Roman Catholic archbishops in South America denounce Protestantism in all its aspects as a veritable cesspool of iniquity. " There are Protestant denominations," said the Archbishop of Lima in 1924 on his return from a visit to the United States and Europe, " which permit indefinite divorce, others adultery, not a few polygamy, abortions, infanticide and many other crimes." He had apparently seen no good thing in the Protestant world which he could hold up as an object-lesson to his flock.

A second reflection which Gorriti provokes is much more vital. The good man puts his finger upon the spiritual source of Protestantism's strength in its best days : family religion, a family altar and a family Bible. South American religion has never possessed either, from the time of the Conquest to the present day. The concentration of religion in a chapel and of Christ in a material substance has robbed the home of the Real Presence. The most significant feature of the *Cottar's Saturday Night* has been lacking in the homes of the people. They have had nothing corresponding to this :

> " The cheerfu' supper done, wi' serious face
> They round the ingle form a circle wide ;
> The sire turns o'er wi' patriarchal grace
> The sacred Bible, ance his father's pride.
>
> .   .   .   .   .
>
> Then kneeling down to Heaven's eternal King,
> The saint, the father and the husband prays."

A contemporary South American writer, Don Julio Navarro Monzó, has recently corroborated the idea of Gorriti as to the influence of family religion upon society. In a little book, *The Religious Problem in Latin-American Culture*, written in 1925, he contrasts the unlovely conditions prevailing in the homes of the rural class in Latin America with the trimness and beauty which he found in the interior of English cottages and in humble homesteads in Massachusetts and Michigan.   He then goes on to say : " There will be few who, like Domingo Faustino Sarmiento (the greatest of Argentine presidents) will be able to find a connection between all this and the old Bible which lies there in a corner of the dining-room, upon a chair or on the window-shelf, and which is read every morning, before the cloth is removed from the breakfast-table.   Few will perceive that all this which captivates us by its simplicity and spontaneity is the fruit of a culture that goes back over many centuries." [1]

At the dawn of South American independence Juan Ignacio Gorriti, with his ecumenical Christian spirit and his moral passion, saw clearly the religious problem of the new republics.   If only a truly national Catholic Church had been formed in the Argentine Republic at the beginning of last century, bringing to fruition what was undoubtedly the immanent tendency in religious circles at the time, how very different might have been the religious and sociological history of the whole Southern Continent !   The " Old Bible " would have gone into the homes from which it has been systematically excluded.   Catholics and Protestants could have lived in mutual appreciation of each other, and both worked for the spiritual welfare of the people.   These lands would have had by this time their own religious reformation.   But . . . the Pope arrived.

(c) *The Coming of the Pope*

It was some time before the Vatican could reconcile itself to the fact that the dominions which former occupants of the Chair of St Peter had given, in Christ's name, to the kingdoms of Spain and Portugal, had

[1] P. 21.

passed for ever from the control of the Peninsula. For a number of years after the last South American country had become free, Pope Leo XII. refused to recognize the new governments. He hoped against hope that, in the course of time, the old order would be restored. It had been, moreover, the traditional policy of Rome to acknowledge no government which came into existence as the result of a revolution against established authority.

The Spanish king, Ferdinand VII., used every means in his power to secure papal influence for the restoration of his lost dominions. He requested the Pope to direct an encyclical letter to the American clergy exhorting them to support Spain. He demanded that no emissary from Spanish America should be allowed admittance to the Papal States. When at length the Vatican showed an inclination to establish friendly relations with the revolutionary governments, Ferdinand asked that he might have the secret right of nominating candidates to episcopal sees in his former colonies. He reasoned that if only, as in the days of the theocracy, he possessed the virtual control of the Church, it would be but a matter of time until he again became " the great, above all the great, the King of the Spains."

The new governments realized, on their part, that it was of first-rate political importance for them to frustrate the machinations of Spain at the Papal Court, and to secure for themselves the adhesion of the Pope. A diplomatic struggle thus began, which lasted ten years, between the young republics and the old metropolis, the scene of which was the Vatican. One after another delegates from Spanish-American countries presented themselves in Rome. Fray Pacheco from Argentina, Archdeacon José Ignacio Cienfuegos from Chile, Don Ignacio Texada from New Granada, the old name for Colombia, and Presbyter Francisco Vásquez from Mexico, endeavoured in turn to win the Pope to the cause of the Revolution, and prevail upon his Holiness to grant investiture to new bishops.   These men, three of whom, it will be observed, were ecclesiastics, form a group of most interesting characters.   The tale of their diplomatic efforts, the stratagems they had to employ to evade the vigilance of the Spanish embassy in Rome and get the ear of the Pope, with the ill-fortune that for a time attended their efforts, is a fascinating romance.[1]

There was a period in the negotiations in which it began to appear as if the new republics might go their own religious way and separate national churches come to the birth.   In 1824, two years after negotiations had begun, the Pope published an interventionist encyclical, in which he called upon all churchmen and loyal Catholics in the New World to repudiate the Revolution and support the re-establishment of the old order.   This ill-starred document awakened a strong reaction in Spanish-American countries.   The Pope was accused of partiality and strong distrust was entertained regarding his designs.   This encyclical, it would appear, is not found in the Vatican archives, and an attempt has been made to deny its authenticity. Such an attempt, however, is futile, as at least one authentic copy does exist.   Moreover, other considerations, which were admirably formulated in 1874 by a Chilean writer, Miguel Luis Amunátegui, prove to the hilt that an effort was made to spread the famous encyclical through the new American republics.

In the same year, 1824, an apostolic vicar, a certain Monsignor Muzzi, visited Chile and Argentina.   His autocratic and disrespectful attitude made the situation worse in Chile, and, later, when he showed the same disrespect of national aims and institutions in Argentina, he was promptly sent out of the country.   The general impression was that he was simply an emissary of the king of Spain.

[1] *Vide* Lucas Ayarragaray, *La Iglesia en la América.*

In the meantime, it had been represented to his
Holiness that there was a real danger of Protestant
propaganda making headway in the old Spanish
dominions. Don Ignacio Texada informed him as
follows : " English, Dutch and Swiss merchants are
coming to America and are spreading their doctrines
and missions, and we have no bishops." The Pope
was disturbed, and agreed that in each country in
South America the Church should be represented by
apostolic vicars who would do the work of bishops
without belonging to any episcopal see. When the
Spanish king objected even to this mediating policy,
insisting always in his ancient right of patronage, the
Pope replied that the privilege granted by the Church
to the Catholic monarchs ceased to be valid when they
affected unfavourably the interests of the Church.

The real crisis came in 1830. A new Pope,
Gregory XVI., was in power. The Mexican delegate,
Vásquez, presented his Holiness with an ultimatum.
Mexico would henceforth admit no more apostolic
vicars. The latter had created great confusion, and
the country wanted regular bishops. When the Pope
asked for delay the bold Aztec priest, true to the
tradition of downrightness for which his race has been
noted, replied that it would be necessary to act
immediately, " in order," said he, " that your Holiness
may be spared the chagrin of seeing me depart from
Rome." Gregory was well aware that if the break
came there would never be another Canossa to heal it.
He yielded. A Bull was issued in 1831, the *Sollicitudo
Ecclesiarum*, by which the Vatican offered to establish
relations with revolutionary governments that gave a
fair promise of stability. In the following year bishops
were installed in Mexico, Chile and Argentina ; and
in 1833 the Vatican granted official recognition to
Nueva Granada, the first of South American republics
to be so honoured by the Holy See.

From the very first, however, the new South

American governments insisted upon their right of patronage, which, they maintained, became legally theirs as the successors of the Spanish, or, in the case of Brazil, the Portuguese monarchy. This right the Vatican conceded, postulating in return the most rigorous protection of Roman Catholic religious interests, to the exclusion of all other faiths. It might be said, indeed, that until nearly the end of the nineteenth century the policy of the Vatican was devoted mainly to securing for itself, so long as it was able, the monopoly of religious propaganda and nurture in the new lands. Its chief arm was the foreign religious orders which now poured into the continent. In 1836 the Jesuit Order was restored and invaded South America afresh. The Order was later expelled from several countries, but slipped back again. In Peru, for example, where the Jesuits have no legal title to residence in the country, they carry on the most powerful private school in Lima, the school in which the last generation of Peruvian politicians received their education. Only after a long struggle were such elemental human privileges as the right of civil marriage, the right to found civil cemeteries and the right of liberty of worship, wrested from church-controlled governments in the western and northern countries of South America. In many cases it was only through diplomatic pressure from abroad that such rights were obtained.[1]

Concordats have been drawn up at different times between the Papal See and various South American republics. Typical among these is the existing concordat with Colombia. Article XII. of this agreement establishes that " in the universities, colleges, schools and other educational centres, public instruction shall be organized and carried on in accordance with the dogmas and morals of the Catholic religion. Religious teaching shall be obligatory in all such

[1] T. Robertson, *Hispanic Relations with the United States*, pp. 322-327.

centres, and the pious practices of the Catholic religion observed." In Article XIII. it is laid down that the Church authorities shall have the right of inspecting public schools to make sure that the stipulations of the previous article are duly observed, that no text-books are being used nor any ideas propagated which are inimical to the Catholic faith, or derogatory to the respect due to the Church.

Reviewing the ecclesiastical situation as it stands to-day, we find that in the course of the last forty years separation between the Church and the State has taken place in Brazil, Uruguay, Paraguay, Bolivia, Chile and Ecuador. Colombia has been faithful to the Church throughout her whole history. Venezuela and Peru, the souls of both of which are liberal to the core, have been proving more and more reactionary and obscurantist, especially Peru. The former country has been lying for years under a brutal dictatorship, while the latter has just recently been released from the shackles of another. On the other hand, Venezuela passed a law not long ago prohibiting the entrance into the country of all foreign clergy, whether Catholic or Protestant; while in Brazil, where Church and State have been separated, a determined effort is being made to reinstate the Roman Catholic Church in its former position as Church of the nation.

(d) A Peruvian Episode

To such an extent was the Peruvian Republic gagged and bludgeoned in recent years that public opinion could no longer express itself. It thus came about that a government, sold body and soul to Rome, dared to outrage the moral consciousness of the nation and the world by issuing the most retrograde educational decree of modern times. The decree in question laid down that no other kind of religious instruction should be given in public and private

schools than that prescribed in the official Roman
Catholic syllabus.   Any private school contravening
this order would be closed and its property and
equipment confiscated.   The novel and reactionary
feature of this enactment lay in the fact that the
obligation to teach Roman Catholicism was imposed
upon evangelical schools.   In Turkey and Mexico
religious instruction has been forbidden in all schools,
both public and private, but in Peru it was not only
required that a religion uncongenial to the state
and ecclesiastical authorities should not be taught
in private schools, but that the religion congenial
to those authorities should be taught.   It was an
attempt on the part of the clerical forces in the
country to take advantage of an abnormal political
situation to re-establish the old Catholic theocracy.
What was aimed at chiefly was the elimination of
non-Catholic educational influences because of the
growing prestige of evangelical institutions among
all classes in the community.

Let it be said, however, to the credit of Ex-President
Leguía, a Mason of the thirty-third degree, who has
since passed away in a Peruvian prison, that the infamous decree did not originate with him.   According
to irrefutable evidence it was sprung as a surprise
upon Sr. Leguía by his clerical minister of education.
The President signed it in an unwary moment, but
convinced afterwards of his error, he set himself
immediately to tone down the application of the decree
to evangelical institutions.

The preamble to the above-mentioned edict contains an extraordinarily significant and revealing
statement which, when read in connection with the
corresponding article in the decree itself, throws a
flood of light upon the past and present of official
religion in Peru, and its relation to national problems.
" Considering," so the document runs, " that the
educational establishments in which are propagated

religions contrary to that of the State carry on a
work that is destructive of national unity which it
is the duty of the State to conserve and strengthen,
and considering that such propaganda is particularly
harmful when carried on among the indigenous
population which should be specially protected by
the State, it is decreed . . . that the government shall
establish special schools for the indigenous population, wherever it deems them desirable, and pedagogical institutes for the preparation of indigenous
teachers in the departments of Puno, Loreto and
Ayacucho." The indigenous population in Peru
numbers 3,000,000 Indians, or roughly three-fifths
of the total population of the country. For the first
time in nearly four centuries something was going to
be done to educate those Indians. And why now?
And why in the particular departments mentioned
rather than in others? Because in the three departments mentioned, and especially in the Department of
Puno around the shores of Lake Titicaca, the American
Adventist Mission had carried on for many years one
of the finest pieces of educational work that is carried
on anywhere in the world among an aboriginal
people. The whole region had been completely
transformed. Thousands of Indians had abandoned
their alcoholic and cocaine habits, becoming respectable and useful citizens. This work had been praised
over and over again in the past by leading Peruvian
politicians and educators. Some years ago, however,
a special emissary from Rome visited the region.
Soon afterwards the work came to an end, and eighty
schools, where over two thousand Indians were being
educated by teachers of their own race, had to be
closed down.

Some years previously a clerical reaction in Bolivia
had succeeded in persuading the government of that
country to close the Adventist schools situated on the
Bolivian side of the lake, and to hand over the work

to Catholic religious orders.   Such, however, was the
popular outcry against the governmental decree that
it was rescinded, and things left as they were.   " *Frailes
no !* " or " No friars ! " was the slogan which re-
sounded through the streets of La Paz.   They have
had four hundred years in which to do this work,
and have not even begun it.   Let them stand aside.
They possess no moral title for such a task.   Such
was the sentiment so resolutely expressed in the
Bolivian capital.

(e) *The Vatican and Argentina*

The relationship between the Argentine Republic
and the Vatican is so anomalous as to merit a couple
of paragraphs apart.   According to the constitution
of this nation, there is no state religion.   At the same
time, the State exercises the right of patronage over
the Roman Catholic Church, and, in return for this
privilege, gives an annual subvention for the support
of that Church in the Republic.   It is also customary
for the President and his cabinet to attend a special
Te Deum in the Cathedral on the anniversary of
national independence.   This anomalous relationship
has been combated at different times by both radicals
and Catholics in the National Congress.   A very
bitter controversy raged some years ago between the
government and the Pope owing to the latter's refusal
to appoint to the Archbishopric of Buenos Aires the
churchman whom the government had nominated for
that see.   It appears that Andrea, the official nominee,
had been accused in Rome of favouring a nationalistic
religious policy which, by co-ordinating Catholic forces
in Argentina, would greatly limit the influence and
income of the powerful religious orders.   The Pope,
who at first appeared to be favourably disposed to the
Argentine prelate, suddenly changed his attitude, and
refused to appoint him.   In view of the resulting

deadlock, his Holiness suggested that a quiet and amicable separation should take place between Church and State such as had been effected in Brazil. To this the Argentine President Alvear is reported to have replied: "If separation comes about, it shall be a noisy one as in France."

In the end, however, the Pope won, and an archbishop was appointed who was satisfactory to both parties. Such an upshot was inevitable in view of the increasing power of the Papacy in Argentina. The chief instrument of this resurgence of papal influence has been the steady entrance into the country of new religious orders. According to the constitution of 1853, no new religious order shall be allowed entrance to the country except by a special decree of the National Congress. But nowadays no government dares put that provision into force. The design of the fathers of the republic in adopting no state religion, while giving the government the constitutional right to control the Roman Catholic Church, was to assure, as Rojas puts it, that the new republic " would not become a Jesuit theocracy or a society plunged into anarchy by ultramontane bodies."[1] " Under this regime of dependence," he continues, " the people are becoming transformed in the direction of spiritual liberty, while the clergy, noted formerly for their culture and broadmindedness, are now becoming atrophied through the inaction resulting upon the state subsidy and the pittances thrown to them by the laity." [2]

[1] Rojas, Introduction to *Relaciones entre el Estado y la Iglesia*, por Dalmacio Vélez Sarsfield, p. 43.
[2] *Id.*, p. 44.

CHAPTER V

THE NEO-CATHOLIC REACTION

THE last thirteen or fourteen years, that is to say, the period since the close of the world war, have witnessed in all parts of the world a great and significant Roman Catholic reaction. This reaction has not been without influence in South America.

Although the Pope entered South American ecclesiastical politics in 1831, it was not until the time of Leo XIII. (1878-1903) that the Vatican appeared to show an intelligent and creative interest in the continent. It is true that Leo's predecessor, Pius IX., had given over the Indians to the spiritual care of Don Bosco, the famous founder of the Salesian Fathers, but he did so without possessing an intimate knowledge of conditions in South America. Moreover, his action was taken against the opinion of the Papal Secretary of State, Cardinal Barnabó.

It remained for Leo XIII. really to discover South America. What surprise and pain the discovery must have caused him! How he must have been shocked at the revelation of a form of Catholicism which had become de-Christianized and was steadily losing influence over the minds of educated people! A materialistic philosophy held sway. The preoccupation of the Pope led to the founding of a large number of educational institutions throughout the continent, under the direction of different religious orders. About forty years ago new church schools began to appear in the capital cities of South America. Some of these grew into large and flourishing institutions, a few into Catholic universities. Shortly before the outbreak of the world war the influence of these schools began to make itself felt in a new generation of writers and politicians.

Since the close of the war, however, more significant movements have taken place in the South American Church than during the whole previous century of republican history. Let us consider what these movements are.

(a) *The Catholic Youth Movement*

For the first time since the days of the early missionaries has South American Catholicism developed an aggressive religious policy and made a serious attempt to adapt itself to the new social conditions. The famous slogan of Leo XIII., "*Allez au peuple*," [1] has been taken seriously. Catholic workmen's clubs have been founded. A Catholic youth movement has been organized in imitation of the Young Men's Christian Association. The usual name given to the different centres forming this movement is " Social Action of Youth." These clubs promote physical and cultural activities. From time to time they meet in national and international conferences. Three main motives appear to bind the members of these groups together, motives which reflect the thinking of a representative section of the community, namely, youth, which, particularly in Latin America, is the bold and ingenuous spokesman of latent community sentiment. In addition to such secondary motives as social and recreative interests, the primary motives are : first, the identification of Roman Catholicism with the Latin spirit and at the same time with social stability ; second, hostility towards every form of Protestant effort, which is invariably represented as the chief agent of foreign, especially North American, imperialism ; and third, political ambition.

[1] " Go to the people."

The first of these motives is a phase of contemporary traditionalism and race loyalty. Whatever is closely identified with the history or spiritual formation of a people is jealously defended. If it can be shown that a given institution is capable of contributing to national security or to the glory of race or nation, that institution tends to become nationalized, at first in public sentiment, later on in official action.

This was precisely the attitude of Charles Maurras and the leaders of *L'Action Française* towards the Roman Catholic Church in France. In his famous book, *La Démocratie Religieuse*, Maurras says in substance, " Politically I am a Catholic; personally I am an Agnostic." He was a political Catholic because he considered that the destinies of the Roman Catholic Church and the French nation were inseparably bound together. The former he regarded as the only bulwark sufficiently strong to withstand the oncoming surge of disruptive forces.[1] In a prologue to a book by his compatriot Marius André, *La Fin de L'Empire Espagñol d'Amerique*, Maurras goes further. " Catholicism," he says, " is ideally and morally organized; Latinity is not. Catholicism is formed, Latinity is not yet formed or conserves no longer its formation." In support of his position he recalls the desire of August Comte, the founder of Positivism, to form an alliance with Jesuitism in order to stem the disintegrating forces of the age. The dread of change and the future brings strange bedfellows together! It is not surprising that in certain intellectual circles, and in the Catholic youth movement in particular, this *zeitgeist* from the Mecca of Latin culture should exercise a very large influence. The renaissance of Catholicism among the French intelligentsia, together with the rapprochement between the See of St Peter and the Italian State, have contributed to lead many cultured South Americans into the ranks of militant

[1] P. 464.

Catholicism. They have returned to the Church for sentimental or patriotic reasons, although at heart they may be neither Catholic nor Christian.

The second motive is a direct consequence of the first. Evangelical Christianity in South America is attacked by the Catholic youth movement, not on objective religious grounds, but rather on grounds of a purely sentimental or political order. Protestantism is considered alien to the Latin spirit. Its introduction into South American countries would, it is alleged, destroy nationality and national traditions. Its progress might even lead to a religious war. All evangelical effort, especially the work of the Young Men's and the Young Women's Christian Associations, is regarded as the precursor of complete foreign domination. Particularly violent are the attacks directed against the United States. A political motive is attributed to religious propaganda. This idea is carefully fostered by French writers of a certain type who, fully conscious of the wane of French influence in South America, lose no opportunity to launch a vicious, vengeful attack at North America.

Recently a new argument has been formulated with a view to combating religious propaganda from the north. The loss of North American trade in the southern continent is attributed to popular hostility towards Protestant religious propaganda. The deduction drawn from this entirely gratuitous assumption is that if United States manufacturers wish to do business with South American countries, and if the North American government wishes to maintain good relations with its southern neighbours, no effort should be spared to anathematize evangelical activity in Latin America. To this subject we shall return later in dealing with Protestantism in South America.

The best and most representative example of an attack on evangelical Christianity by a South American Catholic youth movement is a large volume entitled

Violando la Clausura.[1]   This book, published by the
Association of Catholic Youth in Uruguay, edits with
voluminous comments the reports of the " Conference
on Christian Work," held in Montevideo in April
1925.   It may be said that this conference marked an
epoch not so much in the progress of evangelical work
on the continent, as in the organization of the Roman
Catholic reaction against evangelical Christianity.   On
the one hand, Protestant effort on the continent has
been violently and systematically attacked, while, on
the other, Protestant methods of work have become
increasingly adopted.

The third motive referred to is obviously the least
worthy.   It is none the less real and potent.   The
increased political power of the Roman Catholic
Church in South American lands lures many young
men with political ambitions to join the ranks of
Catholic youth movements.   An interesting case in
point is the history of the powerful Catholic club
which grew up in Lima, Peru, in the closing years of
the dictatorship of Leguía and under its favouring
shadow.   The moment the dictator fell the majority of
the members stampeded in search of cover, and the
organization disappeared as rapidly as Jonah's gourd.

(b) *The Cardinal Ferrari Movement*

Much more significant from a religious point of
view is the Cardinal Ferrari movement.   In 1920, the
year in which Italy was in serious danger of falling
a prey to Bolshevism, the Archbishop of Milan,
Cardinal Andrea Ferrari, founded a new society called
the Company of St Paul.   The purpose of this organization was to meet in a practical way and in the spirit
of Christ the urgent needs of the existing social situation.   The new movement was to be an apostleship of
youth to " enlighten people with the light of truth,

[1] Violating the Entrance Ban.

F

fascinate them with works of love and induce them to honour Jesus Christ the King of the ages and of the human race." It would devote itself to every kind of social activity and work for the good of everybody without distinction. Thus arose a modern monastic order which included in its ranks clerical and lay elements of both sexes and of all ages, and whose members took the vows of chastity, poverty and obedience.

In 1921, a few months after Cardinal Ferrari's death, the first building of the new order was inaugurated in Milan by his successor, Cardinal Ratti, now Pope Pius XI. In 1926 the Company of St Paul was recognized by the Church as a regularly constituted religious institution. The head of the movement is a young and dynamic priest, Don Giovanni Rossi, who had acted as private secretary to the founder.

The growth of this social Christianity movement has been little short of phenomenal. In Italy its membership increased from 7500 in 1922 to 100,310 in 1928. The most varied forms of work are carried on, preferably in the great metropolis. Schools have been founded. Evening educational courses are offered on a great variety of subjects. Hotels are provided for young men and women; excursions and camps are organized; personally conducted tours take crowds of people year by year to the holy places of Christianity.

The religious propaganda of the movement is directed chiefly towards the conversion of people living outside the ordinary ministrations of the Church. To facilitate the work of propaganda a great publishing house has been founded with branches in Rome, Milan and Bologna. Important newspapers, magazines and books are published by this press, the director of whose book department is none other than Giovanni Papini, the celebrated author of the *Story of Christ*.

Outside of Italy the Cardinal Ferrari movement is directing its chief attention to Jerusalem and Latin America. It would appear that the activities carried on by the Young Men's Christian Association in the Holy City of Christianity and in the metropolis of South American lands has led the Company of St Paul to select these places in order to counteract and substitute, if possible, the influence of a movement whose spirit and methods it has been at great pains to imitate.

The new movement has become firmly established in the Argentine metropolis, where its presence has introduced some new and vital elements into the traditional Catholicism of South America. On 24th June 1928 a unique function was held in the Colón Theatre of Buenos Aires to celebrate " *El día del Evangelio.*" [1] In connection with this and similar festivals it is calculated that 100,000 copies of the Gospels in Spanish have been distributed in Argentina. These Gospels, of course, contain notes, to distinguish them from the simple Protestant versions. Work has been initiated for Italian immigrants to Buenos Aires. Very interesting and significant also is the cultural work for men and women carried on in the city. The following extracts are from an announcement in *Criterio* of Buenos Aires, the leading Roman Catholic magazine in South America:

" *Atrium* is an institute for female culture, where a woman finds everything that can interest her for the development and cultivation of her artistic and intellectual faculties."

" *Coenobium* is an intellectual centre for the interchange of ideas and for artistic, literary, social, political, historical and religious culture. The year's programme will be inaugurated with courses of lectures. These will include three different sections. First : comments on the most important book or event of the previous fortnight. Second : an artistic course

[1] " The Day of the Gospel."

for the study of all the manifestations of art in a given century. This year (1929) the Sixteenth Century will be studied. Third : a course of lectures by G. I. Franceschi on ' The Evolution of a Principle (or beginning), its origin, development and transformation, according to the historic and social life of the ages.'

" The members of the *Coenobium* will also take part in the concerts, recitals, excursions, etc., which may be organized for cultural ends."

(c) *New Religious Approach*

The new approach to the masses is admirably illustrated by the title of Father Franceschi's series of lectures referred to above. The Spanish word *principio* is ambiguous ; it can mean either " beginning " or " principle." The obvious subject of the lectures is " The Evolution of the Church." But in view of the rooted prejudice in the minds of people against anything with an ecclesiastical flavour, the subject of the course is disguised.

A still better illustration of the new religious approach is the evangelistic activity of the young Spanish Jesuit, Father Laburu. Laburu visited Montevideo and Buenos Aires in 1926, being introduced to university circles in both cities as a brilliant pupil of Ramón y Cajal, the famous Spanish histologist. After a brief course of lectures on the subject of evolution, given in both universities in turn, Father Laburu returned to Spain, without having engaged in any other activity in the River Plate countries.

The following year he returned. After an initial lecture in the Faculty of Medicine of Buenos Aires he launched an evangelistic campaign in the great Jesuit church of the city. Thousands thronged to hear him. Some weeks later the same method and programme were repeated in Montevideo. The author mingled with the huge audience which listened to the young orator in the Jesuit temple. Intense expectation. The preacher arrives. He ascends the pulpit stairs. Without any ritualistic preliminaries he begins his sermon. He rejects the wordy traditional sonority of pulpit oratory in these lands. His style is tense, his sentences brief and incisive, while his telling illustrations are drawn from the real life of our time, many of them from the scientific laboratory. His plea for the religious life is overwhelming. The sermon over, the orator retires as silently as he has come, and the congregation files out of the church. Had any ritual act been engaged in, a large section of those present would probably have left the building immediately. It was an admirable example of the *Conferencia sin Culto*, the religious address without ritual act or ceremonial accompaniment, which should constitute an essential feature of pioneer evangelism in our day.

(d) *Neo-Scholasticism*

Quite different in character from the Cardinal Ferrari movement, with its predominantly social and evangelistic emphasis, is the Neo-Scholastic movement. This movement, whose seat is also in Buenos Aires, is a projection of the Roman Catholic renaissance among French and Belgian intellectuals, especially of that important group of thinkers, clerical and lay, who, led by the famous Cardinal Mercier, have sounded the return to Thomas Aquinas.

While some Frenchmen have turned in recent years to the Roman Catholic Church in search of a political buttress, others have turned to it in search of an objective and authoritative world-view. A passion for objectivity and authority, together with a strenuous effort to reinstate the intellect in its lost place of honour, are characteristic of the thought of continental Europe at the present time. The idea of a new

" middle age," in which a single great idea or loyalty shall dominate the whole of life, has caught the imagination of many distinguished thinkers.   Modern democracy, modern culture, modern freedom, modern religion, all of which have come to be regarded as self-sufficient ends, are weighed in the balance and found wanting.[1]   One aspect of this aspiration towards transcendental unity and authority is represented by the Neo-Scholastic movement.

As Thomas Aquinas, the father of scholasticism, used the philosophy of Aristotle to develop a comprehensive world-view for his time, the neo-scholastics of to-day propose to use Aquinas as he used the Stagirite, as a point of departure for a world-view adequate to our time.   In the new *weltanschauung* a rational interpretation will be given of universal history, life and culture.   Distinguished representatives of this neo-Thomistic tendency are Jacques Chevalier, R. P. Joseph de Tonquedec and Jacques Maritain.   An authoritative account of the movement, written by some of its leaders, can be found in a religious symposium edited in 1928 by Georges Guy-Grand, and entitled *La Renaissance Religieuse*.[2]

A few years ago the influence of this movement appeared in Buenos Aires.   It led to the founding in 1928 of an extraordinarily able weekly magazine called *Criterio*, in which, in addition to churchmen, a number of brilliant young Argentine intellectuals collaborate. A study of this magazine over an extended period has revealed the fact that its tendency is entirely ultramontane.   It discovers neither the broad intellectual vision nor the spirituality of the French movement. It resolves itself simply into a fanatical defence, not so much of the Catholic faith as of the Roman Catholic institution.

A few illustrations will suffice to indicate the spirit

[1] Vide *Un Nouveau Moyen Age*.   By Nicolas Berdiaeff.
[2] *La Renaissance Religieuse*, Librairie Felix Alcan, Paris.

and tendencies of this movement in Argentina. For several months after *Criterio* was founded a systematic campaign was carried on in its pages against the memory and reputation of distinguished Catholic figures in South American history who had the grave defect of being more Christian than Roman. The great de las Casas came in for his share in this campaign of detraction. But he who most suffered was the famous Dean Funes, the father of the Argentine Constitution, because of his audacity in suggesting, at a certain critical moment in Argentine history, that it might be possible for the country to subsist perfectly well without the intromission of the Papacy.

Liberalism and Protestantism in all their forms are anathema to the members of the *Criterio* group. Some time ago an eminent Spanish Catholic, Osorio Gallardo, happened to make the innocent remark in a public address that he was a Catholic, but a liberal one. Referring to this statement a writer in *Criterio* truculently rejoined : " To be a liberal Catholic to-day is impossible. One must be a Catholic or a Liberal." In an article on North America, published on 12th May 1928, we are told that the " true Bible of North Americans is the telephone guide."

(e) *The Shadow of Loyola*

Early in 1929 a great journalistic scandal occurred in Buenos Aires. A distinguished journalist, Sr. C. A. Leumann, a member of the editorial staff of the newspaper *La Nación*, published an article entitled " The Mother of Jesus." It was a reverent study, but in the course of it the writer used phrases which made clear that he regarded as mythical the ideas of the Immaculate Conception and perpetual virginity of the Virgin. As the result of a violent letter written to the newspaper by Dr Thomas D. Casares, a professor in the University of La Plata and the author of the statement regarding the mutual exclusiveness of Catholicism and Liberalism, Leumann was obliged to tender his resignation to the editor of *La Nación*.

The case had an interesting sequel, related by Leumann himself in an article in the leading Argentine literary review, *Nosotros*. Shortly after the above-mentioned affair the journalist received a pressing invitation to call on a Jesuit father, Mariano Clavell, professor of philosophy in the *Colegio del Salvador*, a Jesuit institution in Buenos Aires. They conversed amicably about what had taken place. Leumann explained that he belonged neither to the Roman Catholic nor Protestant communion, but was a sincere lover of Christ and an earnest student of Christianity. At the same time he defended, with arguments from the Gospels, his position regarding the Virgin Mary, upon which the reverend father held up his hands in horror. Two things, Leumann tells us, impressed him in this interview. The first was that the professor's study was full of Virgins. Some were on his desk, others on the shelves, and still others in different forms on the four walls of the study. The second impressive feature of the interview was the professor's ignorance of the Gospels. The familiar words of Jesus referring to His disciples, " Behold my mother and my brethren," he declared that he had no recollection of having ever read.

Ignatius of Loyola dedicated himself to the service of the Virgin in the little chapel of Monserrat. His followers in the South American metropolis of to-day continue the Virgin cult. They are the strongest force in South American religious life. Although by no means neo-scholastic they stand behind *Criterio*, which is more than anything else their organ. They can bring it about that one may blaspheme Jesus Christ with impunity but dare not write even a serene article about the cult of the Virgin Mother.

It is not surprising, therefore, that whereas from

modern Italy comes to South America a breath of evangelical enthusiasm in the Cardinal Ferrari movement and a breeze of intellectual passion from French Catholicism, the religious influence of modern Spain, through the all-powerful Spanish Jesuit Order, is entirely directed towards the cult of Mary. In the spring of 1929 a Hispano-American Exhibition was opened in Seville. To coincide with the historic event a Hispano-American Catholic Congress was organized in the same town, whose object, according to the official announcement, was to offer an opportunity " for the nations of Spanish and Portuguese origin to meet during the week in Seville for the purpose of glorifying Our Lady the Virgin Mary."

It cannot be too much insisted upon that the spirit and type of South American Catholicism are different in many respects from European Catholicism outside the Peninsula and from the Catholicism of North America. It is related on good authority that Cardinal Gasparri's successor as Papal Secretary of State, a churchman who had spent nine years as *Nuncio* in Germany, made recently the significant remark : " The only type of Catholicism in which I have any faith is the Catholicism to be found in Protestant countries."

Certainly Count Keyserling, the German philosopher, received a rude shock when he visited South America on a lecture tour in 1929. " I have never had such an experience in my life," he said to the author when the latter interviewed him in Montevideo. " During the weeks I spent in Buenos Aires the Catholic authorities never ceased attacking me, and in the most unworthy manner. This is not the Catholicism I have seen in Europe. In Germany I have many friends in the priesthood. They don't agree with me, but they say that, in general, my influence is all to the good. But here they have not given me a moment's respite. This is not Christianity ; I don't know what it is."

PART TWO

A PHILOSOPHY OF SPANISH CHRISTIANITY

CHAPTER VI

THE SOUTHAMERICANIZATION OF A
SPANISH CHRIST

OUR interest thus far has been psychological and historical. The first chapter was a study of the Iberian soul as it has expressed itself in the life of Spain and South America. In the four succeeding chapters we surveyed the course of Catholicism in South America from the time of the Conquest to the present day. We will now attempt an interpretation of Spanish Catholicism as a religious system, with special reference to its naturalization in the South American Continent.

(a) *The Andean King in Bethlehem*

" I have another crucifix of silver, which comes from Upper Peru, the work of some colonial blacksmith, and the figure is that of an Indian whose beard is composed of but three hairs on the extremities of the lips."

" We have an Indian Christ, and this comforts me, since in the three wise men who worshipped Jesus in Bethlehem only the races of the continents which were known at that time were represented. There was lacking in that courtly company the copper-coloured king, the Inca of America. Fifteen centuries later, the man from America arrived at Bethlehem." [1]

In this symbolic way a contemporary South American writer expresses the historic fact that in the sixteenth century the South American Continent became

[1] Ricardo Rojas, *El Cristo Invisible*, pp. 79-80. An admirable translation of this book by Dr. Webster E. Browning has recently been published by the Abingdon Press.

a part of Christendom.   However this incorporation
came about, whether it was the result of violence or
suasion, of expediency or conviction, or an admixture
of all these, the fact remains that the race of whom
the Inca Atahualpa and the Araucanian Caupolican are
historic representatives, was received by baptism into
the bosom of the Roman Catholic Church.

The copper-coloured king came to Bethlehem, but
it would seem as if, unlike the three visitors from the
East, it was the Virgin Mother who impressed him most.
At least he adopted the " young child and his mother,"
and adapted both to his primitive pagan taste.   The
South American Trinity is probably the most original
that exists.   Ricardo Rojas, the distinguished author
whom we have just quoted, describes it in the same
book.   The image of this Trinity, now in his possession, belonged to a colonial chapel : " The Jehovah
of the ages is a Christ ; the Dove of the Spirit is a
Christ ; the Christ who fuses them into a single figure
is a creole of Spanish type, and the Virgin whom the
Three Divine Persons crown with simultaneous sym-
metrical gesture is a pretty Peruvian *chola* with swarthy
face, high cheek-bones and loose black hair." [1]

With this apotheosis of the Virgin agrees an inscrip-
tion which may be read above the door of an old
colonial church in Cuzco, the ancient capital of the
Incas.   " Come unto Mary all ye that labour and are
heavy laden and she will give you rest."   A gorgeously
attired Virgin, *La Virgen de la Merced*, in whose hands,
some years ago, President Leguía of Peru placed a
golden sceptre, is the patroness of Peruvian arms, and
so of the nation's destiny.   Upon the summit of San
Cristobal, the lofty eminence that commands the city
of Santiago, the Chilean capital, stands the most
striking monument in the country.   It takes the form
of a towering statue of the Virgin, the lights on whose
crown flash out at night across the city.   In Argentina,

[1] *Id.*, pp. 117-118.

the *Virgen de Luján* receives popular homage as the patroness of that great republic. The fourth centennial of the miraculous appearance of the Virgin of Guadalupe was celebrated in Mexico last December.

But however much overshadowed by His Mother, Christ too came to America. Journeying from Bethlehem and Calvary, He passed through Africa and Spain on His long westward journey to the pampas and cordilleras. And yet, was it really He who came, or another religious figure with His name and some of His marks? Methinks the Christ, as He sojourned westward, went to prison in Spain, while another who took His name embarked with the Spanish crusaders for the New World, a Christ who was not born in Bethlehem but in North Africa. This Christ became naturalized in the Iberian colonies of America, while Mary's Son and Lord has been little else than a stranger and sojourner in these lands from Columbus's day to this.

(b) *The Religion of a Spanish Christ who was born in Tangiers*

" Many a time," says Unamuno, " has Guerra Junqueiro (a distinguished Portuguese writer) remarked to me : ' The Spanish Christ was born in Tangiers.' " [1] As to the parentage of traditional Spanish Christianity which this famous saying suggests, the Spanish writer is in the fullest accord with his Portuguese literary colleague. In fact Unamuno goes further. He identifies the popular faith of the African Moslem and the Spanish Catholic. In an article written in 1909 for *The English Woman*, he relates a conversation he once had with a Jesuit, which is extraordinarily suggestive. " One day a Jesuit told me," he writes, " that it is impossible to convert Moors and Mussulmans. And I answered

[1] Essay, " El Cristo Español," in *Mi Religión y Otros Ensayos*.

him : 'How can you expect to convert them when they are already converted? Their living popular religion is the same as ours. Our peasants believe in God and in the immortality of the soul, in a heaven in which they will take up again their earthly life, only far from misery, and in which there will be fairs and pilgrimages. All that goes beyond this simple creed they simply admit as ornament. And the substance of this faith is the same as the Moors'. Nothing has any value for us except the doctrines we live by ; and our people live by no doctrine but this. All the business of the *filioque*, and even of the Trinity, are for the Spaniard nothing but theology, science, that is to say, irony and scepticism, an ethical device to aid mental economy. His æsthetic demands are met by the tragedy of the Passion, which pierces his soul because it is a tragedy. And this tragedy strengthens his faith in immortality, a faith which has a tragic basis.' " [1]

Tragedy and immortality. A sense of tragedy and a passion for immortality are still the warp and woof of Spanish popular religion, as they were when America was discovered, save perhaps that during the intervening centuries the sense of tragedy has deepened. These have profoundly influenced the Spanish conception of Christ, and, at the same time, many of the most characteristic view-points of Spanish Catholicism. Apart from them the Spanish Christ and the religion that centres around Him cannot be understood and evaluated.

Christ stands before us as the tragic Victim. His likeness belongs to a classic type of anguished figures in the religious art of Spain. With what realism does Oliveira Martins describe the grim, artistic masterpieces of Zurbarán, Herrera and Rivera : " Squalid monks ; frightful visions ; lacerated Prometheuses, human monsters, tortured by painful forces. These are laid out upon dark canvasses, with

[1] Vol. IV., December 1909, " Spanish Religion."

black backgrounds, pierced in places by blinding spots
of light." [1]   More tragic than the rest are the figures
of Christ.   Bruised, livid, bloodless and blood-streaked
images, twisted Christs that struggle with death and
recumbent Christs that have succumbed to it—those
Tangerian Christs are to be found all over the Peninsula.
They are the quintessence of unrelieved tragedy.

Unamuno has depicted one of these latter.   He
found it in the *Iglesia de la Cruz* of Palencia.   In the
Crucified Christ of Velazquez Jesus is represented as
dying, but in the recumbent Christ of Palencia, cradled
in the arms of Franciscan nuns, He is dead forever.
He has become the incarnation of death itself.   The
only light which gleams upon His awful pallor descends
from a lamp that stands before the Virgin Mother, the
Virgin Mother, " all full of heaven and life."   Says
Unamuno in pensive strain, " This Christ, immortal
as death, does not rise again.   Why should he ?   He
awaits nought but death.   From his half-open mouth,
black as the indecipherable mystery, dissolution flows
towards nothingness, which it never reaches.   For
this Christ of my land is earth.[2]

" This Corpse Christ, which as such does not think,
is free from the pain of thought, from the awful
anguish which made the Other, weighted with grief
in the olive grove, ask the Father to spare Him the
chalice of His woe. . . .

" This Christ is not the Word which became incarnate in livable flesh.   This Christ is desire (*gana*),
real desire which has become interned in earth, pure
will which destroys itself by dying in matter.

" This Spanish Christ who has never lived, black as
the mantle of the earth, lies horizontal and stretched
out like a plain, without soul and without hope, with
closed eyes facing heaven. . . . And the poor Franciscan nuns of the Convent in which the Virgin Mother

---

[1] *Historia de la Civilización Ibérica*, p. 266.
[2] " *Porque este Cristo de mi tierra es tierra.*"

G

served—the Virgin all heaven and life, gone back to
heaven without having passed through death—cradle
the death of the terrible Christ who will not awake
upon earth.   For he, the Christ of my land (*tierra*) is
only earth (*tierra*), earth, earth, earth, . . . flesh, which
does not palpitate, earth, earth, earth, earth . . . clots
of blood which does not flow, earth, earth, earth,
earth. . . .

"And Thou, Christ of Heaven, redeem us from the
Christ of earth." [1]

The prayer which Unamuno breathes into these
concluding words throws a shaft of prophetic light
across the religious life and history of Spain and
South America.

In Spanish religion Christ has been the centre of a
cult of death.   And yet, paradoxically enough, it was
the passion for fleshly life and immortality that created
this interest in death.   The dead Christ is an expiatory
victim.   The details of His earthly life are of slight
importance and make relatively small appeal.   He
is regarded as a purely supernatural being, whose
humanity, being only apparent, has little ethical
bearing upon ours.   This docetic Christ died as the
victim of human hate, and in order to bestow immortality, that is to say, a continuation of the present
earthly, fleshly existence.   The contemplation of His
passion produces a sort of catharsis, as Aristotle
would say, in the soul of the worshipper, just as in the
bull-fight, an analogous creation of the Spanish spirit,
the Spaniard sees and feels death in all its dread reality
in the fate of a victim.   The total sensation intensi-
fies his sense of the reality and terribleness of death;
it increases his passion for life, and, in the religious
realm, makes him cling desperately and tragically to
the dead Victim that died to give him immortality.

The Spanish religious passion for life has not,

---

[1] "El Cristo Yacente de Santa Clara de Palencia," in *Andanzas y Visiones Españolas*.

however, aimed at life in the qualitative Johannine sense; it has been a craving not for regeneration, but for immortality, for " total immortality in its vilest and sublimest meaning." Its supreme dread has thus been death not sin. The sovereign preoccupation not to die is the mainspring of the historic religion of Spain. How impressively it meets us in the religious experience of the Peninsula, and how it colours all life and dogma! There is a story that when Santa Teresa was a little girl of seven, she and her brother, a boy of about her own age, left home one day in search of martyrdom at the hands of the Moors. Teresa's object, as she herself tells us in her autobiography, was to win immortal life in this the surest and simplest of ways. In later years when she had transcended the popular faith, she gave utterance to the same passion in one of the most striking phrases in religious literature: " I die of longing to die." [1] It was death to her, in other words, not to be able to die and so to enter upon a deathless life. She was dying for death.

The same passion makes the Spaniard an instinctive Kantian in his apologetic for God's existence. For Kant there must be a God to ensure that the good will achieve happiness. " If there be no other life, if we die altogether, why should there be a God?" said a Spanish peasant once. To doubt salvation, meaning a happy life beyond death, however bad a life one may have lived, is mortal sin. In the famous drama of Tirso de Molina, *El Condenado por Desconfiado*,[2] Paul the hermit has to go to hell for doubting his salvation, while Enrico, the brigand and assassin, because of his naïve confidence that God in His boundless mercy will overlook his offences—which he very reluctantly acknowledges in order to give pleasure to an aged priest—goes to paradise. Unamuno refers to a similar case in a poem of the Catalan poet, Juan Maragal. The bandit Suralonga is about to die.

[1] " *Muero porque no muero.*"   [2] *Condemned for Distrusting.*

After a sorely unwilling repentance in the face of death, he asks the executioner not to cut off his head until he has said the creed as far as the words, " I believe in the resurrection of the body."

Such a religious attitude tended naturally to produce a type of faith which was utterly devoid of both intellectual and ethical content. The ground of assurance in immortality was not, in the last analysis, belief in a divine revelation, nor in a dogma of atonement; it was a blind faith in the authority and infallibility of the Church which taught it. Popular religious faith in Spain has always been that particular species which in Spanish is known as the " Coalman's faith," [1] and whose formula is the following : " Well, what do you believe ? " a Spanish peasant was asked. " I believe what the Church believes." " And what does the Church believe ? " " The Church believes what I believe." The Spanish mind is not naturally philosophic, nor would the Spanish consciousness tolerate an Aquinas to rationalize its faith. To think for oneself has been considered the sin against the Holy Ghost ! " One has heard it said in this Spain of ours," writes Unamuno, " that to be a liberal, that is, a heretic, is worse than to be an assassin, a thief or an adulterer. The greatest sin is not to obey the Church, whose infallibility defends us from reason." [2]

Even the great mystics, whose religion was entirely distinct from both popular and official religion in the country, were careful to state in their writings that they submitted their opinions and experiences to the superior judgment of the Church. " Don't ask me that," said Santa Teresa once, " I am an ignorant woman. The Holy Mother Church has doctors who will know how to answer." [3]

It was inevitable in such a case where no room was allowed either for apologetics or private judgment,

---

[1] "La fé del Carbonero."   [2] Del Sentimiento Trágico de la Vida, p. 73.
[3] Vida, XXV., 2.

that ritual should attain an exaggerated importance, becoming converted into magic. Not only did the Spanish Catholic accept the doctrine of transubstantia- tion ; the Host became for him the " Bread of immor- tality." He partook of it not to become better through feeding upon Christ ; he ate it as a magic recipe, prescribed by his spiritual advisers, in order to live for ever. Pizarro, Almagro and the friar Luque partook of the same consecrated wafer in Panama in order to seal their pact and assure themselves strength for their enterprise. In other words, Christ in the Eucharist is made use of for private ends. He is taken for the mortal vigour and immortal life He can give, but not as the Lord of Life to whose influence the soul submits. The Sacrament increases life with- out transforming it. The ethical is absent, its place being taken by ritualistic magic.

Speaking of the extreme ritual tendency in Spanish religion, Havelock Ellis remarks very truly and sug- gestively that it " involves a faith in exteriority which is almost fetichism." He then adds in the strain of Unamuno : " It seems to have been a Spaniard, Ramón de Peñafort, who first mentions the pardon of venial sin by aspersion with holy water, and in one of Calderón's plays, the *Devoción de la Cruz*, a man commits every crime yet retains his respect for the cross, the symbol of redemption, and by that at the end he is saved ; he has not violated his tabú." [1]

Philosophically speaking, Spanish Catholicism has passed straight from æsthetics to religion, clearing ethics at a bound. The Tangerian Christ, and the religion that grew up around him, have æsthetic and religious values, but they are both unethical. Who- ever has visited Seville during Holy Week will never forget the scene of woe which the cathedral presents throughout the midnight hours of Easter Friday. Scattered through the immense nave, across which

[1] *The Soul of Spain*, p. 54.

the huge dark veil covering the High Altar throws a
gloomy shadow, women groan and lament the night
long.   But after pealing bells have announced on the
morrow that Christ is risen, the populace rises with
Him from its week of mourning . . . to attend the
first bull-fight of the season !   The lack of an ethic
in Spanish religion constitutes its problem, as it constituted the problem of the religion transplanted in the
New World by the Last Crusade.

Having no necessary connection with either right
reason or right conduct, this religion has best been
propagated by awakening fear.   Men must be fright-
ened into believing.   " The sermon that bears fruit,"
says Father Vieira, a preacher of the sixteenth century,
" is the one which produces pain, when the hearer
trembles, when he goes from the sermon confused and
dumbfounded."   In order to awaken the " Coalman's
faith," and save a soul from death, it might be necessary
on occasion to threaten the body by suffering and
death, and even to sever the golden cord of terrestrial
life.   Thus the rack, as one has put it, " became a
mystic weapon in the hands of Torquemada," and the
Inquisition could be regarded as a means of grace.

A Christ known in life as an infant and in death as
a corpse, over whose helpless childhood and tragic
fate the Virgin Mother presides ; a Christ who became
man in the interests of eschatology, whose permanent
reality resides in a magic wafer bestowing immortality ; a Virgin Mother who by not tasting death,
became the Queen of Life,—that is the Christ and
that the Virgin who came to America !   He came as
Lord of Death and of the life that is to be ; she came
as Sovereign Lady of the life that now is.

(c) *Christophers in the World of Columbus*

Christ came to America.   As we have seen,
Columbus considered his very name prophetic of the

main mission of his life, to take Him to the New World. Some of the early " Christophers " who followed the great Genovese have already passed before us ; *conquistadores* with a Cross on their banners ; martial monks like Valverde ; *encomenderos*, the land-lord evangelists ; the *Anticonquistador* Las Casas, who " bought Christ " at a dear price ; heroic mission-aries like Anchieta ; theocratic empire builders like the Jesuits who went to Paraguay. Besides these there came from Spain and Portugal, or were born in South America itself, thousands of now forgotten names who, as priests, monks or nuns, were " Christophers " by profession. To be able to appraise the religious significance of the life and teaching of these pro-fessional " Christophers," we must regard them from three distinct angles : their personality, their method of religious instruction, and the concrete picture of Christ which they presented to their converts and catechumens.

Many of the Catholic priests, monks and nuns who came to South America from the mother lands, as well as many others who were born in the new lands, were pure and consecrated souls who lived in strict accordance with their conscience and their vision of Christ. Las Casas and Anchieta were not alone. Taking only those born in the New World, we have creole religious types such as Santa Rosa of Lima, through casual contact with whom the Spanish Cavalier Don Ramiro, hero of the famous South American novel, *La Gloria de Don Ramiro*,[1] was con-verted from being a libertine knight into an ascetic monk. Another such was the Peruvian friar, Martín de Porras. " There was in the Colonial epoch," says Dr José Gálvez, " a very interesting creole in the person of the blessed Fray Martín de Porras, in whom is found a sentiment of charity and love extending to all beings, even to animals, and in whom there shines

[1] By the Argentine author, Enrique Larreta.

a kindly Franciscan attitude towards life ; but he is unique." [1]

There lived in Argentina in the early Republican period a veritable saint in the person of Father Esquiu, Bishop of Cordoba. Besides being a cultured man and a great orator, Esquiu was an ideal pastor of souls. So humble and retiring was he that, having learned of his appointment to the Archbishopric of Buenos Aires, he fled into Bolivia to avoid having to take office. A distinguished fellow-countryman has called him " the man most like to the saints who has been born on Argentine soil." And yet even the saintly Esquiu was more of an ascetic than a mystic.

The observation has been made by the Peruvian literary critic, José de la Riva Aguero, that the Colonial period produced no truly mystic figures or writers, but simply ascetics. Another indubitable fact is that the literary output of South American Catholicism has been infinitesimally small. It is extraordinary but none the less true, that the traditional " bearers of Christ" in these countries have not produced, from the time of the Conquest until now, a really great and original book on Christianity.

On the other hand, a very large number of professional " Christophers " in these lands—in South American opinion the greater number—so far from living Christ, have denied Him by their lives. It is difficult to exaggerate the moral conditions which have prevailed in the ranks of the South American priesthood. Until the most recent times, clerical chastity was not the rule but the exception.

A well-known novel by a Peruvian authoress, written towards the end of last century and entitled *Aves sin Nido*,[2] paints things as they have been and to a very great extent still are in this connection. Two

---

[1] Quoted from a paper specially prepared for the author, sections of which can be read in *Christian Work in South America*, Vol. II., Report No. 11.   [2] *Birds without a Nest*.

young people fall in love. On the eve of their wedding they discover, to their horror, that they are both the children of the same bishop. The mother of the young woman is the wife of a simple Indian ; the mother of her lover, the wife of a local village magnate. A priest, Pascual, who plays a leading part in the novel, makes the remark, " Unhappy is the man who is thrown into the desert of the priesthood without the support of family life." When the noble couple who adopted Marcela, the helpless heroine of the story, pass through Arequipa, the capital of Southern Peru, on their way to the coast, Doña Lucía says to her husband Don Fernando : " I have been struck by two things in this town, the number of friars who walk about the streets, and (with a sigh from the bottom of her heart) the surprising number of orphans in the *Casa de los Expósitos*.[1] Oh! Fernando, I know that in the lower classes a woman does not throw away bits of her soul like that. . . . May God forgive my evil thought, but this idea has suggested to me the saddest thoughts, as I remembered, without wanting to, Marcela's secret."

Anyone who is intimately acquainted with South American life knows how common it is for pious Catholics to make a clear-cut distinction between a priest as a man and as a religious functionary. Many will listen to him say mass who would not think of inviting him into their homes.

Passing to the pedagogical method of the South American " Christopher," we find it is distinguished by two main characteristics. It is catechetical and it is sensuous. Religion has been presented to the understanding by means of crystallized definitions and formulas, and to the sentiments in the seductive guise of ceremonial.

An admirable description of the catechetical method of religious education as pursued by Spanish and

---

[1] An orphanage with a revolving box in the outer wall where unwanted infants can be deposited, to be taken in charge by the religious sisters within.

Spanish American priestly mentors is given us by Luis
de Zulueta, one of the most distinguished pedagogues
and men of letters in contemporary Spain.   Zulueta
introduces his description of this method as· employed
within the pale of Catholicism by an anecdote of the
religious education of the famous German writer
Novalis.   The anecdote is so picturesque and symbolic that we cannot resist the temptation of quoting
it.   " Tieck relates," he says, " that on one occasion
when he went to call on the father of Novalis, during the boyhood of the latter, he heard old Herr
Hardenburg shouting and scolding in an adjoining
room.   ' What is the matter ? ' he asked in surprise.
' Nothing,' replied the butler composedly, ' the Governor is giving his son the religious lesson ' ! "

And then he goes on : " We have listened at some
time or other to the monotonous sing-song of a group
of children who automatically recite pages and pages
of the catechism of Christian doctrine.   The mechanism of memory makes lamentable prodigies.   In
monotonous tone they go on repeating series and
lists of words : ten commandments, then other five,
seven sacraments, fourteen articles, other fourteen
works of mercy, seven sins, seven virtues, three
enemies of the soul, three new virtues, other four
more, three powers, five senses, seven gifts, twelve
fruits, eight beatitudes, four last things, nine things for
which venial sin is pardoned. . . . In addition to that,
a string of questions and answers ; how many natures
has Christ, how many persons, how many under-
standings, how many wills, how many memories. . . .
They are giving the children the religious lesson ! "

To which Zulueta adds this observation: " The effort
is great ; great is the fatigue.   What more can be done
to prevent the fulfilment of Christ's yearning in the
Gospels : ' Suffer the children to come unto Me ' ? " [1]

No further comment is needed on this method of

---

[1] *El Ideal en la Educación*, pp. 26-27.

presenting religion and Christ to youth. The consequences it has produced are commentary enough.
Those who have received their religious education by
this method have either been lulled into the " Coalman's faith," or they have reacted radically and
tragically against all religion. In South America by
far the greater number have followed the second path.
The most violent anti-clericals on the continent have
been educated in clerical institutions.

The great masters of the sensuous method have
been the Jesuits. The followers of Loyola made the
discovery that ideas germinate best when the imagination has been surrounded by a sensuous atmosphere.
So they set themselves with the greatest care to prepare
the environment most suitable for the moulding of
thought. As their chief aim was not to transform
personality but to use it for their own ends, they
worked from the outside to the inside. They strove
to dominate and mould the minds of the children and
of primitive people by the sensuousness of art and the
appeal of rewards ; while by political methods they
sought to turn whole societies into vassals of their
will. In the words of the eminent Portuguese historian and psychologist, Oliveira Martins, " they tried
to win the world for God, not with the arms of heaven
but with those of earth ; not by means of preaching
and example but by politics and art." [1]

Rubén Darío, generally regarded as the greatest of
Latin-American poets, was educated in a Jesuit college
in Nicaragua. In his autobiography he gives us the
following illuminating account of his experiences as
a pupil : " I entered what was called the Congregations of Jesus, and wore in the ceremonies the blue
girdle and medal of the members of the congregation.
About that time there was a great scandal. During
the festival of St Luis Gonzaga the Jesuits used to put
a letter-box on the high altar of the church. In this

---

[1] *Historia de la Civilización Ibérica*, p. 379.

box all those who wished to petition or correspond
with St Luis and the most Holy Virgin could post their
letters.   The padres took the letters out and burned
them in the presence of the public, but it was said that
before doing so they read them.   In this way they became masters of many family secrets, and increased
their influence by this and other means.   The government decreed their expulsion, but not before I had the
opportunity of attending the exercises of St Ignatius
of Loyola.   I was delighted with the exercises, and, so
far as I was concerned, they could have gone on inde-
finitely, because of the appetizing viands and delicious
chocolate with which the reverend fathers regaled me."[1]

In the Jesuit ideal of education the love of truth
for its own sake plays little or no part.   According to
Father Miguel Mir, a late member of the Spanish
Academy, and probably the most eminent man who ever
left the Jesuit Order, Jesuit intellectuality has been characterized by two main features : first, " a spirit of independence and opposition to every form of education
different from their own, and, in particular, to that
which they found established and formed by tradition ;
and, secondly, the absence, attenuation or falsification
of the spirit which is scientific in the true sense and
which is inspired by the pure love of truth and by the
disinterested desire to seek it, know it and declare it."[2]

With this agrees a story told by Unamuno, who
as a boy was educated in the school of St Luis
Gonzaga of Bilbao.   A medical friend of his was once
sent for to visit the Seminary of the Company of Jesus
in Oña, in order to attend a novice who was ill.   In
a gallery in the private part of the building his eye
fell on " a tableau representing St Michael the Arch-
angel with the devil Satan at his feet.   Satan, the rebel
Angel, held in his hands . . . a microscope !   A

[1] La Vida de Rubén Darío, p. 29.
[2] Historia Interna Documentada de la Compañía de Jesús.   From the section
" La enseñanza de la Fé."

microscope is the symbol of hyperanalysis." [1]   To
pry too much into the nature and meaning of things
was diabolical, so far as the heads of that establishment were concerned.

The company of professional " Christophers " who
undertook to nurture the new South American lands
in the faith of Christ proceeded very differently and
achieved very different results from the men who
undertook a similar task in North America.   And
here we think not only of the Protestant pastors who
accompanied the *Mayflower* expedition and their
successors, till the end of last century ; we think also
and very especially of the Roman Catholic priests and
monks who went to the French province of Quebec.
Most of the latter were men of the Las Casas and
Anchieta type, with an evangelical sense of their
mission.   They kept out of politics and were deeply
interested in all the problems of the colonists.   Says
Dr Juan B. Terán, the late President of the Argentine
University of Tucumán, referring to this contrast :
" The French Church in North America was distinguished for its apostolic fervour—the French
missionary disdained purely commercial politics, and
by the implantation of agriculture, succeeded in trans-
planting a genuine Christian Church."   As a result
Canadian Catholicism to-day is strong and militant.
In North America the propagation of Christianity,
whether Protestant or Catholic, was characterized by
its strongly ethical and practical character ; Roman
Catholic propaganda in South America has been
characterized, until the dawn of the present century,
by its preponderating emphasis on dogma and ritual.

(d) *The Creole Christ*

If it be true that each Life of Christ is much more the
autobiography of its author than it is the biography of

[1] *L'Agonie du Christianisme*, p. 129.

Jesus, it is equally true that nations tend to delineate Christ after their own image. What kind of portrait of Christ did South American " Christophers " succeed in imprinting upon the thought and imagination of the people ? In what resultant portrait has South American religiosity expressed its conception of Him ? What does the Creole Christ look like and how does He act ? It might be said, in general terms, that the Christ who became naturalized in South America is the Christ who was born in Tangiers, the Christ of popular religious tradition in Spain. It would be an interesting study to consider how far religious life in South America has been a simple prolongation of the religious life of Spain and Portugal, and how far it is different ; how far the Creole Christ is a simple replica of the Spanish Christ and in what respects He has been modified. We shall get further, however, if we consider the traditional Christ of South America in direct relation to the New Testament picture of the Christian Lord as we find Him portrayed in the Synoptic Gospels and in the Pauline and Johannine writings.

The first thing that strikes us in the Creole Christ is His lack of humanity. As regards His earthly life, He appears almost exclusively in two dramatic roles—the role of the infant in his mother's arms, and the role of a suffering and bleeding victim. It is the picture of a Christ who was born and died, but who never lived. The great formative and decisive period of Jesus' life between helpless, unthinking infancy and His virile resolution to die with the untold suffering this entailed, is strangely passed over. Why is it that the only moments in the life of Christ which have received emphasis are His childhood and death ? Because the two central truths of Christianity are Incarnation and Atonement, someone answers. Yes, but incarnation is only the prologue of a life, while atonement is its epilogue. The reality of the former is unfolded in life and guaranteed by living ; the efficacy of the latter is

derived from the quality of the life lived.   The Divine
Child in His Mother's arms receives His full significance
only when we see the man at work in the carpenter's
shop, receive the Spirit in the baptismal waters of
Jordan, battle hungry and lonely with the tempter,
preach the glad tidings of the Kingdom to the poor,
heal the sick and raise the dead, call the heavy laden
and children to His side, warn the rich and denounce
hypocrites, prepare His disciples for life and Himself
for death, and then lay down His life not as a mere
victim of hate or destiny, but voluntarily, and in dying
ask the Father to forgive His slayers.   In the same way
the Crucified, in mortal anguish on the cross, is transfigured when we think that in life He had experienced
the temptations of a strong man and overcame them.
It was the Man who died, the true, the second Man, the
Lord from heaven as a man, such a man as never has
been nor shall be.

The manhood of Christ, however, has made little
appeal to South American worshippers.   Why ?   Because they have known no Christ save one whom they
could patronize.   An infant can be patronized ; so
can a suffering victim and a dead man ; but the Christ
of the Gospels cannot.   He would not receive the
patronage of tears even on His way to Golgotha.
Christ is patronized in the elaborate Nativity festival
at Christmas time, and again in the sombre festivities
that mark the course of Holy Week.   By such patronage pent-up sentiments of parental piety or of tragic,
sympathetic emotion well up and are exhausted.

Jesus Christ has had a religious, or in Aristotelian
language a " cathartic," value for South American
worshippers.   The contemplation of Him has provided them with an emotional safety valve, but they
have not regarded Him as ethically significant.   Their
exclusive interest in Christ's meaning for death and
immortality has led them to ignore the One who by
the lake-side told men how to live.   Because the

reading of the New Testament has been traditionally discouraged and because Christ has not been associated with life and living problems, people in general have not come face to face with that tremendous Leader who was conscious that He had come into the world to be the Lord of Life. It has thus come about that the most impressive aspects of His teaching have never been made a rule of life nor the most impressive aspects of His conduct become an inspiration for living. His words, "Follow me," have been utterly meaningless. His supreme command has afforded no guidance for the daily round, the common task.

The vision of the Risen Christ, on the other hand, whether He be conceived, in New Testament language, as King and Priest at God's right hand, or as living in the souls of Christians, has been no less dim than that of the historical Jesus. His sovereign lordship over all the details of existence, a Saviour King who is deeply interested in us and to whom we can bring our joys and sorrows and perplexities, is neither visualized nor experienced. A most extraordinary thing has happened. Christ has lost prestige as a helper in the affairs of life. He lives in virtual banishment, while the Virgin and the saints are daily approached for life's necessities. The latter are considered to be much more human and accessible than He. And, curiously enough, as an Argentine writer has pointed out, the saints who are most petitioned and whose figures are most frequently reproduced in *estampas*, as coloured pictures of the saints are called, are the lesser luminaries. In popular devotion the great and well-known saints tend to suffer the same fate as Christ. Their very eminence makes them less human and accessible. The common people feel more at their ease and more confident of success, if they present their pleas to the *Santos Menores*,[1] the quality of whose life was less different from their own. The ordinary worshipper

---

[1] Lesser Saints.

is a practical polytheist whose pantheon is presided over by Our Lady. She alone has never lost her crown. The Virgin is the real divinity of popular religion. The Trinity crowns her and the saints lead up to her.

But at what a cost to the Virgin's Son has this evolution taken place ! When the man in the street in Argentina wants to say of someone that he merits his supreme contempt for his poor-spiritedness and pusillanimity, he says, " *Es un Cristo*," or " *Es un pobre Cristo*." [1] How different from the connotation this name is receiving in India, where it has become the symbol of spiritual strength ! Ricardo Rojas, the eminent Argentine writer, from whom we have already quoted, thus describes the popular conception of Christ to-day in his and other South American lands : " Christ," he says, " has been made to appear as an archetype of beggars, a kind of human pariah, a footstool for everybody's feet, a compendium of miseries and a paradigm of indignities." Unto this last has the dehumanization of Christ brought Him.

The Christ, however, who becomes lost to life by a process of dehumanization is later restored as a fetich. His image, His humanity and His name have all been converted into fetichistic realities.

In the Church of Santo Domingo in Lima is a recumbent image of Christ. It is called *El Señor del Sepulcro*,[2] and represents Christ laid in the tomb. This particular image is the chief centre of devotion during Holy Week. Surrounded by a host of burning candles it appears to sweat. The faithful, who file past it on the afternoon and evening of Good Friday, buy pieces of cotton wool which have been dipped in the perspiration. These they carefully preserve as amulets.

Lima possesses another famous effigy of Christ, in

[1] " He is a Christ," or " He is a poor Christ."
[2] The Lord of the Sepulchre.

H

the form of a painting called *El Señor de los Milagros*.[1] According to popular tradition a likeness of Christ on the cross was discovered by a negro during an earthquake which devastated the city in the eighteenth century.   It appeared in a wall which remained standing amid the ruins.   Since that day the sacred picture has been the religious patron of the coloured population of the Peruvian capital, and enjoys an immense reputation as a miracle-worker.

Ica, a principal town to the south of Lima, was the seat of a very sacred wooden image of Christ called *El Señor de Lurin*.   To this image the country people were wont to pray for a good harvest and other temporal blessings.   Some fourteen years ago the Church in which the idol had its shrine was burned to the ground.   No sooner had the fire been extinguished than a frenzied multitude rescued the charred remains of *El Señor* and bore them in procession through the streets, to the sound of the piercing dirge : " God is dead, God is dead ! "   That image was the divinity the people lived by, and by its destruction they were filled with blank dismay.

Such examples might be multiplied around the Continent, particularly from the life of provincial towns. A dehumanized Christ has been given a materialized human likeness to which special virtue is attached.

Less repulsively materialistic, but not less fetichistic, is the rehumanization of Christ in the viaticum and the Sacred Heart.   One of the traditional sights of Lima is the procession of the *Santísimo*, vividly described by José Galvez in his book *Una Lima que se va*.   " The toll of a bell announces that the *Santísimo* is coming to the neighbourhood.   Beneath a dais covered with cloth of gold walks the parish priest holding aloft the Cibarium with its divine food.   Four members of a religious brotherhood support his canopy.   Behind comes a throng, composed mostly of women, bearing

[1] The Lord of Miracles.

lighted candles. From time to time they break into a chaunt. They are on their way to bring the Bread of Immortality to a dying man."

Tradition relates that on one occasion the Pericholi,[1] the notorious paramour of one of the viceroys, was passing along in her rich calash when she met the parish priest bearing the *Santísimo*. Conscious-stricken at the contrast between the luxury in which her sinful self was travelling and the lowly appearance of the procession, she offered her seat to the priest while she joined the sorrowful throng behind. Long years afterwards, when it was proposed that thenceforth the viaticum should be carried through the streets inside a carriage, the ladies of Lima organized a demonstration of protest, while on the banner which they bore aloft were blazoned the words : " *Morir por la religión.*"[2]

The most modern attempt to convert Christ into a popular fetich is the worship of the Sacred Heart. The truly historical and the eternally real humanity of Christ having disappeared from popular religion, the symbol of his material humanity is substituted for it. In 1923 the Republic of Peru was about to be consecrated with great pomp to a huge bronze image of the Christ of the Sacred Heart. The day was fixed for the ceremony. In the presence of the highest authorities of Church and State, the effigy was to be placed in a niche on the front wall of the cathedral of Lima overlooking the main Plaza. The local Press had protested against what was regarded by the majority of citizens as a regression to mediævalism and idolatry ; but in vain. Suddenly, however, on the eve of the ceremony, a formidable protest movement was organized by students and workmen and the consecration ceremony was suspended till a more convenient season.

---

[1] The Pericholi appears in Thornton Wilder's novel, *The Bridge of San Luis Rey.*

[2] *Die for the Faith*, in the chapter entitled " El Viático.

God forbid that any effort to make Jesus Christ more real to human beings, or to keep ever before them the reality of His compassion, should be disparaged. But to materialize in bronze the qualities of which His heart is the symbol will not make the historical Jesus or the eternal Christ more real. The special qualities of Christ requiring to receive greatest emphasis in South American lands to-day cannot be symbolized by His heart. Their best symbol would be His eyes, those apocalyptic eyes which could blaze on occasion like a " flame of fire." Calm and sorrowful reflection obliges us to endorse the opinion of Unamuno when he says : " The cult of the Sacred Heart of Jesus, or hierocardicracy, is the grave of the Christian religion." [1] It is the Christ of the whip and *not* the Christ of the Sacred Heart that South America needs to be confronted with.

Even the name of Jesus has become a fetich. In popular religion it acts as a powerful charm. The autobiography of Rubén Darío affords us a good illustration. The poet is describing the religious experiences of his boyhood. " I dreaded such devotions," he says, " for example, the approach of the festival of the Holy Cross. For, Oh God of the Gods, Thou canst not imagine what a martyrdom it was to me at my tender age. When the day came, we would all assemble before the images, while my grandmother recited the prayer, a prayer which, after several ejaculations, ended with these words :

' Satan, avaunt !
For me you cannot daunt,
Because on Holy Cross day,
I ' Jesus ' a thousand times did say.' [2]

" The truth is that, we had to say the word Jesus a thousand times, and that was unending. Jesus !

---

[1] *L'Agonie du Christianisme*, p. 125.
[2] " *Vete de aquí Satanás,*
que en mi parte no tendrás,
porque el día de la Cruz
dije mil veces : Jesús."

Jesus! Jesus! up to a thousand! and at times one lost count and had to begin again." [1] A pagan parody of the promise that every tongue shall one day acknowledge that Jesus Christ is *Lord!*

Hitherto the true Lordship of Christ has not been acknowledged in South American religion. He has been known as the Lord of the Sepulchre and the Lord of Good Harvests, as the archetype of wounded love and the material pledge of immortality; He has been known, too, as the possessor of a magic name. But He remains to be known as Jesus, the Saviour from sin and the Lord of all life.

(e) *Peace! Peace! . . .*

Peace is one of the great words of human speech, as the reality which it connotes is one of the chief goals of human effort. It is the quest for peace that has given birth to all religion and philosophy. But how diverse the inner moods this word is used to cover! There is the peace of the motionless ocean of Nirvana, and there is peace that is like a river. There is the peace of the egotistical sluggard who whiles away his time amid the sights and sounds and aromas of an unreal world, and there is the peace of the tireless worker who loses sleep and tranquillity, friends and fortune, in an unselfish effort to build a real world of truth and goodness. "Peace, peace," said some popular leaders of old time who were careless and criminally unconscious of their people's danger. "My peace I leave with you," said Jesus, as He braced Himself up for His passion.

Which peace most truly characterizes religious life and experience in South American Catholicism? How has the " peace of God " which is Christianity's inseparable fruit been interpreted in these lands? Let this question be answered by representative

[1] *La Vida de Rubén Darío*, pp. 27-28.

citizens of the Continent, men whose eminent position and serene judgment give them the right to offer an opinion.

We take first the opinion of Dr Francisco García Calderón, who is perhaps the South American writer most widely known and read abroad. He is a Peruvian, and the author of the well-known book *Latin America : its Rise and Progress*. In an article entitled *La Restauración Católica*, to be found in his book *Ideologías*, published a few years ago, García Calderón says as follows : " American (meaning Latin American) Catholicism has become converted into a social formula and an elegant rite. Parasitic practices suffocate traditional belief. Minute precepts are substituted for mystic fervour, moral elevation and the disquietude produced by the thought of destiny and death. According to an Italian critic many of our Catholics pass their lives offering fetichistic adoration to their saints, of whom they ask the gift of a good harvest and a prize in the lottery. An external creed like this is impotent to create morality. Unless there be a religious renaissance to teach how the letter killeth and the spirit giveth life, America, now threatened by Caliban, will become the theatre of impure greed and utilitarian orgies." This opinion regarding the peace born of religious æstheticism, social etiquette and ethical indifference, coming as it does from a man who was educated in a school of French priests in Lima, who has passed a good part of his life in France and Belgium, who is himself a Catholic, and is preoccupied about the future of Catholicism in South America, is particularly significant.

Alberto Cabero is a Chilean sociologist who in 1926 published a large book entitled *Chile y los Chilenos*. He writes as follows regarding the religious life of his country : " The upper classes, especially the women (who have received from childhood up a religious education), limit their religious life to the scrupulous observance of the sacred formulas, to assiduous attendance upon the ritual ordinances of the Church and to the fervent recital of the prescribed prayers. They go to Church through habit. They attend the sacraments, and some of them put on the appearance of Christian piety. The factors that oblige them to adopt this attitude are the need of conforming to the established social order, their personal docility and respect for general opinion, their fear of the unknown. That true religious feeling which demands inwardness and introspection, that mysticism which creates the personal need of getting in touch with a supersensible power and which is a source of perseverance and self-sacrifice, cannot possibly be acquired amid the intellectual and sentimental dispersion which disturbs our life. These are found now only among the few select believers who generally live apart from the world's noise."[1]

Cabero refers particularly to the religious life of women because, while the great majority of the men are everywhere in South America notoriously irreligious, the women have conserved at least the externals of religion. His reference also to the few select believers who find spiritual peace and satisfaction apart from the world's noises is exceedingly suggestive. The highest peace which Spanish or Spanish-American Catholicism has been able to conceive is that of the monastery or of complete retirement from the real world and its problems. As to the piety of the clergy, a very remarkable Spanish priest who has laboured many years in Chile in different parishes made this statement to the author in 1929. "I have met only one person in the ecclesiastical life of Chile who gave me the impression of living a saintly life. She was the prioress of a convent." This good padre was heart-broken over

[1] Cabero, *Chile y los Chilenos*, pp. 375-76.

the state of religion in the country. He made this terrible indictment of the morals of the clergy. " Of some six hundred priests whom I have known in different South American countries I calculate that five per cent. are sexually pure."

Among the prizes for literature bestowed on national writers in the Argentine Republic in 1928, one of the chief was given to Dr Juan B. Terán for two books he had written on Spanish-American history and sociology. Their English titles are : *The Birth of Spanish America* and *The Welfare of Spanish America*.[1] Dr Terán has been for over twenty years President of the University of Tucumán, and is, so far as we know, a Catholic.

Most significant is the heading, *The Irreligiosity of America*, which he gives to one of the chapters in his second book. " For men of the upper class," he says, " religion is a woman's affair. They take up towards it the position of benevolent neutrality. They are not atheists, because to be an atheist is in a way an evidence of having reflected on the religious problem. They are simply indifferent and Epicurean.

" In so far as religion is regarded as an affirmation that the universe has a supreme Cause with whom man aspires to have communion ; in so far as it is a rational and mystic sense of the Deity that requires no ritual forms to stimulate it ; that is to say, in so far as it signifies that kind of pure spirituality which has its analogy in science and art, something that creates imperative duties with no other sanction than that of conscience, while exercising over life the controlling force of a feeling, we may say that Spanish America is that part of the Western World which possesses religion in the lowest degree." [2]

To this expression of opinion we add that of Terán's countryman, Ricardo Rojas, probably the

[1] *El Nacimiento de la América Española*, and *La Salud de la América Española*.
[2] *La Salud de la América Española*, p. 68.

---

most eminent man of letters in all Latin-America to-day. In 1927, while President of the University of Buenos Aires, Rojas wrote a book entitled *The Invisible Christ*, which created a profound sensation in Latin-American lands. To the general religious position of Rojas we shall have occasion to refer in a later chapter. For our present purpose it will be sufficient to quote his opinion regarding religious life as it is. The book is written in dialogue form. In the course of a conversation between a provincial bishop and his guest, who happens to be the author himself, the former makes the remark that " the Christian tradition is a living reality in all the Iberian peoples of the New World." To which his guest replies : " That is doubtless true, so far as concerns Catholic tradition as an external form, but it is not true if we think of Christian sentiment as the inspiration of life." He thereupon proceeds to expound his meaning as follows : " Neither the fetichism of the masses nor the religious affectation of the aristocracy is Christian. The *culto* is practised, but its significance is unknown. Charity among us here is nothing more than an egotistical instinct or worldly vanity. The reconciliation which St Augustine was able to realize in his life between the acceptance of ecclesiastical discipline and the need of understanding God as a lofty expression of truth, searching for Him within oneself, is something which is neither practised nor understood in our country. If I were to write a book to expound my restless musings on this problem of the soul, I should be looked upon with suspicion and hostility." [1]

A little further on he adds: " There does not exist in the whole of Spanish America either a taste for, or the comprehension of, these problems. In some countries, as in ours, for example, there never has been true religious unrest. . . . What is lacking is the 'interiorization' of Christianity as a necessity of conscience."

[1] *El Cristo Invisible*, p. 247.

These two heads of Argentine universities are agreed that South American Catholicism has lacked two constitutive features of the Christian religion. It has lacked inward spiritual experience and it has lacked outward ethical expression. People have possessed religion, but a religion has not possessed them. They have practised religion, but have not lived it. Religion has been neither a subject of intellectual preoccupation nor an incentive to virtuous living. Souls have not been in agony. There has been indifference and there has been peace; but the latter has been that eerie, æsthetic peace which haunts the graveyard; the peace of death, not the peace of life.

Yet, let it not surprise us to find that this peace has its advocates in South America to-day. Some years ago another Argentine man of letters, Manuel Gálvez, wrote a book called *El Solar de la Raza*.[1] It is an evocation of Spain and her traditions, especially her religious tradition. In the first part of the book Gálvez, who is an ardent Catholic, makes a frank confession regarding the contemporary Catholicism of Spain. "There does not exist in Spain," he says, "that religious fervour which the unprejudiced observer may see in France, nor the profound and militant Catholicism of the Belgians, Canadians, Irish, Bavarians and Italians. The mystic atmosphere which one feels in Spain proceeds from past ages when faith was more intense, and not from the Spaniards of to-day who are in general formalists rather than believers."[2] Towards the end of the volume he quotes with enthusiasm some words of the French author Maurice Barrés in his *Colline Sacrée*. The quotation is as follows: "Whoever you be, says the chapel, that is, the Church and her discipline, there is nothing in you, nothing excellent, which prevents you from accepting my assistance. I will put you in agreement with life."[3]

---

[1] *The Native Home of the Race.*   [2] *Id.*, p. 49.   [3] *Id.*, p. 255.

These words of Barrés stir Gálvez to say what is
deepest in his heart about religion.   He breaks into
a glowing panegyric of the education offered by the
Church.   " Only by following a norm, only by
discipline, can we acquire true liberty of spirit.   In-
credulity and doubt are terrible hells.   They lead to
the disintegration and dispersion of the self.   Those
who return to the Church recover soul unity, that is
to say, happiness."   A reference follows to the great
master of peace.   " Ignatius Loyola loved obedience
above all other virtues, and by the profound penetration of his genius he found in it the elixir of our
inward happiness.   For that reason the teaching of
the Jesuits tends to inculcate in children the spirit of
obedience and of discipline.   That is to say, *it tends
to prevent them suffering the torments of unrest, and assures
the return of peace."* [1]

How naïvely unconscious Galvez seems to be that
a close connection may and does exist between the
formalism and lack of mystic fervour which he found
in Spain, and which he well knows to be the rule
in South America, and the obedience and peace of
Loyola !   And is he quite sure that the Order which
is called by the name of Jesus has not succeeded in
creating a religion and an ethic which are equally
hostile to the religion of Jesus and to the faith of
Christ ?

Let him not be surprised either that among his own
countrymen and other South Americans in general
ardent spirits should be found who began to draw
the distinction between Hispanic Catholicism and
Christianity, and who express their preference for one
or the other.   Unamuno relates that he met on one
occasion a South American writer who expressed a
decided preference for the former.   " I shall never
forget while I live," says the Spanish thinker, " what
was said to me by a very famous and much-discussed

[1] *Id.,* p. 257.

South American writer in the course of a conversation on religion. I, friend Unamuno, am a Catholic, but not a Christian. I am drawn to Catholicism precisely by what repels you from it, that, namely, which differentiates it from the other Christian confessions, its pagan ballast, the pomp of its worship, and its casuistry, especially its casuistry, that marvel of Jesuitism." [1]

On the other hand, Octavio Bunge, the author of *Nuestra América*, the best book ever written on South American sociology, indicts as being anti-Christian the religion which had its origin in Spain and which was propagated in the New World. " Spanish Catholicism," he says, " was an anti-Christian Catholicism," while " the mass of the people did not take from Christianity more than outward forms." [2]

A Christ came to South America who has put men in agreement with life, who has told them to accept it as it is, and things as they are, and truth as it appears to be. But the other?—He who makes men dissatisfied with life as it is, and things as they are, and tells them that, through Him, life shall be transformed, and the world overcome, and His followers put in agreement with reality, God and truth? He wanted to come, but His way was barred. . . . But now again spring voices announce His coming.

[1] From the essay on Riva Aguero's book, *El Carácter de la Literatura del Peru Independiente*, Vol. VII. of Unamuno's *Ensayos*.
[2] P. 65.

CHAPTER VII

THE OTHER SPANISH CHRIST IN SPAIN'S GOLDEN AGE

THE Christ who was naturalized in South America is not, fortunately, the only Christ in the spiritual history of the Iberian people. There is a Spanish religious tradition which after a long subterranean history begins to form runnels on the surface again. A study of this tradition will teach us what might have been and what may still be in the life of Spain and South America. No full-orbed outlook on the religious situation in the Hispanic world can pass it by, no constructive religious policy for South America can ignore it.

(a) *The Fountain of a Lost Tradition*

In the religious tradition and present-day life of Spain there is another Christ. He is distinct from the Christ of popular faith and the Christ of official propaganda. We meet Him first in the thirteenth century in Raymond Lull. He appears later in the lives and writings of the great mystics of the sixteenth century. He stands out in bold relief in the thought and work of the great men who in the same century threw in their lot with the Protestant Reformation. We find Him in many a great religious rebel in the centuries that followed. In modern Spain this Christ has found a shrine in the lives of the two precursors of the new Spain that has recently come to the birth, Don Francisco Giner de los Ríos and Don Miguel de Unamuno.

This Christ and the pure religious passion He

awakened in many Spanish hearts in the sixteenth century shine out in the sublimest sonnet in the literature of Spain. No translation can do full justice to the passion that breathes in this matchless poem nor to the terse beauty of its verse ; but the following translation of Professor Allison Peers gives an admirable idea of the famous poem whose author is unknown.

> " I am not moved my God to love of Thee
> By Heav'n which Thou didst pledge me as reward.
> I am not moved to cease to grieve Thee, Lord,
> By thoughts and fears of Hell which threaten me.
> *Thou* mov'st me, O my God.   Mov'd sore am I
> To see Thee nailed upon that cruel tree,
> The scorn of men, wounded despitefully.
> Mov'd am I : Thou dost suffer and dost die.
> Mov'd am I thus, my Lord, to love Thee ; yea,
> Were there no Heav'n at all, I'd love Thee still,
> Were there no Hell, my due of fear I'd pay.
> Thou need'st not make me gifts to move my will,
> For were my hopes of Heav'n quite fled away,
> Yet this same love my heart would ever feel." [1]

Christ crucified is the poet's religious dynamic. He " surveys the wondrous Cross," and his heart is won forever.   Henceforth the love of Christ will be the compelling motive of his life and not the hope of reward or the fear of punishment, either in this life or in the life to come.   Religion is here a quality of life and not the simple prolongation of existence.   It is the passionate response of love and not a sordid

[1] " *No me mueve mi Dios para quererte*
El cielo que me tienes prometido,
Ni me mueve el infierno tan temido
Para dejar por eso de ofenderte.

" *Tú me mueves, Señor, muéveme el verte*
Clavado en una cruz y escarnecido ;
Muéveme ver tu cuerpo tan herido
Muévenme tus afrentas y tu muerte.

" *Muéveme en fin, tu amor, en tal manera*
Que, aunque no hubiera cielo yo te amara,
Y aunque no hubiera infierno, te temiera.
No tienes que me dar porque te quiera,
Porque aunque cuanto espero no esperara,
Lo mismo que te quiero te quisiera."

appeal for things. How different is this from the
sentiment contained in the popular lullaby :

" Give me an alms, my rosy-faced Lady,
   Or I'll filch thee the pearly tears of thy Baby.[1]

In Raymond Lull, the Spanish courtier of Mallorca,
who after his conversion became one of the greatest
Christian missionaries of all time, we discover the other
Christ. How sweetly falls upon our ear the music
of Lull's mystic tome, *The Book of the Lover and the
Beloved.* And again, how richly suggestive his famous
saying, " He who loves not lives not, and he who
lives by the Life cannot die."

For Lull, as for the author of the sonnet just quoted,
salvation is qualitative and not simply the endless prolongation of a temporal series. Christ is for him our
Life, our new, eternal Life. He does not immortalize
life as it is, but transforms it into what life should be.
The evidence, moreover, that we shall never die is not
that we believe in our immortality but that we love.

Raymond Lull is the precursor of a notable group
of mystic writers who flourished in Spain in the sixteenth century. Havelock Ellis has called this group
" the most potent and influential school of religious
passion that the European world can show."

The Spanish mystics were in general great solitary
souls, whose reciprocal influence upon each other, if
we except the friendship between John of the Cross
and the great Teresa, was slight. The intensity of
their religious passion has undoubtedly never been
surpassed, but, by the saddest and most tragic irony
in the history of Christianity, the incalculable potency
of their religious experience and ideas was not allowed
to germinate in the spiritual life of the Peninsula. The
greatest of them, Fray Luis de Granada, John of the
Cross, St Teresa and Fray Luis de León, lived under

---

[1] " *Dame una limosna, cara de rosa,*
       O hurtaréte las perlas que el niño llora."

the constant suspicion of heterodoxy, while all of them, save Santa Teresa, served a period in the prisons of the Inquisition. The great Teresa herself barely escaped confinement, and that only because she was a woman.

These seraphic Christian souls represented a spontaneous reform movement within the Spanish Catholic Church of their day. In their reforming zeal, John of the Cross and Teresa the Carmelite nun trudged through the land founding new religious houses with stricter vows, or reforming old ones. Distrusted and persecuted by the ecclesiastical authorities, and exercising but slight influence over the people, they ended their days in loneliness. In the following century they were canonized. Santa Teresa has become the patroness of Spain. It cannot be said, however, that, outside of a very limited circle, her spiritual passion has been an influence, or her ideas have borne fruit in the religious life of Spain. The same might also be said of the other Spanish mystics of the sixteenth century. Only in recent years have they been discovered and read by educated laymen. Azorín, one of the chief devotees of Spanish classical literature, tells us how it was but lately that he awoke to the beauties of Luis de Granada. The movement and tendencies represented by those great souls, and hundreds of others in their day, became a subterranean current in the religious life of the Peninsula. The work they began remained unfinished at the crossroad of Spain's destiny.

From the writings of these Spanish saints a picture can be obtained of a Christ into whose eyes Spain has never looked, a Christ whose name is Jesus, a Saviour, a Lover and a Friend. It would take too long to give a full picture of the Christ of the Spanish mystics, and His relation to the religious life. We must content ourselves with obtaining some glimpses of Him, as He reveals Himself in the light of the mystics' thought and experience. Supreme devotion to Christ is set forth in every case as the standard of life, and union with Him as the goal of all aspiring.

(b) *The Transfiguring Christ*

The greatest lyric in Spanish literature, and one of the greatest in the world's literature, is the *Cántico Espiritual* of John of the Cross. In it the mystic author interprets the Song of Songs in terms of his own experience. Like Bunyan's *Pilgrim's Progress*, it is a prison production, having been written in all probability during the author's imprisonment in Toledo, to which he had been condemned by the Holy Office. Only the Letters of Samuel Rutherford can be compared to this matchless poem as an expression of mystic passion for Christ.

The beginning of the love drama is described in an exquisite minor poem, popularly known as *En una Noche Oscura*. Night has fallen, and under its silent shadow the soul sets out in search of the Beloved :

" Upon a darksome night,
Fevered with love in love's anxiety,
O hapless, happy plight,
I went, none seeing me,
Forth from my house where all things quiet be." [1]

Her only light and guide was the fire that burned in her breast. But this fire made the night brighter than the dawning, so that it seemed to be the night itself that led her on unerringly to where the Beloved was. Beautiful symbol of the soul's instinct for Christ in the darkness of its extremity. The Beloved is found and hides himself again. In the *Canticle* the impassioned search continues :

" Reveal Thyself, I cry,
E'en though the glory of thy presence kill,
For sick of love am I,

[1] " *En una noche oscura.*
con ansias en amores inflamada,
¡ Oh dichosa ventura !
Salí sin ser notada
Estando ya mi casa sosegada.

I

And naught can cure my ill
Save only if of Thee I have my fill." [1]

When the love-wounded heart hears the voice of
the Beloved hailing her from the heights, and she is
able to rejoin him, all nature takes on a fresh sweetness
and becomes a party to the melody of perfect love.
The beauty of the Beloved is transferred to the world.
In His light the soul sees light and beauty everywhere.
And so she shouts—to quote from the admirable
translation of the *Canticle* by Mr Arthur Symons :—

> " Beloved, see, the hills,
> The lonely valleys clad with forest trees,
> The rushing, sounding rills,
> Strange islands, pleasant leas.
>
> .   .   .   .   .
>
> Beloved, let us sing !
> Clothed in Thy beauty now is every hill." [2]

This spiritual experience that oneness with God in
Christ makes the soul at home in nature, reminds us
of the experience of Saul Kane, in John Masefield's
poem, " The Everlasting Mercy." After experienc-
ing the " burning cataracts of Christ," and the breaking
in of the " bolted door," Kane knew that he had
" done with sin " and that Christ had given him birth
" to brother all the souls on earth." So into song he
burst :

> " Oh glory of the lighted mind
> How dead I'd been, how dumb, how blind,
> The station brook, to my new eyes
> Was babbling out of Paradise ;
> The waters rushing from the rain
> Were singing, Christ has risen again."

All nature had for him now a fresh smell and a
new radiant sheen, " and every bird and every beast

---

[1] " *Descubre tu presencia*
y máteme tu vista y hermosura
mira que es la dolencia
de amor, que no se cura
sino con la presencia y la figura."

[2] " *Mi Amado, las montañas,*
los valles solitarios nemorosos,

las ínsulas extrañas,
los ríos sonorosos,
el silbo de los aires amorosos.

.   .   .   .

Gocémonos, Amado,
y vámonos a ver en tu hermosura
al monte y al collado."

should share the crumbs broke at the feast." To become spiritually united to such a Christ means always to "consider the lilies" with new eyes, and behold with fresh wonder the wild birds' ways.

In the experience described in the *Canticle*, John of the Cross transcends the monasticism and asceticism of his religious environment and even of his own religious life. His poet's soul pursues a Christ who in Luis de León's phrase, "lives in the fields," the Lord and transfigurer of all things that have being.

If we endeavour to follow John of the Cross through the "dark night of the soul," up to the summit of "Mount Carmel," we lose sight of him in the empyrean of love's perfect union. Let us consider only some characteristic utterances regarding Christ which he distils on the way. Christ is for him "the sweetest Lover of all faithful souls." "Keep the likeness of Christ pure and clear in thy soul," he says. In another of his letters occur the words : "Jesus be in your souls, my daughters . . . I will indeed come to you, and you will perceive that I have not forgotten you, and we shall see the wealth that is gained by pure love and in the paths of eternal life, and the godly progress that you are making in Christ whose joy and crown His brides will be. A crown that ought not to go rolling on the ground, but should rather be taken by the hands of Angels and Seraphim and placed with reverence and esteem on the head of their Lord." [1]

Christ is all to St John of the Cross and ritual means little. He begs beginners in the spiritual life to beware of those who "load themselves with images, rosaries and crucifixes, both curious and costly." Let them likewise beware of "those who join in pilgrimages more for their own distraction than for the purposes of true devotion." Nor let them squander in adorning their oratories time that they should spend in prayer and inward recollection.

[1] Carta VI., *Obras del Místico Doctor San Juan de la Cruz*, Tomo III.

(c) *Lover and Lord*

Teresa de Jesús has been well named a " soul of fire." The classic symbol used to represent her is the visionary scene in which her heart was trans-verberated by an angel who plunged into it a fire-tipped arrow. Incandescent passion characterizes her conception and experience of Christ. He is her " Divine Husband." She speaks of Him generally as the " Lord," or " His Divine Majesty." Her sense that He belongs to her is so strong that she thinks of Him in one of her poems as her " captive." His captivity within her heart makes her heart free.[1]

Equally strong is Teresa's consciousness that she belongs to Christ and is inseparably and indissolubly one with Him. This mutual interpenetration receives most perfect expression in her account of a vision in which she beheld her soul to be a clear mirror in which Christ presented Himself to her view. " And this mirror," she adds, " I cannot say how, was likewise all sculptured in the Lord Himself, by a communica-tion of love which I cannot explain." When the soul sinned the mirror became dim, and then the Lord could not be seen in it.[2] In another beautiful passage she describes the origin and activity of the silkworm before it passes into a butterfly as a symbol of the fact that she must die that Christ may be born in her. She was passionately fond of flowers, because they and all natural objects were the handiwork of her Divine Husband.

The Christ of Santa Teresa is a living, active, power-ful and loving Being, who requires that the soul shall have no commerce with sin if it is to have communion with Him. Teresa's seraphic passion did not in-capacitate her, however, in the slightest for the routine affairs of life. She was the most practical of women. The Lord lent His aid, she had learned by experience,

---

[1] *Vide* Chapter I.   [2] *Vida de Santa Teresa de Jesús*, Chap. XL., 4.

in the discharge of the most menial tasks. " Understand," she says to her nuns, " that if your work is in the kitchen, the Lord walks among the pots, helping you inwardly and outwardly." [1]

It is greatly to be regretted, nevertheless, that Teresa, possessing as she did a very spiritual and at the same time highly ethical and practical view of Christ and of religion, should have limited the expression of it to monastic activities. Though she knew a Christ who was for the world, a Christ who was little more than a stranger in her land, she made Him a prisoner in her heart, or in the convents she founded. Of much higher religious value than the transverberation of Teresa's heart are the stigmata on the hands of St Francis, symbols of the cost at which the man of Assisi served men for the love of Jesus. We even find Teresa tinctured at times with a passion for the material Christ of Tangiers, who is earth. She was a devotee of what she calls the " *sacratísima Humanidad de Jesús*." " The Saint understands by this," says a distinguished South American writer, " not the human character of the Master nor His way of life as a man, but the corporeal, physical and material part of His person, a preoccupation which culminated at last in the idolatrous adoration of His fleshy heart." [2]

(d) *The Christ who is Jesus*

In the writings of the Augustinian monk Luis de León, the Christ, whom Teresa de Jesús knew and dealt with only subjectively, whom she kept imprisoned in her heart or in her convents, broke out from His confining walls and became fully objective for both devotion and thought. The Christ of experience became the Jesus of history and the Christ of faith.

[1] " Entre los pucheros anda el Señor," *Libro de las Fundaciones*, Chap. V.
[2] Julio Navarro Monzó, *Santa Teresa de Jesús y la Vida Espiritual Cristiana*, p. 26.

The keynote struck by Luis de León is that Christ must be *known* in the fullest Pauline and Johannine sense. "Know much of Christ," is the counsel he gives. "Man's true and proper wisdom," he says in the introduction to his great work,[1] "is to know much of Christ." This is the highest and divinest wisdom of all. For to understand Him is to understand all the treasures of God's wisdom, which, as St Paul says, ' are shut up in Him.' "

For Fray Luis, religion is the response of man's whole nature to Christ, the response of the intellect as well as of the heart. Santa Teresa, like the Magdalene at the open tomb, would fain luxuriate for ever in a physical experience of her Lord. Fray Luis understands the meaning of the words, " I ascend to my Father." His view of Christ becomes essentially objective. He considers Him not only as the source and centre of all his life, but also as the centre of all life and history and of the universe itself. His Christ is the Lord of created reality.

In *Los Nombres de Cristo*,[2] which the Spanish critic Menéndez y Pelayo calls the most perfect prose monument in Spanish literature, Fray Luis expounds his view of Christ. The book is written in dialogue form. A group of friends meet together to comment on the ideas of one of their number, not, however, within the precincts of a monastery or other religious building, but in a beautiful spot by the banks of the soft flowing Tormes, the river of Salamanca. For, as the author says, " *vive en los campos Cristo.*" [3]

Here is an out-of-doors view of religion. If with John of the Cross the love of nature was no more than a transient poetic mood, or as some critics aver, a purely literary device to imitate the nature colouring of the Song of Songs, with Luis de León nature was a passion. He felt it and loved it as Wordsworth did,

---

[1] *Los Nombres de Cristo.*   [2] *The Names of Christ.*
[3] " Christ lives in the fields."

and many of his incomparable lyrics rival in emotional realism the nature-poetry of the author of *Tintern Abbey*. It was none other than the greatest of Spanish lyrical poets who wrote *The Names of Christ*, and made his personages discourse by a riverside, in a grove made vocal by the song of birds. And yet, oh cruel irony, the book itself was composed during the five years the author spent in a prison cell in Valladolid! He had been imprisoned by the Holy Office for the terrible offence of having translated the Song of Songs into Spanish prose. His master passion was mortal sin in the eyes of his country's religious leaders. He dared to let religious reality loose from the cramping confines of an unknown language and of consecrated walls. " Christ for the world," he sang.

The names of Christ whose significance Fray Luis expounds are either prophetic titles of the Messiah in the Old Testament or symbolic names of Jesus in the New. He deals with fourteen of these. Christ is the Branch, the Face of God, the Way, the Shepherd, the Mountain, the Father of the Future Age, the Arm of the Lord, the King, the Prince of Peace, the Husband, the Son of God, the Lamb, the Beloved, and Jesus.

Among the many rich and suggestive things said about Christ in this great book, let us note very briefly some of the most significant. Jesus Christ the " arm of the Lord " does not represent military strength or warrior courage. " The deeds which Isaiah paints of Him," says Fray Luis de León, " are not the deeds of this war which we see, in which pride holds sway and cruelty is awaked and noise and wrath and rage and fury move their hands. He will not, Isaiah says, break the broken reed. So imagine the vain error of those evil men who turn the world upside down with wars." The symbol of such a Christ would ill become the war banners of Pizarro or Cortez or the Duke of Alva, or the table of the Holy Office in Peru.

As " King," Christ is at once Redeemer and Legislator. By His works and sacrifice He merited the spirit and virtue of Heaven for His people. This spirit and virtue He communicates to their will by " engraving upon it an efficacious and powerful law of love, whereby the righteousness which the law commands is desired and those things which it prohibits and forbids are hated." Religion is thus for Fray Luis the expression of an inward principle of life, while " only the preaching of the Gospel, that is to say, the virtue and word of Christ alone is what has always destroyed the worship of idols." Particularly significant are his words regarding Christ as the " Lamb." " Christ is the universal principle of holiness and virtue. He is the author of everything holy and virtuous that saintly beings possess, and is sufficient to sanctify all created creatures and an infinite number more which God may go on creating. He is, neither more nor less, the victim and acceptable sacrifice for the sins of the world and of other worlds without number." In the most absolute sense Christ saves men.

It is in the last study, however, that we find the fullest and most characteristic statement of Luis de León's conception. Christ is " Jesus." In the significance of the name *Jesus* he finds the clue to the profoundest meaning of Christ and the most adequate form in which to express it. Being " Jesus " Christ is *salud*, that is " salvation," or " health." Fray Luis loves to harp on the idea that Christ is complete health, health which he communicates to men. The Christian life is perfect, spiritual health. The Christian is the perfected man, man who has been healed of his ailments and restored to health by Christ who possesses the remedy for every ill. His nature becomes a " welltuned harmony," a " holy concord." An " ordered peace " fills his soul, while his chief ambition is " to become one with Christ, to have Christ in himself, becoming transformed into Him." Like Paul and Augustine, Fray Luis " would put on the Lord Jesus

Christ." Christ is his all and in all. "I, Lord," we hear him say, "repudiate and get rid of self, I flee from and hate myself in order that, through there being nothing in me that is mine, Thou alone mayst be everything in me; Thou who art my being, my life, my health, my Jesus." At the close of this marvellous chapter, the author exults in the fact that Jesus Christ is also the Logos and that, as such, He is cosmic health. To Him owe their health Heaven's angels and all nature.

The strong ethical emphasis and the stress upon order and equilibrium in the life of the soul which characterize Fray Luis' conception of Christ and Christian living, are an echo of Plato's idea of justice and Paul's idea of the Spirit-filled life. All religious life and doctrine must be submitted to an ethical test. "We may take it for certain," he says, "that any doctrine which does not aim at this end of health, which does not uproot the soul's evil passions, which does not endeavour to create in its secret depths order, temperance and justice, however holy it may appear to be on the outside, it is not holy, and however much it proclaims Christ, it is not Christ." Neither can the most punctilious performance of religious rites, nor the imposition of the severest penances be a substitute for inward spiritual health. For "although one may fast and keep silence and be never absent from the singing of the choir, although he puts on a hairshirt and treads upon ice with bare feet and begs his food and wears his meanest vestment, if, with it all, passions surge within him, if the old man lives and kindles his fires, if his soul harbours wrath, if he is puffed up with vainglory, if he is complacently satisfied with himself, if evil covetousness burns; finally if he manifests hate, envy, hurt pride, emulation or ambition . . . let him be sure that he has not reached that health, which is *Jesus*."

CHAPTER VIII

THE OTHER SPANISH CHRIST IN MODERN SPAIN

WHAT happened in Spain to the Christ who is *Jesus* ? Menéndez y Pelayo, the greatest literary critic that country has produced, published between 1877 and 1881 three large volumes entitled *Historia de los Heterodoxos Españoles*.[1] The monumental work deals with a succession of men and women, chiefly between the sixteenth and nineteenth centuries, who fell under the ban of the official Church in Spain. Some of them were Catholics who laboured for the reform of the Church, or who professed doctrines considered dangerous by the ecclesiastical authorities. Others were men who embraced Protestantism. In the lives and writings of many of these "heretics," such as the eminent Valdez brothers, Juan Diaz and Cipriano de Valera, the Christ of the so-called orthodox mystics lived and spoke.

(a) *Death and Resurrection*

It is not generally realized how near Spain came in the reign of Charles V. to throwing in her lot with the Reformation. But the type of reformation which had most adherents in the nation was of the Erasmian rather than of the Lutheran order. What many Spanish religious leaders longed for was a reformation of life rather than a reformation of doctrine. Their ideal was ethical rather than dogmatic. Erasmus had more adherents in Spain than in any other European country of the day. Charles V. granted him a pension. Luther's break with Erasmus lost the former many

[1] *History of the Spanish Heretics.*

admirers in the Peninsula. Charles himself sincerely desired that the differences of Christendom could be arranged by means of a Council. The Council of Trent was called. In its deliberations the position taken by the followers of Loyola carried the day, and the breach within Christendom became irreparable. Later on the Jesuits and the Inquisition quenched the embers of the reforming spirit. Their task was facilitated by three facts : in the first place, the Spanish reforming tendency was for reform within the unity of Catholicism ; in the second place, the religious consciousness of the Spanish advocates of reform was not possessed by a great revolutionary idea such as Luther's Justification by Faith, or Calvin's Sovereignty of God; in the third place, the doctrines of the Reformation did not take hold of the common people as they did in other European countries where the movement won.

Spain's passion for unity at any cost and her arrogant pretension to be the Lord's anointed to establish the unity of the Holy Catholic faith upon earth, threw her irrevocably into the arms of the Jesuit Order which symbolized and fought for the sole sovereignty of the Pope. The result was the apotheosis of the " Coalman's Faith," and the fulfilment of Loyola's religious ideal of ruling in a cemetery. Religious questioning and unrest were stifled. Until the very eve of the republican revolution the most incredible cases of religious intolerance occurred. Only a few years ago the following incident took place in one of the northern provinces. A simple illiterate woman happened to make the remark in the course of a conversation with a neighbour, that in her opinion, the Mother of Jesus had had other children after giving birth to our Lord. A third party overheard the remark and denounced its author. The woman was summoned before the Civil Courts on a charge of blasphemy and sentenced to several years' imprisonment. News of the scandal crossed the Spanish frontier and several foreign organizations petitioned the King to annul the sentence. All Alfonso XIII. felt he could do was to commute the sentence of imprisonment for one of banishment. The unfortunate woman had to leave her home and go to live in another part of Spain.

Meantime what happened to Christ? Christ, the " sweetest Lover," Christ, the " Redeemer and Legislator," Christ, " who lives in the fields," Christ who is " Jesus," they reduced Him to a material fetich. With what result? Spiritual life and theological interest steadily declined.

Dr Jaime Torrubiano Ripoll, professor until recently of the University of Madrid, a pious Catholic, but a violent anti-clerical, made the following significant statement in an article contributed to the magazine *La Nueva Democracia* for February 1927. "It is in our very meagre production of theological and religious books that our spiritual decadence is most evident. This decadence is all the more visible and hateful when it is experienced by the most religious people on earth." Of the forty-four theological and religious books published in 1926, twenty-four were old books got out in new editions. " Of the twenty-two that remain, what are they?" asks Professor Ripoll. "One is ashamed to tell it," he answers. " Catalogues, harmful devotional manuals that lack literary value, knowledge and piety ; monographs on canon law and rubrics, written in a senile and superstitious spirit. . . ." Only two have any value. One is entitled *Lessons on Apologetics and the Fundamentals of the Catholic Faith* to be used in advanced courses on religion, and the other *Divorce and Catholic Dogma*. Twenty-two books on religion as the literary production for one year of 150,000 Spanish priests and monks. We realize afresh the force of Unamuno's terrible words : " The Christ of this land is earth, earth, earth, earth!"

But although the cult of the Tangerian Christ, and submission to the graveyard ideal of religious life have stifled vital religion in Spain, as in South America, the Other Christ has not abandoned the land. He is to be found among groups of dissenters from the official faith who have sought in one or other of the Protestant Churches in the Peninsula the spiritual satisfaction they crave. He may also be found among an increasing group of Christians who find a spiritual home in neither Roman Catholicism nor Protestantism. Inasmuch as the existence of such ecumenical Christians, as we might call them, is a phenomenon which has begun to appear in the twenty Iberian republics of the New World, let us consider two representative members of this group in the life of modern Spain. A study of the spiritual personality of these two men will enable us to form a portrait of the Other Spanish Christ in the life of to-day. We shall then be in a position to judge for ourselves as to his mission and future in the Hispanic lands of America.

Both are laymen. Their names have already been mentioned. One is Don Francisco Giner de los Ríos, the other Don Miguel de Unamuno. When the history of modern Spain is written, the Spain which after a fresh travail in birth has again brought forth, there will be only one Don Francisco and one Don Miguel, whom the future sons and daughters of this ancient land will call "our fathers." Through the life and work of these great souls the yawning chasm between religion and conduct has been spanned in the modern history of Spain.

(b) *Don Francisco Giner de los Ríos : The Restoration of a Christian Sense to Life*

Don Francisco was an Andalusian hailing from the romantic old Moorish town of Ronda. Coming to Madrid as a young man, in the sixties of last century, he exercised an apostleship among youth which extended over fifty years, first as a professor of law in the University, later as founder and soul of the *Institución Libre de Enseñanza*. This was a co-educational institution for boys and girls carried on independently of both church and state. Giner died in 1915 an old man in his eighties, but conserving to the end the glow and the visions of youth.

Don Francisco Giner introduced a new spirit into Spanish life and education, or perhaps we should say he resuscitated, after it had been dead for many generations, that spirit of hallowed comradeship in the pursuit of knowledge which inspires Luis de León's *Nombres de Cristo*. He was his pupils' friend, and his influence over them was even greater outside the classroom than within it. When he met and talked to them in his home or during long excursions into the country, he reminded some of Socrates and others of St Francis of Assisi.

The Spanish writer Azorín gives a delightful picture of Don Francisco among his pupils. The following words were written in 1915, the year the great teacher died. "Our imaginations take flight and we see a large aristocratic house with a fine library and some spacious rooms. Here live in friendly communion with the muses a noble and scholarly man and some young men full of dreams and hopes. Don Francisco guides them in their reading. He points out to them the beauties of the Latin and Greek classics and reads along with them the great poets of Spain. He educates them, in a word, not with the severely knit brow of a preceptor, but with the sweetness and gentleness of a sincere and passionate friend. After that they walk out together, they go on long excursions, they steep themselves in the landscape and in the odours and colours of the country side.[1]

Don Francisco divided mankind into two groups; his friends and his intimates. The latter were two

[1] *El Licenciado Vidriera*, pp. 157, 158.

dozen young disciples who spent their leisure time
by his side ; the former were all the rest of men. He
was a priest of what he jestingly called " the holy
sacrament of speech." Sooner or later each young
man of his acquaintance was asked the pointed question : " Well, and what do you propose to do with
your life ? " The master strove in this way to stir in
the breasts of his disciples the sense of vocation and
responsibility, a sense which he himself possessed in a
supreme degree but which had been lacking hitherto
in the lives of Spanish students. Life was for him,
as he put it, neither tragic nor frivolous, but serious.

Only those who know from first-hand experience
how very slight and impersonal has been the traditional relationship between a professor and his students
in South American and Spanish universities will be
able to appreciate the revolutionary character of the
relations between Giner and his pupils. They, however, will have no difficulty in understanding how it
could come about, as come about it has, that the
" intimates " of Don Francisco should now be guiding
the destinies of Spain.

The *Institución Libre de Enseñanza* to which reference
has already been made has exercised a supreme educational and spiritual influence on the life of Modern
Spain. Its significance has been admirably described
by Don Fernando de los Ríos, the nephew and
worthy successor of Don Francisco, and the brilliant
Minister of Justice in the new Republican government.
Says Don Fernando referring to this famous school :
" It strives to impart a religious sense to existence. It solves the relation between the spiritual
universal and the liberty of the individual conscience
by the saying of St Augustine, ' Love and do what
you like,' because in acts inspired in the highest love
lies the possibility of supreme unity. . . . It is the
attitude favourable to that religious synthesis achieved
through emotion which continues to be upheld in a

quiet way to-day. This is what throws into relief the importance of that minority in their defence of the unquestionable supremacy of spiritual values and of the religious sense of existence." [1]

In his later years Don Francisco had the joy of seeing founded *La Junta para Ampliación de Estudios*,[2] which, subsidized by the government, carried on three major activities in the cultural life of Spain. It provided scholarships to enable students to study abroad, especially in Germany ; it organized special graduate courses for nationals and foreigners on the history and literature of Spain under the name of *El Centro de Estudios Históricos* [3] ; it founded hostels in Madrid for students of both sexes, to which picked students from all over Spain were admitted. It was a year's life and study in one of these, *La Residencia de Estudiantes*, which operated in the life of the present writer the great cultural revolution of his life, which gave him his passion for Spain and all things Spanish and taught him to expect confidently the renaissance of the ancient land. Don Francisco had just passed away, but his spirit filled the atmosphere.

Giner's personal life was that of a saint. God was very real to him, and he regarded religion " not as a disease nor as a transient phenomenon of history, like war or slavery, but as a permanent spiritual function, which the school should educate." He was religiously, however, a very lonely man. He yearned for a spiritual home and found none. He would fain have continued within a reformed Catholic church, but when the hope of reform vanished he sorrowfully abandoned the Church of his fathers. Luis de Zulueta, an old student of Don Francisco, and one of the choicest spirits in contemporary Spanish letters, gives us a picture of his master's profoundly religious spirit. " How much he must have suffered," says

---

[1] Vide *Religión y Estado en la España del Siglo XVI*.
[2] Board for the Extension of Studies.   [3] The Institute of Historical Studies.

Zulueta, " on having to abandon the Church, tearing
himself away from the community of his people and
its tradition. He did all he could to avoid it. The
young disciple of Krause used to hear mass on
Sundays, and, like his friend Don Fernando de Castro,
he cherished the hope of a renovated Spanish Church.

" That hope, like so many others in the religious
world, was dispelled after the Vatican Council. Don
Francisco considered that he could not legitimately,
without hypocrisy, continue to call himself a Catholic.
Outside the official Church, his religiosity became still
intenser and purer.

" He always spoke respectfully of the Catholic
Church. Wherever he happened to be he was in
God's presence. But at times he would enter some
solitary church, some forgotten chapel of a convent,
seeking perhaps a merely æsthetic emotion, or attracted
may be by the eternal aroma of the old wine-skins,
now empty, which it is not possible—Why, my God,
why ?—to fill with the new wine." [1]

The vision of Don Francisco furtively entering a
forgotten chapel and the anguished interrogatory
parenthesis of Zulueta bring us to the heart of the
religious tragedy of Spain, which is also the religious
tragedy of South America. Within the Church, aroma
of empty wine-skins ; without, an increasing number
of religious spirits, followers of the Other Spanish
Christ, who live in perpetual quest of a spiritual home
by the wayside of life, a kind of " Interpreter's House "
for refreshing and rest ! [2]

Don Francisco was laid to rest in the civil cemetery
of Madrid. The Church of his fathers refused his
bones a resting-place beside those of his loved ones
in one of the historic cemeteries of the city. He was

[1] *El Ideal en la Educación*, pp. 208-209.
[2] Soon after the founding of the new Spanish Republic, Luis de Zulueta
was nominated Spanish Minister to the Vatican. The Pope, however,
refused to accept the nominee of the Government and no subsequent appointment has been made. He is now Minister of Foreign Affairs in the
Republican Government.

K

buried like Christ, outside the walls of his people's religious tradition. Yet with him went to the grave, says Zulueta, " a piece of our national soul." But Don Francisco shall rise again, and Spain with him and in him, at the word, which may not long tarry, of the other Spanish Christ.

These last words were written in July 1929 under the growing impression that the day of Spain's resurrection was not far distant. In the month of April 1931 the dawn broke. What surprised the world was the form in which the revolution took place. It came as the result of a trial of strength at the polls. A group of men came into power who had never occupied administrative positions before but who, filled from early life with a deep sense of vocation and of their responsibility for the future of Spain, had been preparing themselves for that day. Not many days after the last of the Bourbons had crossed the Pyrenees on the way to exile, a Spaniard of the new generation, Doctor Salvador de Madariaga, then Professor of Spanish at Oxford, now Spanish Ambassador in Paris, delivered an address before the University of Mexico on the New Spain. In the course of his lecture he said in substance as follows : At a time when Spain was heading for the abyss and was rapidly being prepared for dictatorship, the country had but one statesman, and he refused to take any part in politics. But what has just taken place in Spain is to a very large extent the fruit of the labours of that one man—Don Francisco Giner de los Ríos.

(c) *Don Miguel de Unamuno : the Resurrection of the Other Spanish Christ*

Don Miguel de Unamuno is a Basque, born in 1864, in the Cantabrian town of Bilbao. He is thus a countryman of Loyola, and belongs, like the latter, to the most primitive stock on the Peninsula. When a boy, attending the Jesuit school of San Luis Gonzaga in his native Bilbao, he used to dream, he tells us, of becoming a saint.

Don Miguel became a saint, but of a different type from that which, as a boy, he had dreamed of becoming, and which the religious tradition of his race, as represented especially by his great countryman Loyola, had consecrated as the *beau ideal* of sainthood. He became a rebel, a saintly Christian rebel, the last and the greatest of Spain's mystic heretics. In Giner we see and hear the Christ who taught his disciples on the hill slopes beside the placid sea ; in Unamuno Him who drove the merchants from the temple, who anathematized hypocritical religious leaders, who bitterly wept over Jerusalem and anguished later in the olive garden and on the Cross, the Christ who rose later from the dead to renew the redemptive struggle in the lives of His followers.

Waldo Frank does not exaggerate when he says : " Unamuno is the strongest moralist of our day. Wells and Shaw have thin voices beside his well-aimed uproar." [1] This Basque professor of Greek in the old University of Luis de León, who reads in fifteen languages and learned Danish in order to study Kierkegaard in the original, who, while intimately conversant with the culture of modern Europe has his roots in the Scriptures and in the great mystics of his people, is one of the greatest of living men. His spiritual formation has also owed not a little to British authors. In early life Tennyson and Carlyle became favourites. The latter's *French Revolution* he translated into Spanish. He is, moreover, one of the very few foreigners who have been able to appreciate Browning. Religious movements and thought in the other European countries have been followed by him with keen interest. Keyserling, whose estimate of Karl Barth has so often been quoted, did not so much

---

[1] Waldo Frank, *Virgin Spain*, p. 282.

as know Barth's name, until he met and talked with Unamuno at Biarritz.

The coming of Unamuno to Salamanca in 1891 had the same significance in the spiritual life of Spain as the arrival of Giner de los Ríos in Madrid more than twenty years before. In the person of the new professor of Greek a fresh breath from widely scattered fields of knowledge swept through the musty cloisters of the mediæval university. The Thames and the Rhine, the Seine and the Tiber, not to speak of the waters of the Ægean and the Galilean Lake, began to flood the smooth flowing Tormes.

For over thirty years the Basque prophet thundered his message in the university classroom, in public halls, and in the written page. Essays, poems, novels, philosophical dissertations flowed from his pen. He vied with his friend Angel Ganivet in discovering and portraying the Spanish soul. He assailed unmercifully the ills which plagued the nation. There was no corrupting cancer which he did not uncover, no popular idol which he did not smash, no living problem which he did not deal with.

In his emphasis on individuality, passion and action, and his supreme contempt of sociology, Unamuno resembles Nietzsche. The prologue to his *Life of Don Quixote*, in which he sounds a clarion challenge to heroic, mystic action, is perhaps the most incandescent piece of prose-writing in contemporary literature. His sense of the tragic and the paradoxical, and the essential dualism of his thought, remind us of Kierkegaard and Dostoievski. In his defence of the heart against the intellect, of the man of " flesh and bone " against bloodless logic, he is a fervent disciple of Pascal. Not even Karl Barth has set in higher relief the basic Christian realities of incarnation, redemption and resurrection than has Unamuno. The famous picture of " Christ," by Velázquez, has occupied the same place in the life and thought of the latter that

Grunewald's picture of the Cross, with the pointing finger of John the Baptist, has occupied in the thinking of Barth.

For his uncompromising opposition to the Monarchy, the Dictatorship and the Church, Unamuno was exiled from Spain in 1925. From the isle of Fuerte Ventura, to which he was sent, he escaped a few months later to France in the little sailing yacht of an English friend.

Many fundamental viewpoints of this Spanish thinker are scattered throughout this book. It will not be amiss, however, to synthetize his fundamental religious position, provided it be borne in mind that our author is the most unsystematic of writers and the sworn foe of logic, and further, that his writings abound in those intimate contradictions which present themselves everywhere in life and human nature.

The thought of Unamuno centres round two main ideas which he clothes with religious significance: the idea of vocation or mission, and the idea of agonizing struggle, especially of struggle to live for ever. Truth breaks and life is fulfilled only upon the road when one is pressing onwards, loyal to the heavenly vision.

Not the distribution of wealth is the great problem of modern civilization, says Unamuno, but the distribution of vocations. A man begins to live when he can say with Don Quixote: " I know who I am." Others may hold him for a madman, but for him life has a meaning. Each task should be undertaken with a religious sense of its importance. If a man's particular task does not satisfy him let him change it for another, but let him work at something into which he can put his whole soul. Let him strive, moreover, to make himself unreplaceable in the lives of those whose interests he serves. To do so will involve utter abandon and sacrifice in the fulfilment of his vocation. " Sow yourself," says Unamuno in one of his poems. " Sow the living part of you in the furrows of life;

leave the dead part in yourself. You will recover yourself later in your works." [1]   Speaking for himself, he would be content though his message should die in the minds of his readers so long as it would, by dying there, help to fertilize their thoughts.

Here was Carlyle's gospel of work and of the meaningfulness of life which Giner de los Ríos was preaching in Madrid. No doctrine could be more important in an environment in which young men drifted through life and where work had been generally undertaken not with a view to service but with the hope of gain. In such an environment Unamuno helped to resuscitate Santa Teresa's famous saying : " *entre los pucheros anda el Señor.*" [2]   The help of the Highest could be obtained for the lowest and most menial tasks. No work was mean when a sense of vocation and of God transfigured it.

His own particular vocation Unamuno has regarded as that of reincarnating Don Quixote in modern Spain and the modern age, standing for the eternally spiritual and jousting with evil wherever he seemed to see it, indifferent to all consequences. He would have his countrymen learn to think on the deepest things of life and destiny. His function has been that of tossing them into God's ocean, he tells us, that they may learn to swim. They must abandon the " Coalman's Faith," and the graveyard peace in which their lives have been spent must be broken. It is necessary that they awake to spiritual unrest. From him, however, let them not expect bread, but only leaven and ferment. It is his to arouse them to creative spiritual strife, to the true understanding of the words of Christ, so tragically misunderstood in the wars of the sixteenth century : " I came not to bring peace but a sword." Men can only reach the peace of Westphalia by passing first through the Diet of Worms. Let the divine warfare

[1] " Siémbrate," in *Rosario de Sonetos Líricos.*
[2] " Christ walks among the pots."

be carried to every home. "Only in Thy spiritual war," he says, apostrophizing Christ in one of his poems, "can we have peace, Thy kiss of greeting. Only in struggling for heaven, Christ, can we mortals know peace. . . . Only let it be Thy peace, Brother, and not deceit."

Unamuno will have none of the Jesuit's peace. "The Roman Church, let us say Jesuitism," he writes in a book published in French during his exile, "preaches a peace that is the peace of conscience, implicit faith, passive submission. Leon Chestov, in *La Nuit de Gethsemani*,[1] says very rightly, 'Let us remember that the terrestrial keys to the kingdom of heaven fell to Peter and his successors precisely because Peter could sleep and slept while God, come down among men, prepared Himself to die upon the Cross.' "[2]

This leads directly to Unamuno's fundamental idea or attitude, that of tragic agonizing struggle. We listen to his deepest soul in those "Psalms" which form a part of the chief volume of his poems. For Unamuno is also a poet, the greatest lyric poet of Spain since Fray Luis de León. His psalms are the utterance of an anguished soaring spirit that beats its wings against the veil in an endeavour to pierce beyond it. Their language reminds us of some utterances of Moses, Job and Augustine. "I want to see Thee, Lord, and then die," he cries. "Give me Thy divine Spirit that I may see Thee." And again, "Why didst Thou kindle in our breast the yearning to know Thee, the yearning that Thou should'st exist, only to hide Thyself from our gaze?"

"My religion," he wrote in one of his early essays, "is to struggle ceaselessly and tirelessly with the mystery of things. My religion is to wrestle with God from the break of day till the setting sun. I can make no terms with the so-called Unknowable or

---

[1] *The Night of Gethsemane.*   [2] *L'Agonie du Christianisme*, pp. 96-97.

with the prohibition : 'beyond here thou shalt not pass.'" [1]

Between Unamuno's head and heart an unending struggle rages. With his heart he experiences God and confides in the hope of immortality. " I believe, Lord," he says in one place, " help Thou my unbelief," and in another in calmer mood, " I believe in God as I believe in my friends, because I feel the breath of His love and His invisible and intangible hand which draws me and leads me and presses me ; because I have an intimate consciousness of a personal Providence and a universal Mind which maps me out my destiny." [2]

But when the dawn of Reason breaks the struggle begins afresh. The heart has affirmed the reality of God and the certainty of immortality but Reason denies both. They become locked in mortal strife, as a result of which both are precipitated into the bottom of the abyss. From the wounds of the heart is born a hope, a tragic hope, which Unamuno calls " transcendental pessimism." Whether God and immortality are real or not, he will live his life in such a way as that, if in spite of all, it is annihilation that awaits him, such annihilation will be an injustice. It is the eternal " Yea " of the prophet, " Though He slay me yet will I trust Him," the " yea " of Frederick Robertson of Brighton, uttered in the blackest hour of his life : " If there is no God or future life, even in such case it is better to be generous than selfish, better to be chaste than licentious, better to be loyal than false, better to be brave than a coward."

In this way Unamuno puts ethics upon a tragic basis. At whatever cost let a man live exultingly in accordance with eternal moral values. He throws down the gauntlet to the Universe. If there is no future for goodness in the nature of things, then the

---

[1] *Mi Religion y Otros Ensayos*, p. 9.
[2] *Del Sentimiento Trágico de la Vida*, p. 193.

nature of things is unjust. Nevertheless, to the last the
true meaning of life must be struggle. So convinced
is Unamuno that struggle, and not victory, is the
essence of life, that he exclaims in one of his poems,
" Seek not light, my heart, only water from the
depths." He wants his insatiable and ardent thirst
of truth to continue forever. " He loves thee not,
Oh Truth, who never doubts," he exclaims. And he
wants no rationalized God, " Far be it from me, Lord,
to encase Thee in an idea." Let the creative strife
go on while life lasts, heart and head in perpetual
conflict. Only let the heart be nourished by creative
peace for this unending ordeal. The fountain of this
peace is the same as the symbol of the strife and the
pledge of victory : Christ Crucified.

Unamuno's longest poem, entitled " The Christ of
Velázquez," is unique in modern literature. The poet
muses in a reverie of devotion upon the Crucified, to
whom he lovingly addresses himself. He solilo-
quizes on the mystic meaning of each feature of Him.
The Cross is at once the divinest of all symbols, " the
symbol and cipher of the eternal," and a symbol of
what true human life should be, " agony " in its
original Greek sense of " wrestling," " struggle."
But it is something more : It is no mere symbol ; it
is the instrument and pledge of victory. He gazes
on the Crucified and says : Thou savedst Death."
" Through Thee that death of Thine gives us life."
Not only endless life but new life. " Death made
Thee King of Life. . . . Thou art the Eternal Man
who makes us new men." Christ's was creative death,
for it was not mere man who died but God in human
nature. " Never," he says in his last published book,
" did God feel Himself to be more of a Creator and
Father than when He died in Christ, when in Him,
in His Son, he tasted death." [1]

The Cross, however, did not put an end to the

[1] *Como se hace una novela*, p. 66.

agonia of Christ.   He agonizes still in the lives of His followers.   Unamuno's idea is that of Paul, whom he calls the " mystic discoverer of Jesus," and who, living in the " fellowship of His sufferings " strove to " fill up what was lacking in them for His body's sake, the Church."   In this connection he quotes the striking words of Blaise Pascal : " Jesus will be in agony till the end of the world ; we must not sleep during this present time." [1]   As with Christ and Christians, so with Christianity, it is a religion of agony.   " The supreme objective of its agony," says Unamuno, must be the redemption of individuals, whom it must convert into agonizing bodies of Christ. " The Kingdom of the Redeemer," he adds, " is not of this world."   So-called Christian civilization is a contradiction in terms.   Christianity dare not identify itself with any particular brand of political economy, democracy or patriotism.   Its specific mission is to make new men, living centres of creative agony. And these it must fashion out of " poor men and rich, slaves and tyrants, condemned criminals and hangmen."

I cannot forget while I live the epoch-making day in my experience when I visited Unamuno in his home in Salamanca during Christmas week in the winter of 1915.   It was the year after clerical influence had deposed him from the rectorship of that ancient university, and several years before his banishment from Spain.   Fourteen winters later, on my way from South America to the Scottish Highlands, I shared two days of his exile in the French frontier town of Hendaye, opposite the Basque mountains, those fatefully symbolic mountains in the life of Spain.   It was the opportunity I had dreamed of for years, to share a brief space of the life of the man who had opened up for me the secrets of the Spanish soul,

[1] " *Jesus sera en agonie jusqu' a la fin du monde : il ne faut pas dormir pendant ce temps la.*"

and whose writings had stirred my mind more than those of any contemporary thinker.

Don Miguel was living a life of great simplicity in a little hotel scarcely a hundred metres from the international frontier between France and Spain. He had fled from the din and publicity of Paris to be near the shadow of his native hills. Every day he would walk for hours along the frontier. The simple town's folk of Hendaye loved that bare-headed, ruddy-cheeked old man who passed daily through their streets, the living model of health and friendliness. The details of his fearless life and of his long struggle for righteousness and liberty in his own country were known to them; they also knew of the Nazarene purity and austerity of his way of living; and they regarded him as a saint.

An incident took place during those two days which is profoundly symbolic of the religious message of Unamuno. A sculptor friend had been staying with him for a few weeks before my arrival. It was the noted artist who had made the bust of the great Spanish novelist, Pérez Galdós. I was invited on the second day of my visit to see the bust of Don Miguel which had just been completed in a plaster cast. It was a magnificent likeness. "But what is that on the breast?" I asked. Engraven on the left side, over the region of the heart, was the figure of a cross! The sculptor told me the story. Before the cast was dry, Unamuno went up to it one day and, with his finger, drew the sign of the cross above the place where his heart should be. "What will the people of Madrid say when they see this?" said the sculptor, startled and a bit chagrined; "don't you realize, Don Miguel, that that cross must necessarily appear in the final bronze?" he said. Don Miguel smiled in silence.

A cross, not dangling loosely down the breast, but engraven across the living crusader's heart of Don Miguel de Unamuno, is the true symbol of the life and faith of this prince of modern Christian thinkers. It offers a stern challenge to Christianity in our time to rehabilitate the Cross in the place where it belongs, at the centre of all life and thought, and to rediscover the meaning of creative agony.   It invites Spanish Christianity to re-study afresh the meaning of that Cross and of that Crucified one that have played so central a part in the Catholic epic in Spain and South America.

PART THREE
NEW SPIRITUAL CURRENTS IN SOUTH AMERICA

CHAPTER IX

THE QUEST OF A NEW WAY

LET us now return to South America. In the remaining chapters of this volume the attempt will be made to sketch the history and appraise the significance of the more representative spiritual movements outside the pale of the Roman Catholic Church which have had a bearing upon life and thought in the Continent during the Republican era.

(a) *Rebels*

With the close of the Colonial period and the establishment of independent governments in the several countries of South America came new intellectual currents. The influence of France and in particular of French radicalism became potent. The spirit of the French Revolution, which had already manifested itself in the political history of the Continent, now made itself felt in the spiritual realm also. In the very first generation after the Declaration of Independence, revolutionary and prophetic figures made their appearance in the sphere of thought. It was particularly in the west coast countries of the Continent, where, as we have already seen, the influence of the Church had been most obscurantist and intellectual repression had been severest, that the new voices sounded their wilderness message.

The most representative figure of this revolutionary dawn, and, without doubt, one of the most representative and prophetic figures in the history of South American thought is a young Chilean, Francisco Bilbao.

In 1844, when but twenty years of age, and a student of the National Institute of Chile, Bilbao achieved sudden notoriety by the publication of a book called *Sociabilidad Chilena*.[1]   The volume revealed the influence of the French encyclopedists and the Bible, but particularly that of Lammenais.   That mystic and prophetic figure of the beginning of last century, the author of *Les Paroles d'un Croyant*,[2] had made a profound and decisive impression upon the mind of the young Chilean.   The result was a book written in the aphoristic, prophetic style peculiar to Lammenais in which his South American admirer delivered a frontal attack against the Church and existing society in Chile.   This youthful Philippic burst like a thunderclap in the cloistered atmosphere of Chilean life, where until then the peace of the sepulchre had been regnant. The unheard-of daring of the youthful author took people's breath away.   He was immediately expelled from college and arraigned before the civil courts. Bilbao's words to the accusing fiscal on the day of his trial will never be forgotten in the history of South America's struggle for spiritual liberty : " Here are two names," he said, " that of the accuser and that of the accused ; two names, intertwined by historic fate, which will live on in the history of my native land. Then it will be seen, Mr Fiscal, which of the two will enjoy the benediction of posterity.   Philosophy also has its code, and that code is eternal.   Philosophy assigns to you the name of retrograde.   An innovator, that is what I am ; a retrograde, that is what you are ! "

The audacity of Bilbao made him a hero with the populace.   A fine of 2500 *pesos* imposed upon him by the judge was paid by popular subscription, the people demanding that the judge should be handed over to them.   A few months after the famous trial, Bilbao left Chile for Europe, taking up his residence in Paris,

[1] *Social Life in Chile.*   [2] *The Words of a Believer.*

where he made the acquaintance of Quinet and Lammenais. His relations with the latter, his already venerated master, were touching and fruitful. During his residence in the French capital he devoted a whole winter to translating into Spanish Lammenais's annotated edition of the Gospels.

Returning to Chile Bilbao founded the " Society of Equality." The principles of this organization were as follows : The recognition of the independence of reason as the authority of authorities ; the profession of the principle of popular sovereignty as a basis of all politics ; and the duty and love of universal fraternity as the essence of the moral life. At the same time he translated into Spanish *Les Paroles d'un Croyant*. His new literary effort produced a storm of indignation. As for the Society of Equality, it was dissolved by the government not long after its foundation. The publication of a pamphlet, *Los Boletines del Espíritu,* led to Bilbao's excommunication by the Church. The great love and admiration of the young radical for the personality and teaching of Jesus come to light in this pamphlet. He stands out as a Christian socialist and a most ardent and uncompromising advocate of liberty. His democratic ideology was based on religion : " The first word of the sovereign people is God, the Infinite and Creative Person through whom we exist and to whom we go. The second word is liberty, and the third word is the communion of all creatures—love, fraternity. God is with us, whom do we fear ? "

In consequence of a revolution in Chile Bilbao fled to Peru. There he became the centre of a group of young idealists, with whom he launched a campaign against administrative corruption. As a result of this activity he was obliged to flee to Ecuador. Upon his return to Peru, Bilbao became attracted by the figure of the patron saint of Lima, Santa Rosa, " a lily among thorns," as he called her. This interest led to the publicity of a series of studies on the life of the Limenian

L

saint, in whom Bilbao sought the American ideal of moral perfection and noble self-sacrifice.

A second visit to Europe marked the beginning of a new era in the life of Bilbao. During his absence a complete change had taken place in the spiritual environment of Paris. His venerated spiritual father Lammenais was dead ; many of his old masters were in exile, while reactionaries held the ground. The works of the German thinkers, Strauss, Feuerbach and Hegel, now began to influence the ardent South American. His political and ethical idealism remained as vital as ever, but the simplicity of his early Christian outlook tended to give way to rationalism.

From Europe Bilbao sailed for Buenos Aires. In the Argentine capital he wrote a number of significant books, under such titles as these : *The Law of History*, *America in Danger*, *The American Gospel ;* and a series of studies on the religious problem, *Masonic Discourses*, *The Religious Revolution* and *Religious Studies*. These studies in religion, it should be said, are entirely devoid of originality and do no more than reflect the ideas of Bilbao's favourite authors. The pantheistic influence of Hegel is very marked. Bilbao's admiration for Jesus remains as great as ever, but the supernatural is entirely rejected.

Bilbao died in Buenos Aires in 1864. His name has now become a banner of progress in the Republic of Chile. The prophecy of the youthful revolutionary at the time of his trial has had the most complete fulfilment. His lasting glory consists, as his countryman and biographer, Armando Donoso, has put it, " in his conviction and daring and his apostleship of republican ideas ; in his hostility to all despotism ; in his purity and disinterestedness." Among his last words is a sentence from a letter to the French writer Quinet: "How beautiful it is to live with infinite horizons ! " Francisco Bilbao might be called with justice the first lay saint of republican South America. To him also belongs the honour of being the first layman on the continent to give serious thought to the religious problem. Even to this day his successors have not been many.

A second continental figure whose memory will also live on as an apostle of spiritual liberty is the Ecuadorian, Juan Montalvo. According to the Uruguayan writer and critic, Enrique Rodó, Montalvo is the outstanding writer of the first century of republican South America.[1] He was, besides, a profoundly religious soul, while at the same time an uncompromising anti-clerical.

About the middle of last century Ecuador lay under the heel of one of the classic dictators of Latin America. This was the famous García Moreno, under whose rule the State became a projection of the Church. The sole liberty recognized was the liberty to do what the Church permitted. Montalvo lifted his voice in revolt, and his exile followed.

Montalvo's most famous works are his *Capítulos que se le olvidaron a Cervantes*,[2] a book which is perhaps the most brilliant and successful imitation ever written of the style and substance of *Don Quixote* ; *Siete Tratados*, in which he deals with sundry political and religious questions; and *Mercurial Eclesiástica*, or *Book of Truths*. The last-mentioned work was published as a result of a controversy with the Archbishop of Quito, José Ignacio Ordoñez. The Archbishop had made a statement which roused the ire of Montalvo. " Our forefathers in better times than ours," said the prelate, " had to lament only those sins into which malice and human frailty had made them fall, and as they kept the faith alive, they truly returned to God ; their repentance was sincere and their conversion real." Whereupon Montalvo concentrated all his ironic and satirical powers in a vial of scorn which he poured forth on the Church, and in particular on the idea that moral sins are a comparatively small affair compared with the conservation of religious beliefs.

[1] Vide *Hombres de América*, by Enrique Rodó.
[2] *Chapters forgotten by Cervantes*.

As compared with Bilbao, Montalvo wielded a more brilliant pen and was a much more systematic thinker. He shared with the great Chilean his profound admiration of Jesus Christ, but he lacked, in our opinion, the apostolic quality and personal purity of the former.

The Peruvian, Manuel González Prada, is another striking representative of this group of rebels. In him, as in Bilbao and Montalvo, the influence of French writers predominates. Renan and Guyau were the chief moulders of his thought. His two chief books, *Páginas Libres*, 1894,[1] and *Horas de Lucha*, 1908,[2] consisting of essays and addresses on literary, political and religious subjects, are for strength and purity of style among the most classic productions in the whole range of South American letters. Only Rodó's *Ariel* can be placed in the same class with them. As a controversialist not even Montalvo could wield the pen with the telling power of the Peruvian writer. Probably no South American has chiselled so many immortal phrases as he.

Prada came into prominence shortly after the Peruvian-Chilean war of 1879-83. He appeared as the stern uncompromising censor of those weaknesses in national life which had led to defeat. The Roman Catholic Church and religion in general came in for a special share of his sledge-hammer rhetoric.

His essays and addresses on religion reveal the classic type of free thinker which the Spanish race produces. A race which throughout its history has had a tendency towards polarization, a native passion for extremes, could not but produce radicals who, in Unamuno's phrase, were " Catholics upside down." [3] For Prada as for Guyau, all scientifically minded people tend to be anti-religious. What is religion but a purely private affair, a matter of individual taste like underclothing ? It has no foundation in the nature of things, " for nature," says Prada, " is all bosom and no heart." Nor is religion needed in human life :

<hr/>

[1] *Free Pages.*   [2] *Hours of Struggle.*   [3] *Católicos al revés.*

in order to walk we do not need to look upwards but forwards.   Besides religion has proved a positive evil. Instead of creating human perfection it has served only as an external varnish to dissimulate vices or as a password for obtaining participation in the repartition of honours, power and riches.   Prada is the mortal enemy of Catholicism.   " The intellectual and moral progress of South American nations is measured by the doses of Catholicism which they have succeeded in eliminating from their laws and customs."   So read the last words of *Horas de Lucha*.   He deeply lamented the coming of religious orders to Peru to establish schools.   That was indeed, as we have already seen, a fateful event in the history of the country.

It never occurred to the Peruvian writer that religion, ethics and politics should and could be intimately related.   He quotes with evident gusto the words of the French author Vacherot, " God hands over politics to men and reserves religion for Himself." Yet Prada was ready to acknowledge the fruits of true religion when he saw them.   In his opinion Protestantism produced a higher ethical type than Catholicism.

Particularly interesting and significant is his essay on Vigil, a Roman Catholic priest, who after being excommunicated for an attack on the Papacy was appointed librarian of the National Library of Peru. For this precursor of his on the road of radicalism Prada entertained the tenderest regard.   Vigil had broken with the Church without ceasing to regard himself a Christian, " because," as he expressed it, " the Gospel is the religion of every good man . . . but the Gospel as it existed in the head and in the heart of Jesus Christ."   When this remarkable priest lay on his death-bed he refused the ministry of the Church. He wished to die as a layman, " in the arms of the good Jesus," as his last words were.

Prada died in 1917.   Since his death his name has become the watchword of militant radicalism in his native country.   The scheme of university extension launched in 1919 by a remarkable group of Peruvian students bore the name of *Las Universidades Populares González Prada*.[1]   The master's martial dictum, "*Los viejos a la tumba, los jóvenes a la obra*"[2] was the battle-cry of the University Revolution of 1919.

It is nevertheless unfortunate that Prada was more of an iconoclast than a prophet.   His gifts of intellect and his skill as a literary sculptor to chisel deathless geometric phrases were superior to his gifts of heart. Unlike Francisco Bilbao, he seemed devoid of sentiment, and his attitude, save in the closest intimacy, was invariably marked by a certain icy unapproachableness. This shy, solitary soul did not possess the necessary qualities for dynamic leadership.   His most famous public addresses were carefully written out and sent to the meeting at which their author was due to speak, there to be read by someone else.   One thing, however, Prada had which entitles him to lasting veneration as a mentor of youth : he possessed sterling honesty and an immaculate life.   Moreover, like Francisco Bilbao, and unlike so many literary iconoclasts in South American history, he remained a consistent and uncompromising fighter to the day of his death.

Last of this race of rebels, and perhaps the most iconoclastic of them all, for the simple reason that his political position gave him the opportunity to put his ideas into practice, is José Battle Ordóñez, the famous president and political *caudillo* of Uruguay.   Under the leadership of Battle Ordóñez this little republic attained international prominence on account of its progressive legislation in social and political matters, earning for itself the name of " the New Zealand of South America."   Battle's party adopted a policy which was not simply anti-clerical, as many South American governments have done, but avowedly anti-religious.

[1] The González Prada Universities for the People.
[2] " Age to the grave, youth to the task."

Some decades ago this famous Uruguayan, whose death took place in 1929, set about eliminating every Christian association from the calendar. Christmas Day was converted into " Family Day," and Holy Week became " Touring Week." Even to-day the newspaper of Battle's political party, *El Día* of Montevideo, never prints the name of God save with a small letter,[1] and then only to make fun of deity, while His Holiness the Pope is referred to as " Señor Ratti, a gentleman who lives in Rome."

(b) *Positivists*

In the seventies of last century another spiritual breeze from France reached the shores of South America in the form of Positivism. The system of August Comte wielded its greatest influence in Chile and Brazil, but particularly in the latter country. In perhaps no other part of the world did the ideal inherent in the Religion of Humanity receive so full an expression as it did in this republic.

The first Positivist Society in Brazil was organized in 1870, its founders being mostly army officers. In 1897 a beautiful temple was dedicated to Humanity in Rio de Janeiro by the members of the National Positivist Church. Over its portals were inscribed the words : " Love the principle, order the basis, progress the end."

While the number of positivists has never been very large in Brazil, some of the most influential men in the country have figured and continue to figure within the group. The famous Benjamin Constant, founder and first president of the Brazilian Republic, was an ardent positivist. This explains how the positivist motto, " Order and progress," came to be blazoned on the national flag. The influence of Positivism as an instrument of political and religious freedom has been particularly great in the southernmost state of

[1] *dios.*

Brazil, Rio Grande do Sul, which has given to the republic the president who now governs it. In Rio Grande personal liberty and faith in the efficacy of popular sanction are carried to such an extreme that men are allowed to function in the several professions without possessing any official title to do so. The public is considered to be an infallible judge of professional efficiency.

The immense minority influence exerted by the Religion of Humanity in some South American countries, and especially in Brazil, has been due to a series of concurrent causes. In the first place, the architectonic and comprehensive character of the philosophy of Comte made a ready intellectual appeal to the South American mind. Comte, moreover, did not attack Catholicism. In his Philosophy of History he did not regard previous religious forms as wrong, but simply as inferior. The Religion of Humanity came as the crown of earlier faiths. In 1826 he had even sugguested a rapprochement between his own system and the Roman Catholic Church. Such a viewpoint made a natural appeal to people born and educated in a Roman Catholic environment, who, while dissatisfied with the Catholic faith, were loath to follow the road of the rebels and renounce it utterly.

A second element in the appeal of Positivism was its emphasis upon humanity as the supreme object of devotion. The idea of religion as a function whereby individual life is regulated and collective life harmoniously combined, an idea according to which humanity itself becomes the new centre of unity and the religion of humanity with its golden rule of love the link uniting all nations, made a natural appeal to a people who are universalistic to the core. South American positivists could enjoy a certain smug feeling of superiority. They belonged to no sect—so-called " sectarianism " being ever abhorrent to the South American mind—they were the heirs of all human and religious values. The walls of positivist temples and of public libraries founded under positivist influence are adorned with portraits of men and women belonging to every age and race who have made a significant contribution to the cause of humanity. It is worth while observing in this connection that the first centennial of Comte's endeavour to effect a religious alliance between Catholicism and Positivism was combined with the celebration of the seventh centennial of St Francis of Assisi.

The third element in the Religion of Humanity which has made it a spiritual power among a small minority in Brazil has been its apotheosis of woman, or rather of a woman. During the year 1845 to 1846 the extreme intellectual character of Comte's system was profoundly modified by his very intimate and Platonic friendship with a Parisian lady, Clotilde de Vaux. Through this intimacy the philosopher became alive to the fact that emotive values are equally inherent in human nature. He realized that a philosophic system must have a place for every phase of human personality. He founded, therefore, a religion which should be at once scientific and human, and have the good of mankind as its goal.

A book published in Rio de Janeiro in 1926 by the positivist writer R. Texeira Mendez, and entitled *O Ano sem Par*,[1] is a religious meditation on the incomparable union to which the founders of Positivism, August Comte and Clotilde de Vaux, owed the fulfilment of their mission. Clotilde is depicted as the inspirer and mother of the Religion of Humanity ; she tends to occupy the same place, at least in Brazilian Positivism, that the Virgin Mary does in Roman Catholicism. Her image, as the symbol of Humanity, appears above the doorway of the new positivist temple in Rio de Janeiro, inaugurated on 5th April 1924, the seventy-fourth anniversary of her death. Clotilde de

[1] *The Incomparable Year.*

Vaux is *Santa Clotilde*, August Comte is *our master*, the *first high priest of humanity*. Another evidence of the historic truth that the concrete figures of religious founders become themselves the object of religious veneration in spite of the impersonal and abstract principles of the faith they may have proclaimed.

Not all South American positivists, however, reached the religious stage. Most have stopped short at the ethical milestone, where Comte himself had made his camp before the " incomparable year." This was the case with the well-known Argentine sociologist and psychiatrist, José Ingenieros, who died in 1925. This brilliant Argentine scientist possessed, as he himself said, no mystic tendency. He deprecated everything of the nature of dogma, both in religion and in science. Truth could only be reached by constant experimentation, by a continual process of trial and error. Effective ethics must be the exclusive result of social experience, and must on that account exclude all *a priori* elements.

During a visit to the United States Ingenieros came under the influence of Emerson and New England Unitarianism. The result was a significant book published in 1917 and entitled *Hacia una Moral sin Dogmas*.[1] This book takes up the position that the principles of morality must be constantly renewed. Religious dogmas must be substituted by moral ideals. The influence of the New England school is pervasive throughout, but Ingenieros laments the religious turn which the Ethical Societies have taken. He affirms his personal lack of religious sentiment, but finds it difficult to forecast the future of religion, the power of which he recognizes. His contention is, however, that for those who are incapable of believing in any religion, while still retaining a mystical temperament, the great interests of political and social renovation must become the practical equivalent of the religions of humanity.

[1] *Towards a Morality without Dogmas.*

(c) Romantic Idealists

The figure of José Enrique Rodó, the brilliant Uruguayan essayist, introduces us to a new and more spiritual tendency in South American thought. The *Ariel* of Rodó, translated some years ago into English, may with justice be considered the Magna Charta of South American idealism. Rodó himself has been acclaimed "Master of Youth"[1] by several successive student generations in Latin America during the present century.

As a master of Spanish prose, Rodó has been unequalled by modern exponents of the language of Cervantes, although the cultural influences which formed him as a writer were practically all French. Like the Peruvian, González Prada, he revelled in Guyau and Renan. Rodó cannot be regarded, however, as a truly original or creative writer. His chief gift consisted in eclectic gleanings from the great masters, which he wove into a series of dazzling thoughts, richly poetic in concept and matchless in form. His was a kind of protean philosophy, the main thought of which was "*reformarse es vivir.*"[2] Here is another echo of the South American reaction against the fixed, the dogmatic and the sectarian.

Rodó's religious position appears in a controversial pamphlet, entitled *Liberalismo and Jacobinismo*, written in 1906. José Battle Ordóñez and his school had carried their religious iconoclasm to the pitch of demanding that every religious symbol, in particular crucifixes, should be removed from public hospitals and other charitable institutions in Montevideo. Rodó, while himself professing no religion, was profoundly stirred by the injustice and incongruity of such an action. "The idea," he said, "that any commission of charity should expel from the houses

---

[1] "*Maestro de la Juventud.*"
[2] "The essence of life consists in reshaping oneself."

of charity the image of the Creator of charity! As well might the bust of Socrates be removed from a philosophy classroom."

In his spirited defence of the Christian symbols, Rodó undertook to explain the historical origins of charity. Socrates went no further than a negative attitude towards the evil-doer. Moral passion in the propagation of ethical ideas was foreign to the Jewish temperament. The spiritual domination of Greece did not bring moral regeneration to the world, for Greece had no sense of human solidarity. In the course of the ages many panegyrics of love and brotherly kindness have been spoken and written. It is one thing, however, to formulate an idea and quite another to propagate a sentiment. Seneca proclaimed lofty moral ideas, but his morality was dead. The morality of Philo and of Kant are icy cold. The true inventor of an idea in the moral world is he who first transforms it into sentiment, giving it active expression in his own conduct. This is what Jesus Christ did. After proclaiming the idea of love He warmed it in His bosom, and went with it to the Cross.

In the course of the polemic Rodó drew attention to a truth which continually presses itself upon the student of Latin-American thought. "Latin free thought," says he, "has a native tendency to forensic declamation. It lacks an intuitive appreciation of religion or of religions." It is extraordinarily difficult for a Latin liberal to write dispassionately on the subject of religion. According to Rodó, the only French writer who was ever able to do so was Renan. The liberalism of the others is always fanatically ultra-montane. To be a freethinker does not necessarily mean to think with liberty. It more often marks one who is neither a thinker nor free.

Rodó reminds one in many ways of his master Renan. Like him he felt profound respect for sincere religious sentiment wherever he found it and what-

ever the dogmas which lent it inspiration.   Man's
preoccupation with the mystery of the universe
he regarded as a constitutive expression of human
nature.   He himself, however, professed no religious
faith.   For him undoubtedly positive religious beliefs
were no more than for Renan, the sound of legendary
bells from a belfry tower buried beneath the waves.
He refused to associate himself with or speak under
the auspices of any organization having a religious basis.
This is but another illustration of that non-committal
attitude already referred to, so common among
South American intellectuals, an attitude inspired by
the dread of sectarianism and of being considered
sectarian.   Rodó's spiritual attitude was essentially
that of the Aristotelian spectator in his ivory tower.

It is not without significance that in recent years a
reaction has taken place, especially in student circles,
against the type of idealism represented by Rodó.
His thinking is rightly regarded as lacking in creative
power.   He spoke about the ideal, but did not point
the way to its realization, while the sad fact remains
that his own personality was in no way a model of
idealism.   The Montevidean teacher did not embody
in his personal contact with youth the idealized
picture of Prospero in his own *Ariel*; and when he
died in Italy in 1916 it was in circumstances so unideal
that his admirers prefer to pass over the final scene.
In the life of the greatest of South American idealists
we discover the tragedy of continental idealism in its
traditional form : between the romanticism of theory
and the stern drab routine of practice a deep chasm
opens.   To bridge this chasm is one of the chief
spiritual problems of South America.

An immensely nobler and more dynamic type is
the Argentine educator, Joaquín B. González, the
founder of the University of La Plata.   In González
begins to appear the influence of the Orient and of
oriental thought in the spiritual life of South America.

From early life he discovered a deep passion for nature and cultivated a kind of poetic pantheism. Beauty he loved in all its forms. He was led to the study of law, he tells us, by the contemplation of the beauty immanent in every concept of justice.

González was among the first South Americans to feel the influence of Rabindranath Tagore, and that influence proved decisive. Tagore was for his Argentine disciple the most fervid and complete of spirits, who " realized in himself the consubstantial and indivisible union of the poet, the mystic, the philosopher, the priest and the master." This interest in Tagore led González to translate into Spanish the *Hundred Poems of Kabir*, the Indian poet of the fifteenth century whose verses Tagore had edited in English. What impressed him most in Kabir was the latter's universality, the same quality which had recommended Positivism to many minds of a previous generation. In his introduction to the Spanish version he descants enthusiastically on Kabir's tolerant and liberal philosophy which tended to conciliate all beliefs into one single supreme belief, that, namely, in the essential qualities which all religions have in common. This common feature manifests itself as a form of high mysticism in the theopathic state which is attained through the synthetic vision of God. The manifestation of love is the true solution of human problems. For in love all the contradictions of existence are fused and lost.

This reference to love leads González to refer with sorrow to what he regards as the supreme problem of his country and his race. This problem is the manifestation of hate, " which," says he, " has been revealed among us with all the features of an historic law." Thereupon he quotes the significant words of the contemporary Spanish philosopher, José Ortega y Gasset, " We, Spaniards, offer to life a heart fortified by rancour, and whatever hits against it is cruelly

hurled away. I should like to propose in these essays
to my young readers that they expel from their minds
every habit of hate and strongly aspire that love shall
again administer the universe." But how can hate
be expelled? we ask. Only through the "expul-
sive power of a new affection." Neither reason nor
lofty ideals nor abstract love can ever drive out the
arch-demon; only a concrete passionate affection
can accomplish that. Nothing less than personal
devotion to the Other Spanish Christ will ever prove
adequate to such a task. Only in the "health" of
the Christ who is "Jesus" will disappear the inherent
tendency to "cruelty" and "hate" among their own
people of which South American writers complain.

Not less romantic but perhaps more specifically
Christian in their view-point are the Peruvian writers,
José Gálvez and Edwin Elmore. Gálvez is a contemporary poet and the author of the South American
Students' Song.[1] A long document on his religious
position, which he prepared some years ago at the
request of the writer, contains a number of significant
statements which reveal not only their author's
spiritual pilgrimage, but also the spiritual pilgrimage
of the South American soul in recent years. Says
Gálvez: "I believe that González Prada, whom I
greatly admired, contributed by means of his irreligious writing to make me a kind of radical. I was
an atheist. Do not smile. I was even somewhat of
a *fraile-fobo*.[2] But afterwards my soul reacted. I
began as a very young man to look much at the sky,
and to look at it without any great astronomic preoccupation. I looked at it with religious, almost
mystic preoccupation."

Here a new note is struck; the goal of human life
cannot be fully reached by the forward look as Prada

[1] He was Minister of Foreign Affairs in the Provisional Government of
Peru which followed the fall of Sánchez Cerro.
[2] A priest-hater.

thought ; the upward look is equally essential. The
sight of "far horizons" will not help one who is
lost amid desert sands where the winds have blotted
out the path. In such a case he must wait for the
stars to come out before being able to renew the
march. Gálvez continues : "I feel the need of
believing, and I do believe in a supreme power ; in
a force which is within me and without me, but as
yet there has not been formed definitely within me
the religion which I need. I believe in its necessity
for every one without exception, and I believe that
my spirit is at bottom truly Christian. Never did
man reach his highest and profoundest greatness so
much as when Christianity appeared. To my way of
thinking it is Christianity which has made humanity
what it already is in part and what it should be entirely.
I am a Christian in my own way, and I think I live
within the essential criteria of the ideology, the sentiment and the norms of Christianity, but I have not
been able to return to its rites."

Edwin Elmore, who had he lived would now be
in his early forties, was an entirely unique and symbolic
figure among the young intellectuals of South America.
It is difficult for the writer to speak about Elmore
without deep emotion. We were both members of
a literary group in Lima which centred around the
well-known South American review *El Mercurio
Peruano*.[1] We had many interests in common. A
special bond of union between us was our mutual
enthusiasm for the person and writings of Unamuno.
But in 1925 Elmore's life of brilliant promise was
cut short by an encounter with the infamous poet
Chocano. The latter assassinated him in the building
of *El Comercio*, Lima's leading newspaper, because
Elmore had dared to write a series of articles in the

[1] This group has been described by one of its members, Dr Antonio
Sagarna, one-time Minister of Education in the Argentine Republic, now
member of the Supreme Court of Justice, in an article entitled "*Noches de la
Protervia*," contributed in 1920 to the Buenos Aires review, *Nosotros*.

public Press attacking the ideals represented by
Chocano and his generation.

In Edwin Elmore appears more fully and richly
than in any modern South American writer the flood
of new influences which in recent years have begun
to play upon the intellectual life of the continent.
Carlyle, Tolstoi, Tagore, Unamuno, Barbusse, Fogaz-
zaro, all made contributions to Elmore's spiritual
formation and crusading passion. In two pamphlets, entitled, " The Clamour of Feeling," and " The
Return to Christianity," we reach the bedrock of his
religious position. " The only thing," he says,
" which can free us from desperation is the faith that
Christ lives, the consoling and vivifying idea of his
constant influence at the bottom of our hearts." He
longed for humanity's return to the " bosom of
Jesus," a reminiscence, probably, of the words of his
illustrious countryman Vigil. " Official Christianity,"
said he, " is the greatest of all crimes."

When death overtook him Elmore was interested
in the project of a congress of South American intellectuals. He longed for the *intelligentsia* to launch a
crusade in the interests of the life of the spirit and
universal brotherhood. To promote this project he
had visited several South American countries, meeting,
however, with but scant support. Edwin had not
yet learned that mere culture does not make crusaders,
while not infrequently it produces spiritual reactionaries. But the memory of this noble quixotic soul
will not die in Latin-American history.

(d) *The Lure of the Esoteric*

We now pass beyond the spheres of scientific positivism and of romantic idealism, and enter through the
portals of the esoteric the specifically religious realm.
One of the features of the spiritual history of South
America in recent decades has been the spread of

M

Spiritualism and Theosophy : the former chiefly among the masses, the latter very largely among the educated minorities. The increasing influence of these two esoteric systems, not only in South America but throughout the world, is symbolic of the advent of a new psychic epoch in the spiritual history of man. " A spiritual epoch, I should have said a psychic epoch," said Maeterlinck in *The Treasure of the Humble*, " is perhaps upon us. It would seem as though humanity were on the point of struggling from beneath the crushing burden of matter that weights it down."

As regards Spiritualism, or Spiritism, as it is sometimes called, its devotees claim that it should be viewed as a preparation for a new attitude towards reality, a passage in human evolution—the beginning of a new world order. F. W. H. Myers, one of the earliest and most famous of those interested in psychic research, speaks of it as a preamble to all religion.

Since the days of the Great War the influence of Spiritualism has greatly increased. The anguish of bereavement turned the thoughts of multitudes beyond the bourne of the visible and tangible in quest of evidence that the spirits of loved ones continued a conscious existence, and even hovered around the dear haunts they had left. The common tendency of our time to reduce religion to ethics and social activities has led many men and women whom ethicism has failed to satisfy to seek a deeper insight into reality. Besides that, so-called Liberal Christianity, with its suspicion of the emotional and its disdain of the supernatural, has proved insufficient to satisfy the spiritual longings of masses of people in this age. On the other hand, scientific research has demonstrated beyond all doubt that whatever be the ultimate explanation given to the new phenomena under investigation, " there is more in heaven and earth than is dreamed of in our philosophy."

It is an interesting and significant fact that Spiritualism began to play an important role in the spiritual
life of South America before it had reached its present
vogue, and before eminent figures in science and
literature had lent it the prestige of their names. The
first Spiritualist Society on the continent was organized
in Brazil in 1873 under the name of Confucius. In the
interval between then and now it has had a remarkable
development. As happened in the case of Positivism,
Spiritualism in Brazil also became a religious movement ; it has even been called " the great religious
movement of Brazil." According to the latest available data, in the year 1919 this movement claimed
271,530 members in the republic. There were at
that time a thousand societies. Most of these met in
private houses for séances and the study of Allen
Kardec's classic. It is interesting to observe that
the movement has never had any kind of national
organization to act as its organic centre. Its spread
throughout the republic was due entirely to the
contagious enthusiasm of its adherents.

Besides the accustomed séances Brazilian spiritualists
have carried on activities of a social and literary character. They have been foremost in works of charity.
Their dispensaries have been open to all and sundry.
The work carried on in these dispensaries, where cures
are effected under the alleged guidance of spirits, have
frequently brought the dispensary authorities into
conflict with public officers of health. Yet, despite
this fact, the ministry of healing and the public
charities conducted by Brazilian spiritualists have
given great prestige to the movement among the
lower and middle classes, and have secured patrons
and donors among the aristocracy.

The following are the principal tenets which have
guided the spiritualistic movement in Brazil. First,
the law of spiritual evolution which ensures universal
salvation through personal expiatory experience and

the purification achieved by suffering. Second, the law of action and reaction which explains suffering, and makes it a necessary and uplifting method of approaching God. Third, charity, that is the practice of beneficence as the only expression of religion. Fourth, the need of guidance by spirits not only in regard to the mystery of death but as a help in dealing with everyday problems.[1]

According to more recent reports the power of this movement is now weakening in Brazil, the South American country in which it has made its greatest progress. It has served, however, the valuable purpose of drawing attention to the reality of a spiritual world in a society which was in danger of abandoning religion. It exalted ethics as the supreme expression of the religious life in an environment where an unethical religion had held sway.

Much more formidable and of consequences destined to be more far-reaching is the spread of Theosophy in South America. Like Positivism this movement has owed its success very largely to its universalistic claims, claims which never fail to appeal to the South American heart. It presents itself, moreover, rather as a philosophy than as a religion, a philosophy which contains in synthetic form the quintessence of all the great religions. It is therefore possible for a man to become a theosophist without completely abandoning his own religion, while membership in such a society will not expose him to the terrible brand of becoming a sectarian. In the second place, Theosophy has come to supply one of the deepest-felt needs in South American life, that of soul culture. Through the practice of *yoga* and of meditation in general, which it inculcates, many men and women have been enabled to attain a remarkable degree of spirituality in the broad sense, that is, control of the lower self. The third feature of Theosophy which makes it extra-

[1] Vide *Christian Work in South America*, Vol II., p. 355.

ordinarily attractive to the South American mind to-day is the fact that it hails from the Orient.

Before considering the activity and present status of Theosophy in South America, a word seems in order regarding the origin and general character of the movement.

In recent years, especially since the World War, the eyes of South America have turned wistfully towards Asia, as they had formerly been directed towards Europe, and more particularly towards France. Whatever system claims to have had its origin in the East wins immediate sympathy and is studied with assiduity. The Theosophical Society was organized in 1875, its founders being a Russian woman, Madame Blavatsky, and an English Colonel, H. S. Olcott. Its avowed objects were : First, to form a nucleus of a universal brotherhood of humanity without regard to race, creed, sex or colour. Second, to promote the study of Arian and other Eastern literatures, religions, philosophies and sciences; and to demonstrate the importance of that study. Third, to investigate the unexplained laws of nature and the psychic powers latent in man. The true creator of the theosophical movement in its present form is the English lady, Mrs Annie Besant. She has given great prominence in the movement to the Messianic idea, and has presented to the world its new Messiah in the person of a young Hindu, Krishnamurti.

It is unfortunate for the Theosophical Society that its origins will not stand close scrutiny. In his book, *Modern Religious Movements in India*, Dr J. N. Farquhar devotes a remarkable chapter to the study of the birth of Theosophy in India. Some very unsavoury facts are revealed regarding the personal character of Madame Blavatsky, and of the number of impostures which were resorted to at the beginning to gain notoriety for the movement. It would appear that the Bible of Theosophy, *The Secret Doctrine*, of Madame

Blavatsky, is by no means the original book it has been claimed to be by theosophists, but is rather an eclectic production based on at least a hundred earlier works. Farquhar points out besides, that Theosophy has made a very slight contribution to our knowledge of the great Indian thinkers of the past.

The movement appeared in South America in the early years of the present century. As was the case with Positivism and Spiritualism most of its early adepts were gained in Brazil. Its first students were men belonging to the Brazilian army and navy who were in the habit of meeting for the study of the *Secret Doctrine*. Since those days, and especially in the course of the last decade, Theosophy has made very great progress in South American countries.

Towards the end of 1928 and after theosophical groups existed in most of the large cities, the continent was visited by the Hindu philosopher, Jinarajadasa, Vice-President of the Society, and a doctor of philosophy of the University of Cambridge. Before embarking on his South American tour Jinarajadasa studied Spanish with such success that he was able to lecture in that language. The reception given him on his arrival at Montevideo was a striking revelation of the friendly attitude existing towards oriental thought. Even more so was it an indication of the extraordinary change which had come over the intellectual climate of the Uruguayan capital, previously regarded as the stronghold of materialism. Jinarajadasa delivered his first lecture to a crowded audience formed of the *élite* of Montevideo in the main hall of the National University. He was introduced by the Minister of Education. José Battle y Ordóñez was still alive, yet the meeting took place in a hall which, according to the by-laws of the university, must never be used by any religious organization or for any religious purpose. The minister who introduced the high priest of Theosophy was probably as

religiously neutral as Rodó, but he had obviously
travelled beyond the latter's determination never to
allow his name to be associated with any movement
having a religious basis.

From Montevideo, Jinarajadasa crossed the River
Plate to Buenos Aires, where his lectures filled the
largest theatre in the city.   He later visited Chile,
Peru, Colombia, Cuba and Mexico, meeting everywhere with the most extraordinary success.   In fact
his tour through Latin America had all the features of
a triumphal march.   During his visit to Lima a most
revealing incident occurred.   The Archbishop had
strictly forbidden all Catholics to attend the lectures
of the theosophist.   The result was the complete
breakdown of ecclesiastical discipline and a signal proof
of the waning power of the hierarchy in one of the
most conservative cities on the continent.   A bumper
gathering in the theatre on the last evening of Jinarajadasa's lectures, and the organization of a huge
demonstration under the window of his hotel when
the meeting was over, was the public's reply to
ecclesiastical interference.

The course of lectures delivered by Jinarajadasa on
his Latin-American tour have subsequently been
published under the title of *Gods in Chains*.[1]   The
book is prefaced by an address delivered at one of the
Montevideo meetings by the Uruguayan writer,
Alberto Zum Felde.   An analysis of this address
affords us the point of view of a representative of
South American intellectuality, not himself a theosophist, regarding the ideology of the system.   The
following are some of his statements : " A great
number of those composing the large audience which
attends these lectures of Jinarajadasa are attracted
especially and almost exclusively by a kind of imag-
inative curiosity.   Jinarajadasa represents the legendary mysticism of the Ganges ; the pagoda with its

[1] *Dioses en Cadenas.*

immemorial acts of worship; the remote nudeness of
the Vegas; the sacred awe of the forests of Ramayana;
the hermetic science of the ecstatic *yogis*; the legend
of the enigmatic Thibet; the Brahmanic transmigra-
tion of souls; the clairvoyant vision of the invisible
mahatmas who inspired the Princess Blavatsky to
write the pages of *The Secret Doctrine*." Zum Felde
then makes reference to the spiritual currents in the
Western world by means of which the West approaches
more and more closely to the East. Theosophy, he
says, is a kind of positivism of the spirit in which
intuition is used as an organ of experimental knowledge
for the purpose of forming a great body of concrete
information concerning the metaphysical realm. Its
approach to reality is thus similar to that of the
physical sciences. The significance of Jinarajadasa's
visit, according to Zum Felde, lay particularly in the
reawakening rather than in the superficial satisfaction
of intellectual curiosity. Its interest was particularly
great in view of the fact that the best thought of Europe
and America was now being taken up with similar
problems. He meant to say that for the first time in
the thought life of South America it was intellectually
respectable to treat the religious problem seriously.

What message did the Hindu theosophist bring to
Latin America? Turning to *Gods in Chains* we discover some of the ideas submitted to the Latin-
American public by one of the world's greatest
exponents of Theosophy. Here are some of his
fundamental theses: "Theosophy is not a new
philosophy created by a new school of thinkers; it
is rather a selection of the best thoughts of the ancient
religions, philosophies and mysticisms. It is a science
of nature. Man is God. In one of the Psalms we
find the words, 'I say, ye are gods!' But we are
gods in chains. The difference between what we are
and what we should be is that between rough and
polished diamonds. The finality of life is to liberate

God from his chains. Liberty comes through experience, through the law of *Karma*, the inevitable con-
catination of cause and effect. Man's daily task should
be to be an agent of the Divine plan. Thus Theosophy
is not so much a Gospel of salvation as a Gospel of
work. Man is not the saint who arises out of the
sinner, but the skilled workman who has ceased to be
an apprentice. Original sin consists in our desire to
receive a reward for what we do. Each man is for
himself the way, the truth, and the life."

Referring to the young theosophist Messiah, Krishnamurti, Jinarajadasa gives the following examples
of his extraordinary spiritual originality. For Krishnamurti God is the "Beloved," as if this designation
for the Divine were not common throughout the
history of Christian mysticism. "Conduct is recti-
tude," and this other most strikingly "original"
saying, "Great deeds arise from the vision of the
goal."

The dangers inherent in the practice of *yoga* are fully
recognized by the lecturer. "This practice," says he,
"is not advisable nor possible for man as long as he
has fixed obligations to fulfil. In India it requires the
absolute abandonment of the obligations and interests
of life." Yet, Christ communed with the Father in
periods stolen from sleep late in the night or before
sunrise, between the tasks of a busy ministry, and Paul
looked into the third heaven between spells of tent-
making! The ultimate ideal of Theosophy is the
balcony ; Christianity can accept no ideal which takes
man off the road.

An estimate of Theosophy by a contemporary thinker
who has himself been deeply influenced by oriental
thought, will help us to focus the significance of this
movement. In the course of the tour described in the
Travel Diary of a Philosopher, Count Hermann Keyserling visited the headquarters of the Theosophical
Society in Adyar, in Southern India. Some of his

observations are both interesting and illuminating.
" Theosophy," he says, " is being crystallized more
and more into a kind of Catholic Church within which
faith in authority, readiness to serve, and obedience
are the cardinal virtues."[1] It may be regarded as an
expression of Anglo-Saxon influence on Indian
thought. In his opinion, all philosophic psycholo-
gists and biologists would do well to concern themselves seriously with occult literature. The practice
of *yoga* is particularly interesting and important. It
has a great value for concentration. The great
Jesuits are *yogis*, but *yoga* is neutral, like gymnastics.
For that reason the knowledge of higher worlds and
spiritualization are not necessarily connected.

Keyserling is convinced, in spite of the protestations
to the contrary contained in the statutes of the Society,
that Theosophy is a special religion. This it must be,
in so far as it wishes to be alive at all. Keyserling
means to say that any organization claiming to be
purely universal and entirely non-sectarian is an utter
impossibility as a dynamic and progressive movement.

Very interesting is the German philosopher's criticism of Theosophy, and of the type of individual produced by it. Here are his own words : " Mankind
is becoming more and more individualized from day
to day ; men are getting more and more conscious
of their individuality, and take an increasing pride in
the personal element. Thus the idea of universality
in all inner questions loses importance and power
accordingly, and general formulæ prove themselves
to be increasingly insufficient. . . . The Theosophical
Society has attempted to save the idea of universality,
and make it serviceable for its own purposes by
including all religions within its own. Far from
strengthening it, this weakens Theosophy. So wide
a basis cannot exist as a monad ; it cannot possibly
give an inner form to any one, which is the real pur-

[1] Vol. I., p. 119.

pose of religious profession.   It is true that Theosophy does not wish to be a profession of faith, but it relaxes this determination against its will, for it must be one in so far as the movement is to endure, since it would be powerless as a purely scientific organization." [1]

As regards the theosophist's interest in occultism, Keyserling concludes that this has a greater scientific than religious value.   The whole process encouraged by Theosophy leads to the externalization of the religious impulse.   Besides, the chief virtues which it preaches, being essentially feminine in quality, have ceased to operate.   In the opinion of this neo-Nietzschian, an historical future awaits masculine virtues only for some time to come.

Reviewing the results of Theosophy in South America, one is bound to say that the movement has been fruitful in good.   It has undoubtedly given many people a power over themselves and their lower natures which they had not formerly possessed. It has tended towards temperance, abstemiousness, personal purity, and an interest in good causes and spirituality in general.   It has aroused its followers to great liberality, so that many theosophists give more generously to their cause than do either Catholics or Protestants to theirs.   At the same time, Keyserling's observation that Theosophy tends to produce a spiritually effeminate type in which passive virtues predominate over active, is apt to be borne out by facts. The very universality of which it boasts will prove increasingly its weakness at a time when the creative forces of the world grow more passionate and men demand an absolute.   One cannot but regard this movement in South America and elsewhere as a revolt of the human spirit against the closed and rigid universe in which many modern tendencies would enclose it, and at the same time as a preparation for a more definite and potent form of spirituality.   An

[1] Vide *The Travel Diary of a Philosopher*, Vol. I., p. 159.

analysis of the present situation would suggest that Spiritualism and Theosophy, and the many minor cults which are in vogue, occupy the same position and discharge the same function as did the strange and numerous cults of the Græco-Roman world at the time when Christianity made its appearance.   One thing is certain ; spiritual unrest affecting all groups, from the lowest social stratum to the highest, is the most characteristic feature of South American life at the present time.   The old sluices have yielded before the surge of new waters from the great deep, as the pent-up souls of men burst forth in a feverish quest of fresh channels for heart and mind.

(e) *Spiritual Antipodes*

Besides the new spiritual tendencies just described, two more have made their appearance in the contemporary life of South America.   These may be regarded as the extreme poles towards one or other of which tend to gravitate those expressions of spiritual life that seem destined to have a future.   Both are grounded upon a specific interpretation of history. According to the one the meaning of human history was fulfilled in Jesus Christ in such a way that only in and through Him can life and history attain their true meaning.   According to the other all previous history has been a preparation for the historic epoch now being inaugurated, in which the proletariat of the world will occupy the position which formerly belonged during successive periods to the aristocratic and bourgeois classes.   A distinguished representative of the former tendency is the Brazilian journalist, Dr José Carlos Rodríguez, who died in 1923.   An equally distinguished representative of the latter is the Peruvian journalist and author, José Carlos Mariátegui, who passed away less than two years ago in his early thirties.

José Carlos Rodríguez was for many years the owner and editor of the leading Brazilian daily, O *Jornal do Comercio*. According to his great friend and biographer, Dr Hugh C. Tucker, agent of the American Bible Society in Brazil, he experienced a religious conversion in early life through reading the Bible. From that time on the Bible became his passion. Until the day of his death, on the border of eighty, he was accustomed to read it carefully and prayerfully each morning and evening. His life was that of a saint. There was no good work in the community in which he did not take a leading part. And yet, strange to say, this Brazilian saint and scholar never came to identify himself with any religious organization, Catholic or Protestant. On one occasion, a devout Roman Catholic asked him about his religious affiliation. "Now, doctor," he said, "please tell me, are you really a Protestant?" The reply was: "I hope I am a Christian!" As to his being truly so, a life abounding in good works was ample testimony.

For many years it had been Dr Rodríguez's ambition to write a monumental work on the Bible. After retiring from active journalism he found the necessary time to undertake this task. During five years he devoted himself to critical research upon the Old Testament, and at the end of that time he produced a book which will remain a monument in Portuguese religious literature. It is a large two volume work printed and bound by T. & A. Constable, Edinburgh.[1] In the preface we read: "Our principal object in this work is to show that the advent of Jesus Christ is the legitimate outcome or end of the old Testament—the historic conclusion of the Divine activity in the life of Israel." The author's chief interest in the Old Testament was that it "leads us to Jesus Christ." He had intended following this work with a small volume on the period between the Testaments, and to write a

[1] *Estudo sobre o Velho Testamento.*

third on Christ and the Apostolic Age.   Death took
him, however, before these plans could be realized.

In two distinct senses is José Carlos Rodríguez a
symbolic figure in the religious life of South America.
He represents that group of people who, like Unamuno
in Spain, have found spiritual satisfaction in historic
Christianity.   Their minds are open to truth wherever
it comes from, they are interested in the new light
which historical studies have thrown upon the Scriptures.   They have discovered a unique revelation of
God in the Christian records, and through the study of
them they nourish their spiritual life.   They have, above
all, discovered the significance of Jesus Christ, and their
passionate devotion to Him leads them to work for the
same objectives for which their Lord lived and died.
Many of them are members of Evangelical Churches,
some live within the pale of the Roman Catholic communion, some have no ecclesiastical home.   The
Brazilian journalist is particularly symbolical of these
last, an increasing number of men and women throughout Latin America who are Christian in their attitude
towards Christ and the Scriptures, but who, for one
reason or another, have hitherto failed to find a spiritual
home within the organized Christian Church.

At the opposite pole stands the militant communist, José Carlos Mariátegui.   For a number of
years before his death, this other José Carlos was the
most erudite and dynamic writer on social questions in
the whole South American continent.   The Peruvian
Sociological Review, *Amauta*, which he edited, came
to have a continent-wide circulation among radical
thinkers and leaders.   Mariátegui had the qualities of
an apostle.   Returning to Peru in 1922, after three
years of observation and study in Europe, he devoted
himself to a brilliant analysis of modern civilization,
giving special attention to the problem of Peru.   He
treated the religious problem with great reverence and
acumen, fully aware of the significance of religious

values, but convinced that revolutionary socialism was the true successor of religion in our day.   In the sphere of economic theory, his thinking was determined by Marx and Engels.   Though for many years a cripple, and with a constitution undermined by phthisic germs, Mariátegai toiled day and night at his desk.   To visit him in his home and listen to that mellow voice pour out in measured accents a militant philosophy of life, so strangely dissonant from the fragile physique of its author, was indeed an inspiring experience.   For Mariátegui Communism was a religion, a religion which he professed and propagated with all the passion of his soul.

The figure of Mariátegui is a symbol of that great wave of social unrest which began to manifest itself among the working and student classes in South America in the second decade of the present century. Reference has already been made to the historic occasion in 1918 when the student body of the old Argentine University of Cordoba rose in revolt. The reform movement spread like wildfire to most of the other university centres on the continent.   One of its chief features was the rapprochement between the student and the working classes.   In several countries, especially in Peru and Chile, the students organized People's Universities for the education of the masses. Mariátegui returned from Europe at the time when this movement was at its height in Peru, and just before a tyrannical government, fearing the projections of the student-workmen *entente* in the social structure of the country, banished its leaders.   Being an invalid, Mariátegui went unmolested, and continued to pour out his soul.[1]

Revolutionary socialism as represented by Mariátegui has taken possession of a considerable number of South

---

[1] An interesting article by Waldo Frank in the *New Republic*, August 12, 1931, entitled " Two Latin Americans," describes the personality of Augusto Leguía, the Peruvian Dictator, and José Carlos Mariátegui, the " Poet."

American youth around the continent.   It is a different
phenomenon from any which has appeared hitherto in
the turbulent political and social life of the Southern
Continent.   In the ranks of the movement are members
of blue-blooded families who have become passionately
and sincerely interested in social problems, and who
have steeped themselves through prolonged study in
the principles of social radicalism.   Apart from the
far-reaching consequences which this movement may
have in the future life of the continent, it has besides a
distinctly religious significance.   Many of its members
believe with Mariátegui that the true present-day
equivalent of the dynamic religions of humanity, which
in their time exercised a great influence upon mankind,
is revolutionary socialism.   For that reason reference
to the ideology of Mariátegui is important.   It will
show in what direction these ardent spirits have turned
to satisfy the religious thirst of their nature.

Mariátegui himself accepted the principle laid down
by George Sorrel in his great treatise on Violence,
that to-day revolutionary myths can occupy the depths
of human consciousness with the same plenitude as
the ancient myths of religion.   Revolutionary action,
says Mariátegui, is only possible on the basis of passionate faith in a myth.   At the present time bourgeois
society finds itself in a state of doubt, in a mythless
world ; only among the proletariat is faith truly found.
The myth of this historical epoch is that the hour
has struck for proletarian domination.   Humanity,
which always needs to feel itself near to a goal, feels
itself to be near one now.   For the proletarian class,
humanity's true representative at the present time, " a
new day of the Lord " has come.   That it is the " final
struggle " is on men's lips everywhere.   The only
true crusaders of to-day are thus to be found among
the masses.   Here alone are conviction and passion to
be met with.   Descartes' *Cogito Ergo Sum* [1] is the watch-

---

[1] " I know therefore I am."

word of a past age ; the affirmation that will bring in the new era is *Pugno Ergo Sum*.[1] Only crusaders are truly alive and have a real future before them.

As a Marxist, Mariátegui considers the ecclesiastical and dogmatic forms of religion to be peculiar to and inherent in the social-economic régime which produced and sustains them. The Communist, says he, is for that reason not interested in mere anti-clericalism, which he regards as simply a diversion of bourgeois liberalism. As for Protestantism, it is Mariátegui's opinion that it has entered Latin America not directly, that is to say, on its own spiritual and religious power, but only indirectly, through educational and social work.[2]

(f) *A Pathfinder*

It remains to be said, however, in order to complete this picture, that not all the social radicals of the new generation in South America are Communists. Still less are they hostile to Christianity. I think of one in particular, the greatest of them all, who has passed through the full cycle of revolutionary thought and activity, including Communism, and has come out convinced that the Russian social experiment can never and must never have a future in South America. This young man, Haya de la Torre, has been the most representative and revolutionary figure in university and labour circles in South America during the last decade. He is undoubtedly the most brilliant figure of the new generation, and one who seems destined to play an important rôle in the future life of Peru and of the Continent as a whole.

Scion of one of the oldest and noblest families in Northern Peru, Haya de la Torre became interested in the social problem in the early days of his student life in Lima. On account of his radicalism his family

---

[1] " I combat therefore I am."
[2] Mariátegui's chief works are *La Escena Contemporánea*, and *Siete Ensayos de Interpretación de la Realidad Peruana*.

N

cut off his support, and the young man was thrown entirely on his own resources. It was difficult to find employment, and for a time he lived on the brink of starvation. A terrible experience of hunger gave him a first-hand experience and insight into the sufferings of a large section of his fellow-countrymen, and he there and then resolved to dedicate his life to the cause of the proletariat. His new sense of vocation led him to prepare himself physically and morally for his life task. Two things were necessary : he must develop his body to be able to stand the fatigues that lay before him, and he must offer a model of right living to the students and workmen who followed his leadership.

At the beginning, Haya de la Torre shared the religious outlook of the young radicals. " Every time I try to pronounce the word ' God ' it nauseates in my mouth," is a statement of his dating from the early days of his student life in Lima. He later made the discovery that in the writings of the Old Testament prophets and in the teachings of Jesus were more incandescent denunciations of oppression and wrong than he or his companions had ever made. It dawned upon him not only that there could be a union between religion and ethics, but that there should be, and that in the religion of the Bible there was. The Book began to take on a new meaning.

Between 1919 and 1923 the young revolutionary, as President of the Federation of Peruvian Students, carried on a remarkable piece of social and educational work among the working-class in Lima and its environs. Not only were the rudiments of education imparted, but instruction was given in hygiene and civics by a volunteer band of enthusiastic young undergraduates. A transformation began to take place in the way of life and outlook of a section of the proletariat. The Indians in the valleys and high Punas of the Andes saw a ray of hope for their future. But a tyrannical, soulless government, afraid of the consequences if the new social movement spread, adopted drastic measures against the leaders.   A few months after Haya de la Torre and his friends had prevented the consecration of Peru to an effigy of the Sacred Heart, he and they were expelled from the country.   That was in the month of October 1923.   In October 1931 he stood as a candidate for the Presidency of his country.

Eight years of exile were the best preparation the future presidential candidate could have had.   His first great experience was in Russia, which he entered as a Communist in 1924, at the special invitation of Trotsky.   He was shown everything from the Neva to the Volga, many things that ingenuous visitors never see.   " What I saw," as he himself afterwards put it, " cured me of Communism forever."   He compre- hended clearly that Latin America required something quite different.   Very specially did he revolt against the Soviet effort to eradicate the religious sentiment.

Broken health followed this Russian visit, and months of rest became necessary in a sanatorium in the Swiss Alps before Haya de la Torre's health was restored. When he recovered he went to London.   A period in England, during which he studied in the London School of Economics, and Ruskin College, Oxford, and came into close contact with members of the British Labour Party, was epoch-making both in the formation of his character and the clarification of his social ideology.   At the same time the organization and ideals of the Chinese Kuo-ming-tang exercised an extraordinarily deep impression on his political outlook. He preferred the Chinese model to that of Moscow.

A very successful visit to the United States, Mexico, and the countries of Central America in 1928 ended in Haya de la Torre's deportation to Germany by American officials of the Panama Canal Zone, when he was returning again to Mexico by the Pacific Coast. The early months of his stay in Germany were months of terrible suffering.   But his iron will remained un-

broken. He corresponded indefatigably with groups
of Peruvian exiles in different parts of Europe and
Latin America, whom he had already organized into
a new party called the *Apra* or *Alianza Popular Revolu-
cionaria Americana*.[1] He supported himself by teaching and writing articles for the Latin-American Press,
engrossed the while in the study of Economics and
the Latin-American problem.

In December 1929, in the course of wanderings
through Europe, I made a surprise visit to my old
friend and colleague of the Anglo-Peruvian College,
Lima. I found him in the Berlin suburb of Charlotten-
burg. It was evening when I knocked at the door
of his lodgings. The door opened, and there was
Haya rigged out in his dressing-gown as though it
were still morning. He had, faithfully as of old,
begun the day by an hour's gymnastic exercises to
keep himself fit. After that he settled down for the
rest of the day to his desk, without having had a
glimpse of the outside world.

More than six years had passed since Haya de la
Torre was exiled from Peru. I discovered that he had
greatly matured, and that his spiritual outlook was both
calmer and clearer. A few weeks previously a group
of Peruvian officers in Europe had been to visit him
to propose that he head a revolution in his native
country. He refused to have anything to do with the
old kind of revolution they had in mind. One of his
first gestures that evening was to take down a small
Bible from a book-shelf. "Look how it is marked;"
he said opening it, "this new book on Latin America
which I am writing is going to be full of quotations
from the Bible." The following evening, as we
strolled together along the Unter den Linden, he
recounted an experience which had come to him during
his last visit to Mexico. The Soviet minister and he
happened to be guests together at a banquet. The

---

[1] Popular Revolutionary Alliance of America.

former made the following statement in his after-dinner speech : " I consider that our social organization in Russia would be the ideal solution of the Latin-American problem. I see, however, one great difficulty in the way of its introduction : the innate mysticism of the people. If only that could be eradicated, the implantation of Sovietism would be a simple matter." When it was the Peruvian revolutionary's turn to speak he turned to the representative of revolutionary Russia : " How dare you, a foreigner," he said to him, " suggest that we eliminate from the life of this Continent that mystic sentiment which is our greatest asset for the future ? Understand, sir, that there are men who propose integrating that sentiment into the coming social revolution in Latin America."

Haya de la Torre is interested in conserving and cultivating true religious values. Quite as revolutionary and socially-minded in his outlook as Mariátegui, he recognizes what the latter failed to recognize : that the human problem is spiritual before it is economic. At the same time Haya de la Torre and the party he has brought into being, the chief fruit so far of the socially-minded and strongly Latin-Americanistic generation which was born in Cordoba in 1918, represent the most constructive revolutionary forces in Latin America to-day.

Rejecting both Communism and Fascism, the *Apra* presumes to deal with the specific problems of Latin-American countries, focusing particular attention upon the question of so-called economic imperialism. The importance of this movement lies in the fact that the new party went to the polls in the Peruvian elections last October, and its leader, although returned from exile only a few months before, and after announcing a most radical programme, came very near being elected president of the country. In the not remote future this party will come into power. It can be taken for granted that the tendency it represents will

be followed in other parts of the Continent where the
Cordoba generation with its continental outlook begins
to make itself felt.   There are evidences that a new
era is about to break in South American politics.   A
new Ayacucho is being dreamed of, which will bring
to the Continent economic and spiritual independence,
as the last battle of the Revolutionary War brought it
political independence more than a century ago.   It is
fully recognized, however, that for the present situation in the political, economic and spiritual realms, the
people themselves have been more to blame than any
outside forces.   For that reason the spiritual problem
will have a place alongside the economic and political
in the mind of the future leaders of the Continent.
At the same time the understanding sympathy of
Christian leaders, especially in the United States and
Great Britain, will be sought in the great approaching
struggle.   If this is ungrudgingly given there will be
no danger of South America following Russia in its
spiritual attitude.   If it fails to be given the future is
a red question mark.

As for religion, in so far as it represents a purifying
and creative force, it will be treated with sympathy,
but clericalism and parasitic religion will be combated
as it has been in Spain.   The next government
in Peru will undoubtedly decree the separation of
Church and State in that Republic.   It would not
be surprising, however, were the attempt made to
sever the connection between the Peruvian Church
and Rome.   Haya de la Torre has expressed the view
that a free and independent Catholic Church in that
country would inevitably pass through a spiritual
reformation, and make a decisive contribution to the
national life.   There is not the slightest doubt but that
the advent of a series of national churches in South
America, liberated from the influence of Rome and the
Jesuit Order, would mark the opening of a new day
in the spiritual history of the Continent.

CHAPTER X

SOME CONTEMPORARY RELIGIOUS THINKERS

IF in the sphere of life South American Catholicism did not succeed in producing a true mystic, in the sphere of thought it failed to produce a religious literature. In the space of nearly four centuries the clergy have produced no religious work of note. As for the laity, whatever may have been the sentiments of individual men of letters among them, religion has not been considered a suitable subject for the exercise of literary talent.

In recent years, however, a decided change has taken place in the intellectual attitude of both clergy and laity towards religion and the religious problem. The former have awakened to the necessity of offering a reasoned defence of the dogmas of the Church; the latter have been impressed by the new attitude of European and North American thinkers towards the whole subject of religion. The death of philosophical materialism as a respectable creed in the leading universities, the arrival of idealistic currents from Europe, the recognition of the fact that religion is regarded in the great centres of learning as a human phenomenon worthy of serious intellectual consideration, blended to the growing consciousness of personal spiritual needs, have operated a complete change in the outlook of South American thinkers. In almost every one of the leading magazines, such as *Nosotros* of Buenos Aires, a serious article appears from time to time on a religious topic. From an attitude of iconoclastic hostility to religion followed by a spirit of utter indifference to it, representative thinkers have now turned to a serious investigation of the religious problem. Religion has at least come to signify a psychological phenomenon with projections of a vital and far-reaching sociological character.

In the course of the last decade writers of distinction have appeared throughout the Continent for whom religious studies have had supreme interest. Among the minor figures may be mentioned Nuñez Regueiro, the Uruguayan Consul in the Argentine port of Rosario. Regueiro, who occupies a chair of philosophy in the university of that town, has written several books of a religious-philosophical character. Protestant in origin, he possesses considerable philosophical culture, united to a truly religious spirit. He reveals an undoubted grasp of some of the main problems at issue ; but unfortunately his literary work has been marked by great abstractness and obscurity, so that his books are neither easy nor interesting reading. His influence has in consequence been slight.

Another interesting figure is Clemente Ricci, Professor of Greek in the University of Buenos Aires. Ricci is the author of a number of studies on the historical origins of Christianity He himself, however, is neither a Christian nor a man of any religious faith whatever. That being so, his work has been lacking in passion, possessing little more than a technical value in the spheres of history and linguistics. The figure of Ricci is extraordinarily interesting nevertheless, representing, as it does, the beginning of a new direction in South American cultural interests.

(a) Gabriela Mistral : a Liberal Catholic

In Gabriela Mistral we have a representative South American authoress, who is at once a sincere Catholic, and a frank and ready exponent of the faith that is in her. This Chilian poetess came to fame following a review of her volume of poems *Desolación* by

Federico de Onís, professor of Spanish in the University of Columbia, New York. She is now recognized by literary critics to be the leading contemporary poetess in the Spanish tongue, whether in the Old World or in the New.

Gabriela Mistral began life as a simple primary school teacher in a country district of Chile. An echo of her teaching days and experiences occurs in a beautiful prose prayer, *Oración de una Maestra*,[1] which for the sentiment it contains and the language in which it is clothed, forms one of the choicest passages in modern Spanish literature. We venture to translate some of its chief paragraphs as follows : " Lord, Thou didst teach, forgive me for teaching, for bearing the name of teacher which Thou didst bear upon earth. Give me supreme love for my school. . . .

" Grant, Master, that my fervour may be enduring and transient my disappointment. Take from me this improper desire for justice which still disturbs me, this base suggestion of protest which rises within me when I am hurt. May I not be pained by the lack of understanding nor saddened by the forgetfulness of those whom I have taught. . . .

" Make me more a mother than mothers are, that I may be able to love and defend as they do what is not flesh of my flesh. May I succeed in making of one of my girls my perfect stanza, and in her bequeath Thee my most enduring melody against the day when my lips shall sing no more. . . .

" Show me the possibility of Thy Gospel in my time that I may not give up the daily, hourly battle in its defence. . . .

" Friend, come with me ; sustain me ; many a time I shall have no one but Thee at my side. When my doctrine is purer and the truth I teach more scorching, the worldly will abandon me, but Thou wilt then press me against Thy heart, Thy heart which knew so well

[1] *A Teacher's Prayer.*

the meaning of loneliness and abandonment. Only in Thy look shall I seek the sweetness of approbation."

Here is the Other Spanish Christ, and here the attitude toward life which His fellowship engenders : a sense of vocation, a passion for human beings even the humblest, loyalty to truth, disregard for popular opinion, a life spent under the guiding eye of the Divine Friend. In this prayer of a village schoolmistress a new note sounds in the religious life and thought of South America. The Christ who " lives in the fields," who " moves among the pots," whose name is " Jesus," the bestower of health, the Christ who died and now lives, has entered the school-room where his presence is much more needed at the present time than in thousands of costly churches which have been erected to his dead memory.

So far Gabriela Mistral has not given systematic expression to her thoughts on religion. She has, however, in a number of articles and letters made a profession of faith, and indicated its implications for the life and culture of the present time. In a long letter to the Argentine educator, Julio Barcos, a copy of which has come into the writer's possession, she discusses very frankly the educational theories of her Argentine friend, pronouncing herself resolutely opposed to the so-called " neutral " school which he advocates. " There can be no such thing as religious neutrality in education," she declares. " Only stupid people can make the claim to be absolutely neutral on the great issue of life and religion. As for ' neutral ' schools, they inevitably become instruments of the teaching of irreligion as has happened in countries like France." What is needed is the development of private schools where religion can be taught freely according to the faith of the school authorities. This involves, however, the finding of suitable teachers with a religious sense of vocation. The kind of teacher needed for the school of the future must have " grace," which the poetess interprets to mean a " certain God-given joy in creating." Were such " grace " to descend from on high the mantle of Don Francisco Giner de los Ríos would fall upon every man, and that of Doña Gabriela Mistral upon every woman, who devote themselves to the sacred task of educating youth in South America. .

One of the most interesting articles of Gabriela Mistral on the subject of religion appeared in the *Nueva Democracia* for January 1931. At her suggestion the editor instituted an inquiry among representative South American writers to elicit their opinion concerning the Bible. She herself took the lead in formulating her own. As a girl of seven, so she informs her readers, she began to read the Bible. Her grandmother, who was a *católica biblica—rara avis*, adds Doña Gabriela—taught her some of the Psalms of David. From then till now she has been a constant reader of the Scriptures. The periods in her life in which her daily reading of the Bible ceased, coincided with her times of spiritual declension. " My passion for the Bible," says she, " is perhaps the only bridge which unites me with the Anglo-Saxon race, the piece of common soil on which I find myself at home with this race." Then she adds, " Some day not far distant I hope to see the essential Book in every South American Catholic home—the Book which can as little be done without as our faces, which is as logical a necessity as our names—just as I see it in every North American home, where it meets us with its holy and familiar countenance." These words, which are an echo of the sentiments expressed nearly a hundred years ago by the Argentine priest and patriot, Padre Juan Ignacio de Gorriti, and of similar sentiments more recently expressed by the contemporary Argentine writer, Julio Navarro Monzó, give the reasoned and passionate opinion of a cultured and patriotic South American lady of our time, that the greatest need in the spiritual life of the Continent is the presence of the Bible in every home.

(b) *José Zorrilla de San Martín : an Orthodox Catholic*

Zorrilla de San Martín is beyond doubt the most venerated figure in South American letters to-day. He is the author of two epic poems, *Tabaré* and *La Leyenda Patria*, which will keep his memory fresh in South American letters throughout all time. He is also a prose writer of great power and classical beauty. In his prime he was an orator of the first rank.

Zorrilla has given chief expression to his religious sentiments and ideas in a volume of addresses delivered in his prime,[1] and in a couple of small books entitled *El Sermón de la Paz* and *El Libro de Ruth*, which belong to the period of old age. It is not, however, his thoughts on religion that constitute the most interesting and original aspect of Zorrilla as a writer, but rather his own religious personality. That a leading professional man of letters should never lose an opportunity to give expression to his deep and sincere religious sentiment is a unique phenomenon in South American literary history. It is interesting to note, in this connection, that when Zorrilla was a young man, the Catholic Church in Uruguay was the object of bitter opposition. A Young Men's Catholic Club was formed, of which he was one of the founders. It was under the auspices of this club that most of his addresses on religious topics were delivered.

The religious thought of Zorrilla de San Martín contains nothing that is original and much that is commonplace. It does little more than breathe loyalty to the Church, her dogmas and her authorities, and to the fundamental Christian spirit. Yet some of his favourite and most frequently expressed ideas may be of interest. Addressing his fellow-members of the

---

[1] *Conferencias y Discursos.*

Catholic Club, he calls himself "your brother in the cause of Christ." Time and again he reiterates his consecration to the service of Christ in his native country. Faith he describes as a "blind church organist," it is a "gratuitous gift of God, a reflection of his glory, a luminous breath of his infinite piety upon the piece of clay which forms my heart." Merely to admire Jesus Christ he regards as no more than naiveté. It does not constitute religion or anything like it. His fine Christian spirit and wide sympathy come out in the following statement : "Our religion, our church, our community of the faithful, is not primarily a doctrine or a system but an organism, a living mystic being made up of body and spirit. We are not Christian men because we profess this or that metaphysical or moral doctrine, but because we are part, let us say cells, of that organism. Those who belong to the soul of the church, although not to its visible embodiment, are more numerous than we imagine, infinitely more."

Had the spirit and faith of Zorrilla de San Martín characterized even a minority of cultured men in South American lands during the years since their incorporation into civilization, the religious history of the Continent would have been entirely different. Unfortunately, such a type as Zorrilla has hitherto been noted by its absence. He himself stands out even to-day a unique and solitary figure among the older generation of contemporary writers.[1]

(c) Ricardo Rojas : a Literary Christian

The year 1927 was a red letter year for Argentine and South American letters. Don Ricardo Rojas, one of the leading literary men of the Continent, celebrated in that year his twenty-fifth jubilee as a writer. He

[1] Since these lines were written José Zorrilla de San Martín has passed away.

did so in a very unusual way. After having devoted himself with success to literary and historical studies during a quarter of a century, he celebrated his silver jubilee by the publication of a book on Christ. It was the first time in the history of South American literature that a front-line literary man had written a book about Jesus. That in itself was remarkable, but more remarkable still was the fact that the writer in the course of the volume should have pronounced himself a Christian, while refusing to have himself labelled by any ecclesiastical or denominational title.

It was not the first time that Rojas had expressed his interest in religion. Here and there throughout his works one may discover casual and sympathetic references to the subject. Attention has already been drawn to the introduction with which he prefaced his edition of the *Reflections* of Juan Ignacio Gorriti. From youth up he was devoted to the quest of religious certainty. *El Cristo Invisible*,[1] however, is in reality his first systematic book on the subject. His motive in writing this book was to testify that he had at length discovered a true foundation for his faith. It appears that, in the course of an illness, he came to the conclusion, like many another modern, that in order to be truly a man he must needs come face to face with the Man and define his attitude toward Him. The resultant volume is a long dialogue which took place in one of the mountain regions of Argentina, between the author and a friend of his, a Roman Catholic bishop. The dialogue form as a literary device is rather unfortunate. One gets the impression that the book is rather a long monologue. The author's episcopal interlocutor is entirely lacking in individuality, and is really no more than a convenient foil to give sharper relief to Rojas' own ideas.

Taking the book as a whole, its place in literature

---

[1] An excellent English translation of the *Invisible Christ*, by Dr W. E. Browning, was published in 1931 by the Abingdon Press.

will not depend by any means upon the originality of its ideas. For Anglo-Saxon readers, for whom an admirable translation has now been provided, it can have but slight religious interest. They will learn little that they did not know before about Christ and the Gospels; as a matter of fact, the volume contains a great many curious mistakes in its biblical quotations. It is lacking, moreover, in the highest form of religious passion. Unamuno made the remark in a letter written to Rojas himself that in his opinion *El Cristo Invisible* was much more of a literary than a religious effort. Rojas is not a crusader like Unamuno, nor an apostle like Don Francisco Giner de los Ríos. He is a man of letters with religious interests to which he gives expression, and then passes on to fresh pastures.

The really interesting thing about this book is that it should have been written by Ricardo Rojas at an epochal moment of his career as the sincere expression of his religious experience and ideas, and further, that the author should have related Christ to the life and destiny of his country. In this regard its significance and value are simply incalculable. It inaugurates a new and more Christian era in South American letters, and has done more than any other volume to stimulate interest in Christ and the Bible. Writing in *La Razón* of Buenos Aires, towards the close of 1927, the Argentine journalist, Baltasar Cañizal, made the following significant statement: " Looking at what I call the desert of the Bible in Argentina, a desert more extensive than its boundless pampas, the *Invisible Christ* of Ricardo Rojas, by the simple enunciation of the theme of which it treats, acquires immediately the importance of an exemplary and transcendent work."

Turning therefore to this literary landmark, let us endeavour to crystallize those aspects of it which have deathless significance in the history of South America's spiritual pilgrimage. Most significant of all is the alleged object the author had in writing it. He wanted

to consider Christian sentiment as the inspiration of
life. This is the key to the whole volume. Christianity, as we have already seen, had failed to translate
itself into living, life-inspiring sentiments in the religious history of the Continent. Rojas' main object is
to recount a concrete example of deep religious unrest
which found its satisfaction in a spiritual relationship to
Christ; a relationship which not only satisfied heart and
mind, but which pointed the way towards a new order
of human relationships. Unamuno has emphasized
the element of tension in the kind of spiritual health
which the Christ who is " Jesus " introduces into life.
Rojas lays emphasis on the element of harmony. Let
us glance at the dialogues in order.

The theme of the first is the Image of Christ. Here
the author describes how he set out in quest of the
authentic image of the Master; a profoundly symbolical
pilgrimage in the religious life of South America.
Delicately woven into a Socratic web of ideas is the
strand of a prose lyric, the autobiography of a religious
seeker. " Born in the bosom of a Catholic family," he
says, " with no immediate ancestors who were not
Catholics, I was baptized by order of my parents
according to the orthodox mode of old-time South
America. I kept the commandments of the Roman
Catholic Church during my childhood, and even when
my philosophical liberty separated me from Catholicism, I never ceased to feel myself profoundly Christian
in the broadest sense of the word." " Catholic
idolatry," he adds, " alienated me from its worship, but
its images reconciled me to evangelical truth." The
image of Christ in particular fascinated him. He must
discover the authentic likeness if that were possible.
His eyes would fain look into the very eyes of the Lord.
He became a kind of knight of the real image. During
a visit to Europe he wandered far and wide in search of
the Christ-likeness. " I visited the Catacombs, study-
ing the most archaic images of Christ. After that, I

went through oratories, libraries, museums, searching
everywhere for representations of the God-Man in the
miniatures of the missal and the sculptures of ancient
basilicas. I carried on these rovings, not for the
vanity of knowing the historic truth, but for the need
of possessing the mystic truth."

He came to realize, however, that the Christian
Church possesses no authentic effigy of her Founder.
The image of Jesus has been remodelled throughout
twenty centuries according to the race, region, epoch,
culture, school and temperament of individual believers.
Yet, something has remained unchanged and unchange-
able : the Cross. " The Cross," says Rojas, " has
come to take the place of the human image of Jesus."
In the life of a true Christian, therefore, the ineffable
sacrificial love symbolized by the Cross must be central.
Christ Himself remains invisible, but His action will be
evidenced each time He creates in a human life a fresh
Bethlehem for His birth, and a fresh Calvary for His
resurrection. The whole Christian drama is thus
recapitulated in each Christian life. A reminder of
Pascal and Unamuno.

In the two following dialogues, entitled *The Word of
Christ* and *The Spirit of Christ*, Rojas continues the
narrative of his search. Having discovered the ideal
symbol, or archetype of the true life, he must now
devote himself to the discovery of an authoritative
programme of action and an adequate source of inspiration. Knowing the true road to take, where shall he
find light to guide his steps and strength to carry him
to his goal ? Both these he finds in Him who said He
was the Truth and the Life as well as the Way. It
dawns on the reader at this point that the dialogues are
really a commentary on that jewelled text of the Fourth
Gospel—" I am the Way, the Truth, and the Life."

While the image of Christ had always fascinated our
author, the Gospels appealed to him very little in the
early years of his search. He sought elsewhere the

o

voice of authority. This is a profoundly Catholic
experience. The time came, however, when those
"four poems about Christ" appeared to him in a
wholly new light. The historical criticism of the
Gospels gave him the authentic image in a transfigured
form. "Scientific criticism," he says, "so far from
invalidating the Gospels, has made them more human
and forceful. Considered simply as historical documents they have recovered an authority which they had
lost in the eyes of the incredulous. As a result of
modern exegesis it would be as arbitrary to have doubts
regarding these documents as it would be to doubt all
written sources of antiquity. If our scepticism leads us
to suppress Christ, we might as well suppress Tiberius
also and all the other personages of His epoch."

The figure of the historical Jesus, as distinct from
the liturgic image whose lure had originated his spiritual quest, impressed him with its extraordinary virility.
He saw through the utter unreality of the hellenized
portraits that Strauss and Renan had drawn of the
Galilean. Neither was Jesus the "archetype of
beggars," which He was depicted as being in South
American religious tradition. He was the true Super-
man, a fact which Nietzsche failed to comprehend.
Henceforth Christ became our author's only authority
and the Gospels his only law. The essence of the
Master's message he found to consist in no programme
of political reform; it was of an intimate and personal
nature. It became evident to him, however, that Jesus'
concept of the Kingdom of God had a social as well
as a personal aspect. It was a state of society as
well as a state of the soul. Man had to be redeemed
and the earth to be pacified and be brought under the
reign of justice, work and love. The last and greatest
posthumous miracle of Christ is thus His word or
message, "because of the number of souls which it
has purified, which it has consoled, which it has raised
into holiness in every region of the planet." This

wonder-working power is the only proof needed of the authenticity of the Word of Christ.

But let no one think that Christ has no further message for the world. In a passage of great beauty Rojas expresses his wistful longing that our distraught earth may soon listen to a new message from the Master: "The Master described the Kingdom of Heaven as both a realization on earth and a gracious state of the soul. For twenty centuries humanity has gone on achieving this realization, in the individual through spiritual progress and in the race through political progress. The process has not ended, and the time for a new mystic hope for the world is coming. Humanity goes on its way distracted, like the incredulous Cleopas on the Emmaus road in the gloaming, and perhaps the Risen One is coming in an invisible form to give a new message to souls." Such a passage voices the increasing longing which we find in South America for the advent of a spiritual religion adequate to the needs of the heart.

In the third dialogue the author deals with the *Spirit of Christ*, true fountain of inspiration and power. He relates how for many years of his life he had sought to quench his spiritual thirst at the fountain of philosophy and oriental lore. He read Genesis and the Koran, Plato and Kant, the mystic doctors and poets from Pythagoras to Swedenborg. But he remained unsatisfied. His reason found nourishment in those pages, his imagination pleasure, but the living sense of God did not succeed in becoming incarnate in his life. In the *Bhagavad-Gita* of Hinduism he thought he found at length the oasis he was seeking in life's desert. He was initiated by the teaching of Krishna and the revelation of Arjuna into the scale of ascending *yogas*. He profited much at the time from those studies, but in the end he discovered in the Gospels and the "Spirit of Christ" the soul satisfaction he had so restlessly pursued.

The " Spirit of Christ " is for Rojas a mystic reality.
It means much more than the influence or way of life of
the historical Jesus, approximating much more closely
to the Pauline conception of the eternal Christ who
dwells in each Christian soul.   " The body of each
man," says Rojas, " can and should be the dwelling-
place of the invisible Christ " ; and again, " Christ is a
fountain of living water that overflows the immobile
vessels that contain it in order to fertilize the spirit of
man."   " The Master said : ' Come unto Me and
drink.'   That is what I do.   But in order that we may
live in Him and He in us it is necessary to make alive
His message."   This last sentence states the religious
problem of South America and our time, a dynamic
relationship between mystic experience and ethics.
The solution is life on the Road along which Christ still
moves on His redemptive way.   To make alive His
message is to be on the Road, but we can only keep up
the prophetic march if He is there beside us.

In the course of these dialogues, but especially in
the last, Rojas makes frequent references to religion
in South America.   He gives expression, at the same
time, to his ardent dreams for the future religious
mission of his own country.   He deeply mourns the
fact that his countrymen, in common with South
Americans in general, have woefully neglected religion.
The Catholic tradition as an external form exists, he
says, in these republics, but not so Christian sentiment
as the inspiration of life.   In this respect he contrasts
Argentine most unfavourably with Anglo-Saxon North
America.   He has made the discovery that in the latter,
in spite of the abounding paradoxes that make it such
an enigma to the people of South America, there are
many business men who pursue wealth with a mystic
passion.   Their sole object in making money appears
to be that of being able to donate their gains to great
human causes.   He has been impressed also with a
number of public leaders in the United States who have

not been ashamed to quote and practise the principles
of Jesus in their political and civic life. Such men,
says Rojas, South America has not hitherto had, but
greatly needs.

An expression of the growing sense of destiny which
has begun to throb in Latin-American thought appears
in some of the closing paragraphs. According to
Rojas, his beloved Argentina possesses an asset that
may constitute an unconscious preparation for a great
Christian destiny. The land enjoys the fullest religious
liberty, and throughout its ample borders there exists
a sense of brotherhood among all the races that have
found an asylum there. That hate which is the bane
of Europe and that fanaticism which is the bane of
Asia are transcended. In this our author discerns
the influence of the spirit of Christ, " the Master of
Brotherhood." " And who can tell," he adds, " but
that we are also destined to create a new religious
unity, by the transcendence of foreign cults?" Striking illustration of the universalism of the South
American spirit.

Our author dreams. He dreams of the activity of
the invisible Christ as a transforming spiritual and
social influence. He dreams of the Christianization
of Latin America in order that it may fulfil its true
Messianic destiny of realizing the hitherto unrealized
dreams of Europe and Christianity. " The association
of citizens," he says, " in a democracy like ours can
form a religious brotherhood in the fullest sense of the
word. The afflicted world is awaiting amid the darkness a message of hope, and how great would be our
joy were that message to reach it from this Latin
America of ours."

(d) *Julio Navarro Monzó : a Christian Literator*

If Ricardo Rojas is the first South American writer
of recognized literary standing to write a book on

Christianity, and so the first to catch the imagination of intellectual circles as a religious writer, to Julio Navarro Monzó belongs the honour of being the first among first-rate minds on the Continent to make the religious problem the subject of continuous and systematic study. If for Rojas a book on Christianity was but the culminating moment of his first literary jubilee, with Navarro Monzó religion is a passion for which he has sacrificed all other interests.

During the last decade this Argentine has probably written more extensively on the subject of religion than any other living writer, unless it be Kagawa. Not only by his books has he brought the religious problem prominently before the South American public, but in the course of prolonged apostolic journeys through many Latin-American lands he has had the opportunity of dealing with Christ and religion before representative audiences in theatres and university auditoriums. When Count Keyserling visited Argentina in 1929 one of the things which most impressed him was the extraordinarily high quality and the penetrating insight shown by the reports of his lectures in the great Buenos Aires newspaper *La Nación*. According to his own statement in a letter to the editor, those reports contained the finest account of his lectures which had appeared in the public press in any part of the world where he had been. Their author was Navarro Monzó. When the two men met, the German philosopher found that this Argentine journalist was as erudite or more so than himself in all matters pertaining to the history of religion.

Navarro Monzó was born in Portugal in 1882. His father was a member of the Portuguese diplomatic corps, and as a boy young Julio had occasion to visit different lands in Europe and Africa. For the part he played in the Portuguese revolution he was obliged to leave the country, and shortly thereafter emigrated to Argentina. For a number of years he occupied an

important position in one of the government departments. In this capacity he played a part in drafting a
new electoral law for Argentina. Simultaneously with
his official position he collaborated as critic of art on
the staff of *La Nación*. Navarro Monzó's literary contributions made a deep impression by their high tone,
their penetration, and their severity. Ten or twelve
years ago he came into friendly contact with some of
the officials of the Young Men's Christian Association
in Buenos Aires. So favourable was the impression
he made upon the latter, and so high the opinion he
himself formed of the Association as a platform for
the proclamation of religious ideas, that in 1922 he
became a member of the continental staff of this organization as a special lecturer and writer on religion.
Since that time book after book has flowed from his
pen, while at intervals he has undertaken lecture tours
through the leading cities of the Continent.

In order to understand the religious personality and
outlook of Navarro Monzó, it is necessary to begin,
where he himself does, by referring to a profound
religious experience through which he passed in 1916.
In that year the government official and distinguished
art critic was converted to Christianity. He had, of
course, been born and bred a Roman Catholic, but like
Latin youth in general he had grown utterly irreligious,
and, on his own confession, had given full rein to his
lower passions. Partly through reflection upon the
tragedy of the war, partly in consequence of the death
of a dear child, his thoughts turned seriously and def- .
initely toward the subject of religion. Very different
was his experience from the romantic quest of Rojas.
I can do no better than quote his own words regarding
this critical and creative period of his life. The passage occurs in his first book on religion written in the
year of his conversion and entitled : ' *El Renacimento
Místico ante la Tragedia Europea.*' [1] "This book," says

---

[1] *The Rebirth of Mysticism in presence of the European Tragedy.*

he, " is the fruit of experience rather than of meditation and investigation.   The author is the product of
his environment and his epoch.   He drank the chalice
of their abominations to the dregs, until he had con-
sumed them.   Then the Lord one night on Holy
Friday, before an image of the ever interceding Holy
Virgin, Mother of God, touched his heart for the
thousandth time perhaps, but this time with success,
and the hardened sinner who had so many times
proved unfaithful to divine grace began to think about
his errors.   As love was awakened within him he
began to think also of the miserable state in which the
human race was lying both morally and materially.
The operation was slow, because we ourselves must
lend our human co-operation to the grace of God, and
the rebellious flesh still opposed itself, as it does still
to this day, to the work of the Holy Spirit.   In prayer,
however, my soul found strength to go forward.   God
does not fail him who calls upon Him, and the Light
descended little by little upon this troubled heart so
unworthy of it.

" This book, which is no more than a poor and
partial expiation for the sins of its author, is the result
of all this, written in an environment and for an environment in which, as in all Spanish-speaking lands,
it cannot but displease believers and unbelievers.   The
author can only hope to reap from it a harvest of
despite and loss of friends.   God, who seems to have
inspired it, doubtless knows why He did it.   In Him
the author puts his trust.   He is his hope ; He is his
strength." [1]   No deeper note had ever been sounded
in South American letters.   This was not literary pose,
but the passionate utterance of a broken spirit which
had been healed.

If Navarro Monzó now began to take up the study
of religion it was because religion had taken up and
transformed him.   About this time he began to attend

[1] Pp. 185-186.

the services of the Greek Orthodox Church.   He found
there, however, no permanent religious home, although
he often speaks of the spiritual impressiveness of the
Orthodox liturgy.   About the same time he became
intimately acquainted with that prince of Christian
educators and philanthropists, the Rev. William Morris.
He became a frequent attender at the Anglican services which Morris conducts, and between the two
men there grew up a deep and constant friendship,
which has been one of the most sweetening and stabil-
izing spiritual influences in the life of Navarro Monzó.
With the members, and especially with the ministers
of other Protestant communions, his contacts have
not invariably been so happy.   They have failed
to understand and appreciate him; he has been too
impatient with them.   As a matter of fact, he has
spoken and written on more than one occasion in
very scathing terms of Protestant work as carried on
in Latin-American countries.   A true son of his race,
Navarro Monzó does not always judge institutions
calmly and objectively, but rather in the light of personalities connected with them who are for him
simpáticas or *antipáticas*.   Not that one needs to have
Iberian blood to display the same trait !

Sad to say, this truly great soul has hitherto followed
the course of José Carlos Rodriguez in Brazil, and
in a sense that of Ricardo Rojas and a multitude of
others ; he has found no spiritual home in any organized religious communion.   His spiritual life has been
fed by the prophets of the Old Testament, by the words
of Christ, and particularly by the writings of St Paul
and St John.   Outside the Scriptures he has found
spiritual companionship in the great Spanish mystics,
in Plotinus, in St Francis of Assisi, in Eckhart and
Jacob Boehme, and latterly in George Fox and the
Society of Friends.   As the result of a visit to England
and the United States in 1924, Navarro Monzó came
into touch with the Quakers.   He found himself very

much at home among the followers of George Fox. The type of religious meeting conducted by the Society of Friends made a deep impression upon him, and he formed the idea that the future of Christianity in Latin America lay in the organization of similar meetings throughout the continent. Ever since then he has been in the habit of uniting a small group at his home on Sundays for silence, meditation and prayer.

The new quiet and leisure which were made possible for Navarro Monzó in 1922 by his connection with the Young Men's Christian Association, have borne fruit in a period of intense literary activity. The great majority of his books have been published by the South American Federation of the Young Men's Christian Association. The first volume belonging to this period is a book entitled *Principios Básicos de la Civilización*.[1] Here the author sets forth the beneficent results of Christianity in the life of the world, and indicates ways and means for the application to society of the sociological principles inherent in the Christian religion. This was followed by a book of a very different kind, *Horas y Siglos*,[2] a Pan-Christian liturgy composed of selections from the Scriptures, and containing prayers from Roman Catholic, Orthodox and Protestant sources. Then followed a series of twelve brochures on the *Evolution of Religion in the Ancient World*. The introductory volume of this series is one of the most important efforts of our author. It takes the form of a full discussion of Latin America's religious problem.

After dealing rather fully with the evolution of religion among the Hebrew people and in the Græco-Roman world, the series closes with a study of Christianity in which both streams are united. The perfect union takes place in the Fourth Gospel. The Gospel of John, with its conception of the Logos become flesh, offers the highest synthesis hitherto attained of the subjective and objective elements in religion. Our

---

[1] *Basic Principles of Civilization.*   [2] *Hours and Ages.*

author takes the view, now difficult to hold, that this last of the Canonical Gospels, to which Hellenism contributed the interpretative categories which made it possible for Christianity to subsist and propagate itself in the Græco-Roman world, is at bottom the dramatization of an idea.   It was written, he holds, to illustrate the Neo-Platonic, mystic principle of the ascension of the soul through purification, illumination and union. From such a scheme of thought all catastrophic and apocalyptic elements are naturally excluded as not belonging to the essence of Christianity.   Perpetual progress in a straight line is assured.   Evil does not belong to the essence of reality, even to the essence of empirical reality, nor can reaction belong to the essence of progress.   The process of reality is susceptible of perfect comprehension ; what is needed is understanding rather than faith.   South America's leading religious thinker has clearly become heir to that romantic type of evolutionary idealism so popular in the past generation of thought, and which is now being widely challenged by new voices and new thought forms.

Navarro Monzó's next literary effort was a book which he himself considers to be the most fundamental he has written.   It bears the title of *El Camino de Santidad*,[1] and consists of a genetic study of religious phenomena from their crudest forms up to Christian mysticism.   This was soon followed by *La Revolución Cristiana*,[2] in which, after a fine preliminary study on Nietzsche and Christianity, the fundamental principles of the latter as a revolutionary movement are set forth. His last important work appeared in 1930, *Las Metafísicas del Cristianismo*.[3]   It is, in a sense, his most ambitious effort, the book in which he feels he has been able to formulate a satisfactory metaphysic for Christianity.[4]

[1] *The Way of Holiness.*   [2] *The Christian Revolution.*
[3] *The Metaphysics of Christianity.*
[4] Since these lines were written our author has published a new volume, *La Actualidad de Jacobo Boehme* (*The Present day Interest of Jacob Boehme*).

A study of the books of Navarro Monzó, and of the innumerable articles and pamphlets he has written, reveals a richly stored mind of extraordinary acumen, perfect intellectual sincerity and passionate earnestness. In all he writes one discovers the universalistic tendency, the love of rapid generalization and the fondness for the historical method which characterize the South-American mind. The influence of Heraclitus, Plato, and especially of Neo-Platonism, stands out strongly in his earlier idealogy. The conception of absolute values occupies a prominent place. His later thinking is entirely dominated by the categories of modern vitalism. He appears as a thorough-going monist to whom every form of dualism is abhorrent. The idea of monistic evolution in the most absolute sense holds the field, while genetic categories determine his basic view-points. So completely has he been dominated in recent years by the above-mentioned idea that he now champions a position which he calls metaphysical " Temporalism," according to which God Himself is in process of becoming. His former Platonic position with its absolutes is thus logically abandoned, although he would probably not be prepared to accept some of the inexorable deductions which follow from his new standpoint.

The most systematic expression which Navarro Monzó has so far given to his new religious metaphysic is contained in the book already referred to, *Las Metafísicas del Cristianismo*. A brief analysis of this book, which in certain fundamental respects goes far beyond and even differs from view-points contained in former volumes, will be of interest. In the introductory pages our author expresses the downright conviction that he has reached as absolute and significant an insight into life and reality as that which Buddha proclaimed in his famous sermon at Benares. " The problem which so tormented me," he says, " the problem of evil, the problem of the meaning of life, has now no secrets for me. . . . If I had to fall dead now, I should die peaceably," he adds, " after having fulfilled my mission in life, after having pronounced the final word." [1] The importance which Navarro Monzó himself attaches to this book more than justifies our special examination of its contents, for it is introduced to us in language which is ordinarily associated with a new revelation.

Among present-day thinkers who can make any claim to philosophic capacity, there are only two sets of categories, says our author with impressive dogmatism, with which to conceive the universe : the categories of materialism and the categories of pantheism or *panentheism*. Deism, under which, extraordinarily enough, he appears to subsume Theism in all its forms, has now no importance for thought. While the Fourth Gospel represents the highest conceptual expression which Christianity has yet received, it cannot, says Navarro Monzó, be regarded as the last Christian Gospel. Our age requires a new Gospel, and modern vitalism in science and philosophy makes it possible for us to formulate such a Gospel. Christianity must come to terms with the categories of modern culture, as it did with the categories of Greek culture in the early days of our faith. The idea of enthusiasm associated with Dionysus, that of intuition which forms the core of Bergson's thinking, Keyserling's emphasis on comprehension, offer us elements for the formulation of a modern Christian Gospel.

Navarro Monzó then proceeds to the formulation of his view-point. " Christian thought," says he, " has been hampered in the past by the ideas of eternity and of an eternal God employed as positive concepts. Eternity must be regarded as a purely negative idea. Existence appeared only with the appearance of consciousness, all that preceded consciousness being non-existent in a philosophic sense. What is ultimate in the universe is energy. God Himself is the product of

[1] " *La palabra definitiva.*"

cosmic energy. He has had a beginning and must be regarded as finite. His being is enriched and strengthened by the co-operation of human wills. The cosmic drama began with the passion of conscious energy, or God, to realize all its potentialities in the process of becoming." Let us listen to our author's own formulation of the New Gospel for our time. " Christianity is above all else the religion of the Divinity who becomes incarnate ; of the Divinity who suffers in the struggle against the inertia of matter ; of the Divinity who battles for an ideal. Christianity shares the deathless hope of the ancient prophets who dreamed of the coming of a better world. Christianity is, in a word, a religion which, in spite of everything, has never become stagnant, which has always been open to new inspirations. Perhaps, on this very account, to-morrow may witness the writing of a new Gospel, which like that of St John in its own time, may prove to be a synthesis of the philosophic thought and the religious faith of a new epoch. Perhaps some day in the great Church of the future united in liberty through the bonds of fraternity, may be solemnly read something similar to these concepts." [1]

Then follows the modern equivalent of the Prologue to St John's Gospel, which although lengthy we will quote in its entirety :

" Before the beginning was Force, and Force was Unconscious, for which reason it could not yet be called Existence.

" But the Unconscious became Conscious, and this was the beginning of all things.

" The potential began to become actual, and becoming aware of its latent energies has continued to create the universe by means of which it expresses itself.

" First was Energy, then Intelligence, thereafter Life which created and moulded the material by means of which Intelligence reveals itself.

" In Energy was present Intelligence, but Energy did not become Action until it became intelligent.

[1] *Id.*, p. 131.

" Energy is the Father, Intelligence is the Son, Action is the Spirit.

" The Son is superior to the Father, the Spirit is superior to the Son. For the Conscious is superior to the Unconscious and every thought is inferior until it is translated unto Action.

" Action proceeds from the Father through the Son. Without the mediation of the Son, Action would be Unconscious and could not be called Action. It would be Unconscious Force preceding all existence.

" These three have existed from the beginning, and without their conjunction the beginning would not have been possible.

" But Energy in itself alone is not God nor are Intelligence nor Action in themselves God. However, the three united constitute the Divine Unity.

" This Unity existed from the beginning and this Unity is God. Man was created in the image of the triune God, bearing in the depths of his being the consciousness of his origin.

" Material on account of his body, living, thanks to the Spirit, intelligent by means of the Divine Intelligence, man is the miniature image of Force, of Intelligence and of Action, which are the essence of universal existence.

" And the Conscious One put man upon the earth so that he should be lord over it and collaborate with Intelligence in order to establish the Kingdom of the Spirit upon earth.

" But at the beginning of his history, man did not yet have knowledge of his origin and adored that which he ought to master.

" Intelligence was in the world, and the world was made by it, but the world did not know it.

" Until at length, after many who possessed a glimpse of Intelligence there came a Man according to the Divine Consciousness in whom Consciousness was incarnate.

" He was not born of the flesh, nor of the will of the flesh, but having knowledge of His Divine origin, submitted Himself to it.

" And He became united with Intelligence by means of which all things were made.

" He has given to all those who follow Him the capacity to call themselves and feel themselves sons of God.

" Who have not been born of the flesh nor of the will of the flesh but of the Spirit ; first-fruits of a new humanity to whom the mission has been commended of establishing the Kingdom of God upon the earth." [1]

As our present interest in the religious philosophy of Navarro Monzó is necessarily expository, namely,

[1] *Id.*, pp. 131-133.

that of presenting to our readers the view-point of the
first South American writer who has discussed the
religious problem in a fundamental way, we shall limit
ourselves to such observations as will set in clearer
relief the philosophical position of our author and its
leading implications.   By accepting the idea of a finite
God, the " young fighting God " of H. G. Wells,
Navarro Monzó has put himself in line with a number
of modern thinkers who limit God's power, in order,
as they think, to save His morals.   It is natural that
such an ideal should present itself in a tragic and chaotic
time like ours.   It is a conception, says Dean Inge in
his recent book on Ethics, which tends to emerge in
times of national trouble.   It is by no means necessary,
however, to postulate the finitude of God in order to
account for evil, nor need we de-absolutize Deity in
order to assure ourselves of the presence and sympathy of
a Divine Companion who is the champion of goodness
in the universe.   No one has proclaimed the otherness
and absoluteness of God so strongly as Kierkegaard.
Yet, when the great Dane thought of the measureless
sympathy of God, he pictured Him upon a throne of
sorrow.   The root trouble of such philosophizing as
we have been considering is its fear of the paradox in
dealing with ultimates.   It succumbs to the temptation
to simplify the problem unduly by affirming a hasty
and categoric either—or.   But reality smiles at our
logic.   It should give us pause to discover that the great
Bible thinkers who proclaimed so insistently the transcendence and infinitude of God, reached the limits of
human language in their endeavour to portray His
redemptive love-passion as an operative force in the
world.   The Cross lies at the heart of the universe and
of Christianity.   " Christ," to repeat once more the
word of Pascal, " is still in travail in the heart of His
people," and will be till the Kingdom is " handed over,"
when " God will be all in all," beyond the bourne
and din of tragic strife.   On the other hand, Navarro

Monzó's sketch of a new philosophy of Christianity, fails to discover a real place for the concepts of love and grace as applied to God and of faith as applied to man. It could not be otherwise, because the ghostly abstractions called Energy, Intelligence and Action can never engender these primary Christian realities in their bloodless wombs! The "New Gospel" possesses no dynamic. Only intellectualized spectres could ever chant its dialectic symphonies in the "Great Church of the Future." South America and our time need another Gospel than this. Quite other categories are required for the formulation of an adequate Christian world view, which is one of the most pressing needs of our time.

The undue employment of biological categories to interpret reality and Christianity within it is responsible for the latest developments in the thought of the South American thinker. The apotheosis of Vitalism leads inexorably to "Temporalism." If, moreover, the whole and not simply the parts is in process of change, as the philosophy of our author implies, there can be no fixed points, no absolute values. Utter relativism becomes regnant, and stares us starkly in the face, while the respective rôles of God and man become inverted. It is to be regretted, though it is not surprising, that the first religious philosophy to appear in South America should be the expression of that Romanticism which marks the swan song of a thought era which is dying. The truth is that the Renaissance period has not been able to forge categories which are adequate to the expression of the Christian Gospel. A fresh start is necessary as we cross the threshold of a new age, an age in which physics and astronomy claim to have more right than biological romanticism to discuss the constitution and history of the Cosmos. "If Jeans and Eddington are right," says Dean Inge in one of his most recent utterances, "the emerging, evolving, improving God is not God at all, for surely a God

P

under sentence of death is not God. Modern pantheism is built on the sand." The time has come when absolute identity must give place to real difference, the category of continuity to that of discontinuity. The fact of sin must be faced afresh, and the romantic view of human nature needs to be relegated to the myths. The cycle with its emphasis on the apocalyptic must be rehabilitated as a truer expression of the march of history than the straight line. In all discussion regarding the constitution of the universe, mathematical and ethical categories must be given as full consideration as the biological categories which have recently exercised a dictatorship in thought. Let it never be forgotten withal that the basic Christian facts will eternally elude rationalization. Faith, not reason, must transcend the opposition between the harmonious ball and the rugged Cross.

Much more challenging and suggestive are the views of Navarro Monzó on the practical application and propagation of Christianity. His forte is in the sociological rather than in the philosophical sphere. His historical-mindedness and incomparable knowledge of history, together with his burning ethical passion and loyalty to the figure of Jesus, give great value to his observations regarding the expression of Christianity. With fine poise he emphasizes the function of the ethical and the religious in the coming Kingdom of God. " I hope," he says in an interesting compendium of his religious position entitled *Confessio Fidei*, " that by means of the efforts of the disciples of Christ cooperating with the supreme will of goodness which was manifested in Christ and which rules the universe, the Sermon on the Mount will become the moral, social and political code of redeemed humanity." He points out elsewhere, however, that the Sermon on the Mount cannot be regarded as a code of ethics which ordinary people can follow. It expresses rather the spiritual code in accordance with which men and

women will act naturally and spontaneously after they
have passed through a supreme mystic experience. In
other words, religion is needed to produce the highest
ethic.

One of Navarro Monzó's favourite thoughts is that
of the " New Reformation." " We are on the eve of
a total renovation of the world," he says in the epilogue
to *El Camino de Santidad*. In *La Revolución Cristiana*
he gives his views of the Reformation to which he
looks forward. It will be a continuation of the work
of Erasmus rather than that of Luther. On its intellectual side it will reinterpret all the traditional Christian ideas : God, prayer and the Cross of Christ. On
its spiritual side it will be characterized by a new
" Bohemianism," in which people, especially youth,
will sit fast and loose to material preoccupations, and
live by the implications of the teaching of Christ that
God will take care of those who seek first His Kingdom
and righteousness. Modern Christians must recover
that indifference to temporal needs which characterized
the group which followed the Master, and the later
group which surrounded St Francis. Christianity is an
adventure, and requires the formation of a spiritual
aristocracy. The best way to propagate it is by con-
tagion and radiation. It must also be a lay movement,
adds Navarro Monzó, because the process of human
history tends towards an increasing laicization. " And
who knows," he asks in the epilogue to which we have
already referred, " but that the Spanish race which
produced the orders of preachers of St Dominic of
Guzman, the spiritual militia of Ignatius Loyola,
the interior gardens of Santa Teresa de Jesús and of
John of the Cross may have new surprises to give the
world ? " His meaning is that the new order of things
which will completely revolutionize conditions of life
as they are, may very well be promoted by representatives of the Spanish race.

Particularly challenging is Navarro Monzó's treat-

ment of the religious problem of Latin America. The
basic difficulty of civilization in the Iberian lands of
America, he considers to be the fact that they were not
prepared for democracy when they won their political
liberty. Neither they nor official religion within their
borders have ever passed through a renovating spiritual
crisis. In a word, they have not had a " Reformation."
Men were not brought face to face with God, which is
the indispensable antecedent of democracy. " Democracy," says he in his penetrating study, *El Próblema
Religioso en la Cultura Latino-Americana*, " has been expressed and can only be expressed by men who believe
in one only God, the common Father of the human
family, and for that reason in human equality and fraternity." [1]   For him, therefore, the problem of Latin-
American democracy is inseparably bound up with the
problem of religion. These lands must have their own
religious reformation. But what form should this take
and how will it come about? Neither the Catholic
Church nor the Protestant churches can produce this
reformation, says he. Latin-Americans must " drink
in pure fountains, those of primitive Christianity."
There was a time, he tells us, when he cherished the
hope that an inner reformation of Catholicism would
be possible, but the attitude of the Pope towards
Modernism completely disillusioned him. He then
thought of Greek Orthodoxy, but a similar disillu-
sion followed. The Protestant churches, according to
Navarro Monzó, offer no hope either, partly because
they are Protestant, and partly because they are
churches. It is his opinion that Protestantism will
never be able to exert a widespread, vitalizing influence
in Latin lands, because it is not congenial to them.

This latter contention of Navarro Monzó will be discussed in the following chapter. The observation is
meantime in order that our distinguished author discovers a constitutional antipathy towards Protestant-

[1] P. 47.

ism in its ecclesiastical aspect which has increased in recent years. In his first religious work, *El Renacimiento Místico*, he makes this statement : " We see in Protestantism only cold reason, discussion and verbose pietism, and when within its pale appears some would-be visionary like Jacob Boehme, it is not in order to speak to us of the mysteries of the love of God for the human soul, but to raise the proud problem of why man is so small an affair in the universe ; concluding by opposing God to God." [1] It is interesting to note that since then, Navarro Monzó, as a result of his increasing intellectualistic interest in religion and the religious problem, has discovered a profound admiration for Boehme, whom he now regards as a pivotal figure in modern religious thought.

It is our author's conviction that " religious sentiments may evolve and become transformed in a certain way, but not be radically altered." Christianity must be presented as an ideal and not as a doctrine, still less as an organization. " The Church of the future will certainly have a sentimental rather than an intellectual basis. It will be more affective than disciplinary. It will be a school of spiritual perfection and a fountain of moral power—and that will be enough." [2] While speaking thus, Navarro Monzó has in mind the propagation of small religious groups on the model of the Society of Friends, groups not promoted from the outside, but which from the beginning will be autochthonous and self-propagating.

But how can such a movement be launched, things being what they are ? " The man who must save Latin America," says Navarro Monzó, " will have to be a saint and not an intellectual." In a passage of great beauty and significance he indicates what he considers to be his own mission and its limitations. " If I cannot be successful," says he, " in the high ambition of touching the souls of men, I hope at least to interest

[1] P. 99.　[2] *El Problema Religiosa en la Cultura Latino-Americana*, p. 113.

their intelligence, and so remove, if it were possible, mountains of preconceptions which to-day make them hostile to all religion. . . . The task of removing moral obstacles and of leading souls by means of repentance to the Eternal Fountain from which life flows perennially, is certainly reserved for another voice stronger and purer than mine. . . . But my mission, my poor personal mission, has a precarious character. It is that of a voice of one crying in the wilderness, ' prepare ye the way of the Lord.' " [1]

It is no small mission either. In student camps and university auditoriums, in theatres, clubs and Y.M.C.A. buildings this South American prophet has made his audiences aware of the reality of the religious problem and the religious life. He has loyally focused attention upon the significance of the historical personality and teachings of Jesus Christ. He has insisted that in Christ's Person the Word became flesh. If anyone should lament that in his books and lectures he has tended to bring men face to face with religion rather than with God, with the vision of absolute moral values rather than with the concrete figure of the Christ challenging men to personal commitment to Himself, let him remember Navarro Monzó's own estimate of his special rôle, and thank God for the loyalty and sincerity with which he has discharged it.

[1] *Id.*, pp. 117, 119, 120.

CHAPTER XI

THE ADVENT OF PROTESTANTISM

A DISCUSSION of evangelical Christianity in South America has been reserved to the end. The reason should be obvious. An adequate treatment of this religious movement, the most widespread and aggressive non-Catholic movement on the Continent, as well as the most warmly debated both inside and outside these countries, demands the kind of perspective which it has been the object of previous chapters to build up. Our excursion into racial psychology, into the history and philosophy of Spanish Catholicism, and into the new trends in religious life and thought, has prepared the way for an appraisal of Reformed Christianity in South American countries.

(a) *Precursors*

There was a time when it appeared as if the struggle between the Reformation and the Counter-Reformation was to be carried on simultaneously in the Old World and in the New. About the middle of the sixteenth century some leading French Protestants conceived the idea of organizing a Huguenot colony in Brazil. The scheme had the backing of John Calvin and Admiral Coligny. Two distinct expeditions were organized, one in 1555, the other in 1558. The attempt was made to wrest Brazil from the Portuguese, and to establish the Protestant Calvinistic Faith. Fourteen students of theology specially chosen by Calvin and the Geneva clergy accompanied the second expedition. Unfortunately for the success of the project those French colonists, unlike their English co-religionists who landed in the following century in New England, had to deal not with an aboriginal, but with a European people. More unfortunate still, Villegagnon, the admiral in charge of the expedition, proved a traitor to the cause he led by turning Catholic, earning for himself the bye-name of the " Cain of America." In 1567 the French expeditionaries were driven out of " Antarctic France." While religious motives were not absent, the whole enterprise savours somewhat of an attempt to do with the Pope what the English buccaneers delighted to do with the King of Spain : singe his beard. The true Protestant missionary movement was not yet born.

Early in the following century the Dutch took possession of Bahia in Northern Brazil. The expedition was accompanied by a group of missionaries. Penetrating southwards the expeditionaries occupied little by little an extensive region of the country. Some of the missionaries learned Guaraní, the chief aboriginal tongue, and instructed the Indians in the Gospel and in the arts of industry and agriculture. In 1664, however, the newcomers were obliged to abandon the country after twenty years' partial occupation.

Nearly two centuries passed before Protestant Christianity again became represented in South America. Its appearance coincides roughly with the dawn of the revolutionary period. To the British and Foreign Bible Society belongs the honour of having introduced South America to the perennial source of Christian thought and experience. Not with a sword, but with a Book, did the new Christians appear. Between 1804 and 1807 the Bible Society published twenty thousand copies of the New Testament in Portuguese. The greater number of these were distributed in towns along the Brazilian Coast by merchants and seafaring men interested in the distribution of the Scriptures.

grants, most of them Lutheran, arrived in Brazil, and received permission to build churches. Their descendants and successors of to-day, scattered through the great states of Southern Brazil, form a community of a quarter of a million evangelical Christians. In 1825 two hundred and fifty Scotch colonists sailed from Leith for the River Plate. Before long they erected their own chapel in Buenos Aires. This church, which celebrated its centenary three years ago, has had a remarkable succession of eminent ministers, and has exerted a most beneficent influence in the life of the English-speaking community throughout the Argentine Republic. Many of its members have been among the most public-spirited men which the foreign colony of Argentina has produced.

Some fifty years later, shortly after Italian forces had taken the city of Rome, a group of Waldensian immigrants arrived in Uruguay. They were accompanied by a very remarkable pastor, who proved himself to be a statesman as well as a shepherd of souls. A large number of Waldensian congregations are now scattered throughout Argentina and Uruguay. The pastor referred to, the Rev. Armand Ugón, died a few years ago at a patriarchal age, leaving behind him a colony of ten thousand souls in the two River Plate Republics and a family of twelve sons and daughters, the majority of whom took up a professional career, and are now among the leading citizens of Uruguay.

The beginning of the specifically missionary phase of Protestant activity is associated with the name of a Scotchman, James Thomson. Thomson is one of the most interesting and mysterious figures in the religious life of South America during the past century. He arrived in Argentina shortly after the Revolution. The moment was particularly favourable for the propagation of new religious ideas and the introduction of a new religious spirit. The absence of the Jesuits, the open-mindedness shown by many of the clergy and by the civil and military leaders, the disfavour with which the Vatican regarded the work of the In-surgents, the new desire to become related to the great currents of the world's life, were factors favouring the propagation of Protestantism.

Thomson came to the River Plate with a double commission. He was an agent of the British and Foreign Bible Society, and had, besides, the representa-tion of the famous Lancastrian Educational Society. In his former capacity he reminds us of that other remarkable Bible Society agent, George Borrow. In his latter, he is the first of a remarkable group of Protestant educators from Great Britain and the United States who have left an indelible impression on the cultural life of the Continent. The career of this solitary apostolic figure, and the impression he made upon the governments of four South American re-publics, is sufficient testimony to the possibilities that were latent in the situation.

The educational projects of Thomson received the warmest support from the new Argentine authorities. In the Lancastrian system the older pupils became the mentors of the younger in the elements of education. Such a system was specially adapted to a new country where teachers were entirely lacking. With the un-qualified support of the government and of many members of the clergy, the movement made great pro-gress. A normal school was founded in Montevideo to prepare teachers. In Buenos Aires, where the first branch of the Society was organized, a hundred schools were soon functioning with an enrolment of five thousand pupils. The text-book used for instruction in reading was the Bible. The appreciation of the Argentine Government for the services rendered by James Thomson to the cause of education was expressed in a most unusual way. Before leaving Argentina for Chile, in response to a pressing invita-tion from the new government of the latter country,

the Scotch educator was made an honorary citizen of
Argentina with full citizenship rights. The reason
given for this signal honour is symbolic of the attitude
of a warm-hearted people towards " cultured foreigners
who are interested in the progress and prosperity of the
country."

In Chile Thomson's efforts were scarcely less successful, only that in this country he had to struggle
against the influence of the Roman Catholic clergy,
who, as we already know, were much less liberal than
their confrères on the other side of the Andes. A request by the government that Thomson should bring
skilled workmen and agricultural labourers to Chile
was blocked by the Roman Catholic hierarchy, on the
ground that the new immigrants would probably be
Protestants. The government, however, showed its
appreciation of the services of the educator by repeating
the honour conferred upon him by Argentina, making
him an honorary citizen of Chile.

In Peru, to which Thomson turned in 1822 on the
special invitation of the Liberator San Martín, a Lancastrian school was established in a convent specially
vacated for the purpose. Political and other conditions, however, made the efforts of the peripatetic
schoolmaster missionary less successful than in the
other two republics. So, after circulating a large
number of Biblical portions, he passed on to Colombia
by way of Ecuador.

Colombia is generally regarded as one of the most
fanatical and cloistered of the South American group of
nations. Yet it was here that Thomson met with his
most signal success as a missionary. He was able to
organize an indigenous Bible Society in the Colombian
capital. The president of the new society was none
other than the Minister of Foreign Affairs; ten of
the twenty members forming the executive committee
were Roman Catholic clergy; while the first meeting
was held in the university chapel. The scheme had,

besides, the approbation of five leading government officials. It was not long, however, before a shadow projected itself over the enterprise. The hierarchy reported the matter to Rome. In the course of time a reply came from the Vatican forbidding all priests and faithful Catholics to belong to the Colombian Bible Society, and ordering at the same time its suppression. Nevertheless, the movement for the dissemination of the Scriptures had already got under way, and special editions of Bibles and Testaments were published. One of the most interesting Spanish Testaments in existence is dated 1837, and bears the name of a publishing house in Bogotá. Had it not been for the intervention of the Vatican on this occasion the Catholics of Colombia might have sent copies of the Scriptures to all parts of the Continent, fulfilling almost a century in advance the dream of many liberal Catholics of to-day, that the Bible be placed in the hands of the people. From Colombia Thomson passed on to Guatemala and Mexico.

(b) *Foundations of the Modern Missionary Movement*

Evangelical Christianity as a permanent and creative missionary movement among the South American people dates from the forties of last century. The names of its founders are symbolic of three different religious types who have exerted a permanent influence in the spiritual life of South America.

The first of these pioneers is an officer of the British Navy, Captain Allen Gardiner. The prelude to the modern era of evangelical mission work in the Southern Continent is one of the most heroic and tragic stories in the history of Christian missions. After several futile attempts to establish mission work in different countries of South America, the intrepid Christian captain sailed in September 1850 with six companions for the lonely isle of Tierra del Fuego. The group had provisions for six months, at the end of which a ship was to visit them. Through a regrettable mistake help did not arrive until September 1851. The rescue party made its appearance twenty days too late, and found only the bleached bones of the missionaries. When the tale reached Great Britain the conscience of Christian people was aroused. Another expedition was organized in 1854, one of the first members to volunteer being a son of the dead leader of the former band. The members of the second expedition were massacred in 1859. The attempt, however, was not given up to evangelize the Fuegians, who, according to Darwin, represented the lowest human type in existence. A young Anglican clergyman, who took the torch from dead hands, succeeded in winning the confidence of the natives. Such a transformation was brought about in the course of a few years that Darwin, on his second visit to the island, wished to have the privilege of being listed a subscriber to the South American Missionary Society which had introduced light and life among the dwellers of the lone southern isle. No great missionary movement could possibly have had a more spiritual and inspiring beginning. Gardiner is the luminous prototype of a large group of men and women, who since his day have given their lives unreservedly for the redemption and uplift of the aboriginal peoples of the Continent.

The second symbolic name is that of an American, David Trumbull, who arrived in Chile in 1845 in connection with the Seamen's Friend Society and the American and Foreign Christian Union. Although Trumbull's work lay particularly with foreign seamen and with members of the English-speaking community in Chile, he was interested in general evangelization, and his influence became decisive in a number of community movements. To him was due very largely the law of religious toleration and the provision of civil cemeteries. In order to identify himself more completely with his adopted country, Trumbull renounced his American citizenship and became a Chilian. When he died in 1889, a whole nation mourned one of its greatest sons. David Trumbull will be remembered forever as the precursor of a long succession of Protestant missionaries, who for Christ's sake and the purest love of men have identified themselves closely with the several South American nations to which they have gone in such a way as to dispossess themselves entirely of all mere foreignness, and become part and parcel of their adopted country.

The third figure is that of Dr Robert Kalley, a Scotch physician, who, in 1855, arrived in Brazil from the island of Madeira, from which he had been obliged to flee on account of religious persecution. Soon after his arrival he was successful in founding a congregation in Rio de Janeiro. Though Presbyterian himself, Kalley organized his converts according to the Congregational system. The new group was independent and self-supporting from the beginning, and is known to-day as the Fluminense Church. Kalley is the forerunner of the evangelistic missionary to national groups, while the work he established represents the foundation stone of the South American Evangelical Church, the walls of which, made of living stones, are now rising in different parts of the Continent.

The intervening years from 1855 to the present have witnessed the entrance in quick succession of evangelical missionaries and missionary societies into the different South American countries. Some representative data regarding the course of this movement will help us to focus its character and significance. Let us begin with Brazil, the country in which its roots have gone deepest, and in which its fruits are most evident. The first missionary society to obtain a permanent footing in the country was that of the American Presbyterian Church which established work in Brazil in

1859. The Presbyterians were followed by missionaries from the Southern Methodist, the Southern Baptist, and the Protestant Episcopal communions.

The year 1867 is an important date in the religious history of Argentina, because that year the first evangelical sermon in Spanish was preached in the country. The missionary who delivered the historic sermon was Dr John Francis Thomson, a young man of Scotch parentage, who had been taken to the Argentine Republic at the age of ten. This veteran, though blind and stricken in years, still lives on in Buenos Aires. He it was also who first carried the evangelical faith across the River Plate to Uruguay. Unfortunately, Thomson's preaching was of an extremely polemical and anti-Catholic character which, if it aroused great enthusiasm at the beginning and attracted many leading citizens of the country, produced later a decidedly anti-religious reaction among those same people.

The sympathy with which the presence of Protestant workers was regarded in Argentina is illustrated by the fact that an American missionary, Dr Goodfellow, was invited by the famous Argentine President, Sarmiento, to contract a number of normal school teachers in North America who should establish normal schools in the country. Within a few years, sixty-three teachers arrived, and in 1871 the first normal school in Argentina was founded in the city of Paraná. This is the earliest instance of many which were to follow of a commission being given to a Protestant missionary in South America by a government or a national institution in order that he might make some direct contribution to community welfare.

The establishment of missionary work in the west coast countries was more difficult because of the greater fanaticism existing there. Before the end of the century, however, Chile, Bolivia, Peru and Ecuador were all entered by Evangelical missionaries. The story of the occupation of Peru is full of romance.

One of the pioneers, an Argentine colporteur called Penzotti, lay for nine months in a dungeon in the Peruvian port of Callao for the offence of selling Bibles. He was released only when his detention became an international scandal. Some years later two English missionaries, one of whom was suffering from smallpox, had to flee from the old town of Cuzco and undertake a many weeks' journey across the mountains to Lima. The first Protestant emissary to enter Bolivia was a colporteur from Argentina. He was assassinated in 1880.

Some eighty years have passed since evangelical Christianity began to take root in the Southern Continent. To-day it is represented in one form or another in the ten republics, while in some of these, particularly in Brazil, it has become one of the chief spiritual forces in the national life. Let us glance at some landmarks of the movement.

(c) Landmarks

All the types of activity usually associated with the modern missionary movement are represented in South America. The great Bible Societies, the British and Foreign and the American, have striven to bring the Christian Scriptures to the attention of all classes throughout the length and breadth of the Continent. These remarkable organizations have consistently adopted the ecumenical Christian position of refraining from publishing and distributing any literature save the simple text of the Bible. The work of the colporteur prepared the way for the evangelist. The Protestant preacher, a foreigner to begin with, and later a son of the soil, found his way into the cities, villages and scattered hamlets of the Pampa, Sierra and the great Selva. He went with the Word, but he also went as a living incarnate word. He held his preaching services, but he also endeavoured to express his

Q

Christianity in a form which had tangible community value. Others followed him who gave permanent expression to the spirit of Christ in institutional form. Mission farms, hospitals, schools made their appearance.

The mission farms, when established, introduced many agricultural improvements ; they disseminated useful knowledge among the peon and peasant classes, attending at the same time to the spiritual needs of these. The evangelical farmers became the successors of the old *Encomenderos*. One of these, an American-Presbyterian, Hunnicutt, is one of the most loved and valued foreigners in Brazil.

Although medical missions have not been developed to the same extent in South America as they have been in Africa and the Orient, very largely because of the excellent medical service in the larger cities and the restrictions imposed upon foreign medical practitioners by South American governments, most valuable and significant work has been done by Christian doctors in many needy parts of the country. In Paraguay a self-sacrificing Scottish missionary physician has become a national and much-loved figure because of his devotion to human needs. In a remote outpost of civilization in the Peruvian montaña or forest region another Scottish medical missionary has been appointed health officer by the government. It had been found difficult to secure the services of a national doctor willing to bury his life in that remote community nineteen days' horseback ride from the coast. In the Peruvian capital a Christian doctor from the United States, working under the auspices of the Methodist Episcopal Mission, has won nation-wide reputation because of his skill and his Christ-like dedication to the cause of healing.

Buried in the Peruvian wilds in the virgin forests of the Amazon are three English ladies, two of them nurses and one a teacher, whose work will live on as one of the most heroic and purest examples of Christian missionary devotion in modern times. The leader of this little band, an English lady, Miss Annie Soper, after having rendered valuable service in the Peruvian capital in the organization of a school for nurses in connection with the city hospitals, founded along with a friend an independent work in the Peruvian interior. The influence of these ladies has radiated Christianity through a wide region, and only a biographer is required to add to the annals of Christian missions one of its noblest figures.   Christ-like personalities like Annie Soper belie the allegation sometimes made by Hispanic writers that Protestantism, while it has produced well-ordered societies, has given to the world no missionary heroes.

One of the most characteristic and influential aspects of Protestant work in South America has been educational.   A large number of first-class schools and colleges have grown up around the Continent.   Some of these have exercised and are exercising a profound influence upon the cultural life of the several countries where they are established.   In addition to the contribution they have made to the formation of Christian character in their alumni, they have set standards of educational efficiency and ethical idealism.   It is difficult to overestimate the influence such institutions are wielding at the present time in the spiritual life of these rising nations.   It is no insignificant fact that the new liberal President of Colombia is an ex-pupil of an evangelical school in his native country.   Haya de la Torre, at the time of his exile from Peru, was an enthusiastic and valued member of the staff of the Anglo-Peruvian College in Lima, an institution which was founded in 1916 by the Free Church of Scotland Mission to Peru. The tradition of this school has been one of the closest identification with national life and thought.   At the present moment both the Secretary of the University and the Secretary of the Faculty of Letters are members of its Faculty.   These and others continue to give their services to the institution not

because of the meagre emoluments they receive, but
because they believe in what the school stands for, and
are anxious through it to make a contribution to their
country.   A recent statement of the interim Principal
of the Anglo-Peruvian College, Mr W. S. Rycroft,
illustrates the community attitude towards this institution, which is but typical of what is equally true of
similar institutions in other South American countries.
" Recently," writes Mr Rycroft, " one of our teachers,
a well-known writer, was appointed secretary to the
Rector of the University.   At first I thought he would
resign his position in school, and expressed my mis-
givings to another teacher, who at once replied : ' Oh
no, he will not resign, because it gives one a moral
standing in the community to be on the staff of the
Anglo-Peruvian College.'   He left his classes in other
schools but is still teaching in ours."

The most remarkable piece of educational work in
South America is fruit of the more than thirty years of
Christ-like service and the keen educational vision of
the Rev. William C. Morris, an Anglican clergyman in
Buenos Aires.   Thirty years ago Mr Morris founded a
school for poor children in the Argentine Metropolis.
The work grew and the number of schools was multiplied.   In 1930 six thousand two hundred children
were being educated in the Argentine Philanthropic
Schools, and three hundred and thirty orphan boys and
girls were housed in the new orphanage called *El
Alba*.[1]   In the course of those years a hundred and
forty thousand Argentine children have passed through
the *Morris Schools*, as they are familiarly known.   The
work has been supported by private contributions by
Argentine citizens and by public-spirited foreigners
resident in the republic.   In recent years the schools
have also received a considerable subsidy from the
National Government.   "All for my God, my Country
and my Duty," is their motto.   The walls of the class-

[1] *The Dawn.*

rooms and the school patios are covered with the most suggestive mottoes. In the pamphlet containing the report for 1930 one reads two mottoes of Mr Morris' which have been the inspiration and secret of his life-work. One is, " He educates best who loves most," and the other, " The most valuable treasures of a country are its children."

It is not too much to say that William Morris is the best-loved man in Argentina. For thirty years he has not taken a vacation. He individualizes to such an extent in loyalty to his Master's spirit that with his own hands he is accustomed to try new shoes on the feet of the little waifs whom he has fathered. One of Argentina's leading educators in recent years, Dr Antonio Sagarna, is an ex-teacher of the Morris schools. Inspired by the life and work of Morris, Sagarna when a young man gave his services volun-tarily as a teacher. He later became National Minister of Education. When William Morris passes away the schools will become the property of the nation, and he himself will go down to history as one of the most Christian and creative citizens of the great republic.

Recent years have been marked by the appearance of a new spirit of co-operation among the many Protestant missions working in South America. In 1916 a historic congress was held on the Isthmus of Panama. It was attended by representatives of the National Evangelical Churches and of the Mission Boards working in Latin America. For the first time a complete survey was made of conditions in the Latin-American world and a plan of action agreed upon, whereby the evangelical heritage in its spirit and its fruits could be shared with these countries. The chief outcome of the Congress was the formation of a com-mittee called the " Committee on Co-operation in Latin America " with headquarters in New York. This committee has been a supreme and creative influence in stimulating and co-ordinating the various aspects of missionary activity in the Southern Continent. Under its auspices a monthly review has been founded called *La Nueva Democracia*, under the editorship of a distinguished Spanish intellectual and ex-monk, Dr Juan Orts González. The influence of this review has been very considerable in a number of Latin-American countries through its treatment of current topics of continental interest from a Christian viewpoint. The secretary of the committee, Dr Samuel Guy Inman, has probably done more than any living man to create a better understanding and mutual appreciation between the United States and the Latin-American group of nations.

Nine years after the Panama Congress a similar convention met in the city of Montevideo to deal specifically with the South American area. This conference was a testimony to the growing power and influence of Protestant Christianity in the Continent. Spanish and Portuguese were the official conference languages. The part played by nationals was very much greater than at Panama. A number of distinguished men and women from different South American countries, but not belonging to the evangelical communion, attended as guests. They gave the conference the benefit of their ideas on the general religious and cultural situation of the Continent, offered their frank criticism of the Protestant movement, and at the same time expressed their interest in what was being done by it. Statistics showed that in the course of nine years the total evangelical community had more than doubled its membership. The consciousness was borne in upon all that Protestantism had become an indigenous continental force.

Three years later, at the International Missionary Council meeting in Jerusalem, Latin America was admitted within the sphere of the Council's interests. A decision of the Edinburgh Missionary Conference of

1910 to exclude these countries from the purview of evangelical missionary activity was thus reversed. Two things were recognized at the Jerusalem meeting which had not been recognized before. First, that the religious situation in Latin-American countries was such as to demand the presence of evangelical Christianity in the interest of the good name and progress of the Christian faith; second, that evangelical Christianity had become indigenous throughout Latin America. In view of this latter fact it was agreed that the indigenous churches of Latin America should henceforth be represented on the Council by three full members.

(d) *Some Indigenous Movements*

In illustration of what has just been said regarding the nationalization of evangelical Christianity in South America, let me refer to some indigenous movements which will help our minds to focus the significant and potent character of this new religious crusade. One thinks first of a remarkable religious movement which began in Chile in 1910 through the preaching of an ex-member of the Methodist Chilian Mission, and which is known generally as the Pentecostal Movement. At the beginning its meetings were characterized by extravagant phenomena. The new converts developed, withal, an incandescent religious passion, and the movement spread through town and village at an amazing pace. Its adherents now number between ten and fifteen thousand, or more than double the number of adherents belonging to both Methodist and Presbyterian Churches in the country. Those who have studied this movement closely say that it has produced the purest type of morality in its members. From a beginning among the outcasts of society it has gradually tended to reach people higher up in the social scale. Extravagant phenomena tend to disappear from the gatherings, and the members, while losing none of their incandescent zeal to save other lives, have become more normal in their emotional experience and more disposed to co-operate with fellow-Christians of other groups in the interests of the common cause.

This movement is a testimony to the fact that no mere dogmatism nor ethicism can make its way among the South American masses. The future lies with the production of religious passion centred in a re-interpretation to the people of the significance of the Cross and the Crucified. Very frequently the Anglo-Saxon missionary in his reaction against dogmatism and the sombre character of Spanish Catholicism has not done justice to the meaning of Golgotha. He has thus failed to satisfy those religious needs and longings which produced in the religious history of the Iberian race both the Christ of Tangiers and the Christ of Velázquez. Spanish religion has centred in blood; the Iberian spirit has been preoccupied from time immemorial with the problem of blood. The watchword of this new movement in Chile, " La Sangre del Cordero," [1] could be read some years ago on rocky boulders at the side of highways and rail-roads throughout the country.

A second significant movement has taken place in the ranks of evangelical Christianity in South America. Foremost among the evangelical youth movements in the Continent are the two Federations of Uruguay and Argentina. The time has now arrived when evangelical youth in these two countries recognize the value of their religious inheritance and their personal responsi-bility to introduce it into the streams of life in their respective nations. A remarkable group of young men and women form the membership of these Federations. Many of them occupy important professional positions. The Federations stand for three great ideals: They are determined to work for a united evangelical front which shall eliminate in the course of time the

---

[1] " The Blood of the Lamb."

denominational differences in the Protestant family ; they endeavour to express the principles of Christianity in such practical ways as shall demonstrate the social value of religion ; they give the greatest prominence to evangelism, and in different ways bring the Word of Christ to bear upon the problems of life and thought. No one can study this youth movement at close quarters without becoming convinced that a great spiritual future lies before it.

It is in Brazil, however, that Evangelical Christianity has reached its highest development and made its greatest contribution to national life. The remark was made in an earlier chapter that the Brazilian Republic had probably the greatest absorptive capacity of any country in the world. No country has been so hospitable to foreign ideas. It is here that Spiritualism and Positivism have had their greatest triumphs. It is here also that the evangelical faith has found its most propitious soil. It is difficult to explain why this should be. One thing, however, should be taken into account ; Brazil has grown more rapidly than any of the other republics of South America. The ethnic elements which compose its population are more numerous and varied than in any sister republic. Traditions and religious fanaticism have been less strong. At the present moment the population of Brazil numbers almost forty millions, and in a very few years this republic will be the largest and most populous Latin state in the world.

The native hospitality of Brazil to new ideas and newcomers was taken advantage of by the Protestant missionary movement. The movement has been fortunate in being represented throughout its history in this republic by men and women of great spirit and vision. From the very beginning the missionaries worked for the nationalization of the cause they represented. As years went by eminent leaders began to appear in the national evangelical churches. In no country in South

America and in few countries in the world is the co-operative movement so perfect and effective as it is in Brazil. This has been largely due to the efforts of a remarkable Christian statesman, Dr Erasmo Braga, a Brazilian evangelical of the third generation. It is calculated that the Protestant community in the republic now numbers almost one million souls. Brazilian evangelicals have recently organized a missionary society to the motherland of Portugal and another to the Indians of the hinterland. The Federation of Evangelical Schools which came into being a few years ago is the largest private school federation in the country. No longer do foreign missionaries dominate the religious life. They work as simple partners of their national comrades, making their own contribution to the progress of the movement as a whole. Some years ago when a noted evangelical pastor died in the city of Rio de Janeiro, the municipality, in order to perpetuate his honoured memory, called one of the city streets by his name. Symbolic of the spirit and future of evangelical Christianity in this great republic is a beautiful garden city which is being built in the mountains. It is designed to be a rest home for Christian workers, and to form a centre for conferences and retreats of the National Evangelical Churches. The soul of this Brazilian projection of Keswick and Northfield is in its name—*Uamuarama*—"the haunt of the allies."

In the month of June 1932 an historic event will take place in the religious life of South America. The World Sunday School Convention will convene in the city of Rio de Janeiro. For the first time in the history of the Continent will a world gathering be held on South American soil. It is not without significance that the first ecumenical assembly to come to South American shores, to the shores of a continent destined by spirit and position to become the most ecumenical in the world, should convene under the auspices of evangelical Christianity, and for the purpose of promoting the Christian nurture of childhood and youth.

(e) *An Ecumenical Expression of the Protestant Spirit*

In the preceding sections of this chapter attention has been devoted exclusively to the history and development of Protestantism as a church movement. The fact needs to be emphasized, however, that the Protestant spirit in South America has had a lay as well as an ecclesiastical expression.   This has taken the form of the two Christian youth associations known respectively by the names of the Young Men's and the Young Women's Christian Associations.   In South America these organizations have taken on a decidedly ecumenical character.   While expressing the essential Protestant spirit in a religious sense, they have striven to transcend consistently both Protestant and Catholic ecclesiasticism.   By making a simple declaration of personal faith in Christ the basis of active membership, they have made it possible for Protestant church members, for liberal Catholics and for sincere Christians who have found no spiritual home in either of these communions, to figure on their governing boards.

The first Young Men's Christian Association in South America was founded in Brazil in 1900 by a secretary from North America.   The growth of the movement since that time, so far as institutional expansion is concerned, has been relatively small.   At the present moment it is represented in five of the South American countries by eleven local associations.   On the other hand some of these local associations have grown into very large and influential institutions. This is particularly true of the Association of Buenos Aires.   Moreover, the influence of the movement throughout the Continent has been out of all proportions to its institutional growth.

In the early years of its history the Young Men's

Christian Association specialized in physical education and social activities. It found that the development of such activities offered it the best point of contact with the community. While the formation of groups for the study of the Bible and the living problems of youth was not neglected, major attention was devoted to introducing a new spirit and aim into sport and healthy recreational activities, and in providing an attractive and pure environment in which youth could spend its leisure time. Both Associations have been pioneers in the introduction and popularization in South American countries of new games and recreational activities which are now widespread. Anyone who is intimately conversant with the problems of youth in these lands and the temptations which encompass leisure time, can appreciate the great spiritual value of the work done by the Young Men's and Young Women's Associations by means of their physical and social activities.

In recent years, however, important new developments have taken place, especially in the Young Men's Christian Association. Chief among these has been the emphasis upon welfare work, and the equally strong emphasis upon the Association's responsibility towards the great unchurched masses of the Continent. In regard to the former emphasis, some remarkable pieces of work have been done for abandoned and delinquent boys. One thinks particularly of the noble and unselfish effort carried on in east-end districts of Buenos Aires by Argentine secretaries, who are giving their lives in Christ-like service for city waifs. Most notable among such pieces of service has been that of a young Argentine, educated in one of the Association colleges in the United States, who so impressed the Government authorities by his development of a home for delinquent boys in Buenos Aires that he was set in charge of the largest reformatory in the republic. In the course of one or two years the organization and spirit of this institution were entirely transformed. It was not long before it became one of the legitimate glories of the country. An American educator who paid it a visit made the remark that while in the United States there might be some institutions equally good, there was certainly none better.

Such activities as these have won for the Young Men's Christian Association the gratitude and good-will of more than one South American community. They have set a standard for disinterested social work ; they have expressed the Christian spirit in a new and dynamic way; they have won to the Association fellowship men who were longing for an organization through which they could express their ideals for the community. Through contact with and participation in work such as this, many South Americans have been led to a new appreciation of the religious spirit which made it possible, and at the same time into a sym-pathetic study of the Christian faith. A leading Argentine educator, who at the beginning of his con-tact with the Young Men's Christian Association strongly advocated the elimination of the name Chris-tian from the official title if the movement were to succeed among Argentine youth, came to recognize later on that that name symbolized the Movement's soul, and pointed the way to what Argentina most needed : a Christian sense of life.

The religious emphasis has received increasing pro-minence during the last decade, so much so that it has come to constitute the leading preoccupation of Association leaders. These awoke by degrees to the fact that the movement to which they belonged oc-cupied a unique and strategic position for bringing the significance of Jesus Christ before the attention of South American youth. Accepting their responsibility in this direction they developed spiritual activities along three main lines. Summer camps were organ-ized in chosen spots in different countries, by the seashore, in the woods, by the side of mountain streams. The names of Piriapolis in Uruguay, of Ymcapolis in the Argentine Sierra de la Ventana, of Angol in Southern Chile and Chosica in the Rimac valley in Peru, are sacred in the memory of a large group of men and boys in South America who found there in the bosom of nature the greatest discovery that men can make : their naked selves and God. Who that has attended one of these camps will ever forget the Night of the Open Heart, with which each came to a close, when impressions were exchanged by all, and a supreme spiritual experience confessed by not a few ?

Through its Continental committee in Montevideo the Association has published a number of valuable books on Christianity and the religious problem, which have circulated extensively throughout the Continent. The chief writer of this series has been the eminent man already discussed, Don Julio Navarro Monzó. Chief, however, among the Association's spiritual activities has been the promotion of lectures on religion, and the provision of simple fellowship meetings for people with deep spiritual preoccupations who have failed to find satisfaction in the existing churches. The Association has thus had to fulfil a double religious function in recent years, in each case of a pioneer character. In Y.M.C.A. buildings, in schools and universities, in theatres and public halls throughout the Continent, lectures have been given on the most vital problems of life and religion by men specially enlisted and set apart for that work. Men and women who otherwise would never hear a religious message because of their antipathy to all ecclesiasticism have flocked to these meetings. So great is the prestige of the Association platform in some countries that when Dr Stanley Jones visited South America a few years ago he discovered that he could obtain his best audiences and meet the people he most wanted to get into touch with by speaking under the Association's auspices. He himself was probably unaware of the extent to which the possibility and success of his own meetings were contingent upon the preliminary work done by the Association in accustoming the unchurched to listen to religious lectures.

In addition to this apologetic and evangelistic function, the Association has found it necessary to provide a simple informal equivalent of a church meeting for people who belong to no church, or are essentially antipathetic to everything of an ecclesiastical order. For such as these it has become a kind of " interpreter's house " by the wayside for spiritual refreshment and guidance. It is obvious that such a function must be of a transitory and not of a permanent character, in as much as the Association can never be transformed into nor undertake the full functions of a church. Its specific rôle in this regard must be that of offering spiritual nourishment and orientation, in the hope that those it helps along the Christian road will ultimately find their own spiritual home.

What is the future of these ecumenical organizations in the South American Continent ? Their task has been probably more difficult in this part of the world than in any other. In the East and elsewhere they have simply shared the prestige or the ignominy attaching to the general Christian movement. In South America where Christianity was already known, but where the very name of Christian and especially that of Protestant had unfortunate associations attached to it, in the thought of Catholics and non-Catholics alike, they have had to avoid two invidious extremes. On the one hand, they have had to be careful not to function as a simple adjunct and prolongation of Protestant ecclesiastical activity, which would dub them as purely sectarian organizations among the people they wished to serve. On the other hand, they have had to guard constantly against universalizing their religious position to such an extent as to become completely innocuous as creative Christian agencies. Their constant spiritual problem has been that of combining universality with power, bearing in mind that the purely universal is generally sterile. In a very real sense :

> " You must be a fanatic, a wedge, a thunderbolt,
>   To smite a passage through this close-grained world."

This, however, can be said that both these organizations have been able to respond in a remarkable degree to an environment in which both for psychological reasons and unfortunate historical circumstances, sectarianism and organized religion are taboo among the vast majority of the thinking population. They have succeeded in transcending the clash of sectarian interests ; they have created a much-needed expression of religion in action ; they have rehabilitated religion and Christianity in the thought and life of many men and women, focusing everything in Christ ; they have provided means of spiritual nurture for not a few pilgrims on life's road. Should they continue to be what they are, to do what they have done, or should they be and do something different in order to make the supreme spiritual contribution which the present situation requires ? The discussion of the problem here raised is reserved for the following chapter.

CHAPTER XII

A CRITIQUE OF PROTESTANTISM IN SOUTH AMERICA

THE criticism may be offered of the preceding chapter that the writer has treated the subject of Protestantism in South America with undue warmth and approbation, without the detachment necessary for a completely objective and impartial presentation. He accepts the criticism, but hastens to reply that detachment is impossible where burning spiritual issues are concerned. Still less is it possible in a case in which the religious problem of South America has been the chief preoccupation of one's life, and when one has found within the general movement just described the sphere in which the greatest contribution could be made to the spiritual life of a continent. He hopes, nevertheless, that it will be possible in the present chapter to consider as dispassionately and critically as possible the general question of Protestant effort in South America.

(a) *The Validity Question*

The Protestant missionary movement in South America has been combated on various grounds. Quite recently a new ground of opposition has been formulated which, being the most specious, will be considered first. In an early chapter reference was made to the allegation sometimes heard in these days that the presence of Protestant missions in Latin America constitutes a positive menace to relations between the United States and the Latin-American republics. Protestant propaganda from the United

States, it is said, is particularly prejudicial to trade relations between the North and the South. Nothing could be more utterly untrue. Latin-American merchants have too shrewd a business sense to allow religious sentiment to enter the sphere of commercial interest. Were it not for the present depression in the interchange of commodities between the several countries of the Americas, a situation due to many other factors which are perfectly well understood, such a *canard* would never have been voiced. On the other hand, Anglo-Saxon missionaries in Latin America have been and continue to be among the best exponents of the culture and spirit of their respective countries. But for them and the institutions they have founded, Latin-America would have very shallow and precarious data to go upon in order to judge of the cultural life of North America. It requires no very intimate knowledge of Latin America to discover that in many of these countries, even in the highest intellectual circles, it is frequently doubted whether the North American people possess serious cultural interests at all. Read in this connection the *Ariel* of José Enrique Rodó where it is alleged that the United States is Caliban. Recollect in the same connection the statement appearing in a Roman Catholic review of Buenos Aires that the North American's Bible is the telephone guide.

In point of fact, Roman Catholic writers, seconded by a prejudiced type of French literator, have been interested in spreading throughout the Southern Continent the most erroneous ideas regarding North American life and culture. Evangelical missionaries, on the other hand, have done more than any other social group to promote a true appreciation of Latin-American life and culture in the United States and of North American life and culture in the Latin-American world. More than that, there have been cases in which North American missionaries have actually had to suffer at the hands of powerful commercial interests in

their own country on account of their spirited defence
of the interests of Latin America.   It is a fact of history
that it was the influence of Mexican Protestants and
of American Protestants interested in Mexico which
shattered the iniquitous plot hatched by powerful
industrialists, and sponsored by a disreputable newspaper organization, to induce the Government of
Washington to adopt an interventionist policy in
Mexico. So far as the Latin-American public is concerned, the representatives of evangelical Christianity
are regarded as the most trusted friends of the countries
where they live and work.   It will not be amiss to
quote here a section of the letter sent by Gabriela
Mistral to the Congress on Christian work in Montevideo.   Being unexpectedly prevented from attending
the congress, the Chilian poetess and educator wrote :
" Christianity, do not forget, is the only link between
the United States and Spanish America.   Only in the
Word of Christ do we meet and enjoy a common
emotion ; the rest is pure tragedy of difference."

The second ground of attack is much more classic in
character. Protestantism, it is alleged, is utterly foreign
to the Latin spirit, and for that reason can never become
a natural expression of the religious life nor a creative
element in the cultural development of a Latin people.
The question immediately arises : What is a Latin
people ?   Who are members of the Latin race ?   To
what extent can it be alleged that Spaniards and Portuguese are ethnically Latin ?   Above all, how far can
it be said that the majority of the population in most
Latin-American countries are Latin by blood ?   The
fact is that the inhabitants of the Iberian peninsula and
of their ancient colonies in the New World, while their
culture is essentially Latin, are themselves Latin only
to a very slight degree. Ethnically speaking Latinity is
largely a myth both in Spain and Portugal and in so-
called Latin America.   Many intellectuals in these
republics consistently refuse to employ the term Latin

America in referring to this part of the world, preferring Ibero or Hispanic America.

But in our search for truth in this vexed question of the alleged inherent opposition between Protestantism and Latinity let us leave out of account for a moment the Peninsula and Latin America. France is generally considered to be the centre of Latin culture. Paris has been for a century the Mecca of Latin-Americans. Yet to what extent can it be said that France is Latin? Let me read in this connection some observations of M. Jacques Arnavon, a distinguished French intellectual and diplomatist. When Monsieur Arnavon was French Minister to Brazil he wrote a letter to a mutual friend in Montevideo, in which he dealt with the conception of Navarro Monzó that Protestantism is essentially uncongenial to the Latin mind. According to this French thinker, himself a Catholic, it is a great mistake to group together a number of nations and call them Latin. " It is not possible," he says, " to classify Celtic France among the Latin countries. There is more in common between a Frenchman and an Englishman, a Dutchman or a German than between him and a Neapolitan *lazzarone*, a Lisboan *changador*, or a South American." [1] " But in any case," the writer goes on to say, " the Reformation of the sixteenth century possessed expansive power only in its Genevan form. . . . Where did this Reformation come from? From France in which a government subventionized by Philip II. and the Pope quenched it. In 1560, however, it was on the point of triumphing. With a bolder Coligny and a less frivolous Francis I. the Reformation would have prevailed. Its failure in France was entirely casual and unnatural. The proof of this we find in the fact that those forces were entirely artificially repressed, and therefore exploded later in another form in the French Revolution." If the admission be accepted that France and French Switzerland are not ethnically

[1] This letter was written on 13th October 1927.

Latin, in which case, of course, the conclusion follows
that the Protestant Reformation in its most potent
form was born outside the Latin world, it must at least
be admitted that John Calvin was profoundly Latin
in his culture, and that he is the father of the tongue
which for the last century has been the chief instrument
of higher culture in the Iberian peninsula and Latin
America.

What can be said of the Protestant Reformation in
Spain in the sixteenth century ? The same that happened in France happened in the Peninsula. A large
proportion of the best people in the country, people
who were Latin by culture, were in favour of the
Reformation, some in its Erasmian, others in its
Lutheran, form. The reforming movement, however,
was quenched in blood by the Inquisition. Such a
thorough extirpation of a religious movement as took
place in Spain in the sixteenth century was only possible,
because the new ideas had not taken hold of the masses
as they had done in Germany, Holland, and Great
Britain. It cannot be alleged, however, that there is
anything in the essential nature of Protestantism which
is not congenial to a Latin when once he has been truly
awakened to religious concern, when he affirms his
native love of liberty, and is not prepared to follow
blindly the voices of authority and tradition. It is
perfectly true, as we have already seen, that the natural
reaction for Latins is from the naïve credulity of the
" Coalman's Faith " to the most fanatical radicalism.
The eminent Spanish critic, Menendez y Pelayo, went
so far as to affirm that for a Spaniard the only spiritual
alternatives possible are unquestioning loyalty to the
Church or utter agnosticism. Historically this pen-
dulum swing has been an all too notorious fact. The
possibility, however, of such a violent reaction has
largely been a consequence of the absence in the
Iberian world of Protestant Christianity as a mediating
and creative influence.

Nothing has been more needed, nothing is more needed to-day than a true expression of Protestant Christianity in these countries. This does not mean that what is wanted is a replica of Protestant institutions which have grown up in Anglo-Saxon countries, still less a projection into the Latin world of the sins of Protestant denominationalism. The fact must be emphasized that Protestantism is essentially a movement, a religious attitude, rather than an institutional system or a collection of dogmas. Its positive character needs fresh emphasis. Dean Inge, in his recent admirable study of the subject [1] makes the pertinent remark that it is ignorance which seeks to restrict the term " Protestant " to the attitude of an objector. " Protestantism," he says, " is essentially an attempt to check the tendency to corruption and degradation which attacks every institutional religion. It is the revolt of genuine religion against its secularization. It is always in intention a return to an earlier simplicity and purity." He quotes approvingly in this connection the statement of Harnack that " Protestantism is a re-discovery of religion as faith, as a relation between person and person, higher therefore than all reason, and living not upon commands and codes, but in the power of God, and apprehending in Jesus Christ the Lord of Heaven and Earth as Father."

It is difficult to conceive anything more necessary in the spiritual life of the Iberian world than that personal religious concern which Protestantism kindles, than that insistence with which it directs the thoughts of men to the unique revelation of God contained in the Christian Scriptures, than the affirmation that in and through Jesus Christ any and every man who so desires can approach and enjoy communion with the Eternal. To say that such an expression of Christianity is not congenial to people in general in the Latin world because it makes too great demands upon them, is in

[1] *Protestantism.*

itself the supreme proof that it is urgently needed.
This in any case can be said : the particular type of
Catholicism which has hitherto dominated the Iberian
Peninsula and the republics of Latin America has no
spiritual future. It is totally inadequate to that transforming task which is the inherent function of Christianity. It is very true, of course, that in the Protestant
world also the vision and power of the Christian
religion have very largely been lost, while to the living
soul of Protestant faith many contingent accessories
have been added. It is painfully true that one can find
in some parts of Latin America types of Protestant
missionary work which cannot fail to alienate thoughtful minds because of the bigotry and sectarianism which
they produce in their adherents. These facts, however,
must not blind us to this other : that a great new thrill
begins to pulsate through the Protestant world. The
consciousness grows apace that Christianity is Christ,
and that He who is central in the Scriptures and in
history, in experience and in the cosmos, must be made
Lord of all life and thought.

So far as the majority of Protestant workers in Latin
America are concerned, the conviction is steadily growing that their function is to bring to the people not a
system, but a personality, one who bears the marks
of the Other Spanish Christ. It is obviously inevitable that Jesus Christ should be presented in connection
with religious forms and organizations which had their
birth elsewhere. There is no reason, however, why the
re-discovery of Christ in Latin America should not
create an institutional expression which shall be both
a living member of His universal body, and at the same
time the kind of body through which young cosmo-
politan peoples, sealed forever with the hall-mark of
Iberia, may express their religious life and forge their
spiritual destiny. But only through the action of a
strong ferment in the religious life of the Continent
can an indigenous reform movement be brought about.

The principal concern of every lover of Latin America should be not whether the Continent will become Protestant, as we with our institutional-mindedness understand Protestant, but that it shall become Christian. Protestantism is in the making, it has not yet wholly found itself. Christianity is an ultimate, an ultimate which is Christ.

Such an interpretation of the mission of Protestantism destroys the third ground of opposition to evangelical missionary effort in South America. It is alleged to be immoral and unchristian to propagate one form of Christianity where another has held sway. To which we reply : so far as concerns the interests of the Roman Catholic Church itself the most beneficent event which has taken place in South America in recent times has been the Protestant movement. This is the opinion of many thoughtful Catholics. When a prominent French abbé who visited Mexico last year was asked his opinion as to the Protestant missionary movement in Latin America his reply was : " The best thing that could happen in the spiritual life of the Continent would be an increasingly strong Protestant movement ; that would oblige the Church to put her house in order, and get ready to fulfil her mission."

Quite apart from this, however, it cannot be permitted that these lands, into which new influences are constantly pouring, should continue to become de-christianized and decatholicized as they are now becoming, without an effort being made to introduce them to the pure springs of Christian thought and tradition. To neglect such an imperious Christian duty would be to leave them a prey to the non-Christian influences already considered, and which are becoming increasingly potent, and so to prepare the way for a violent reaction against all religion such as has taken place in Soviet Russia, and is now taking place, to a lesser degree, in Spain.

(b) *The Evangelical Task*

Our chief difficulty is not to justify the presence of
evangelical Christianity in Latin America, it is rather
to feel the reasonable assurance that it will be able in
loyalty to its intrinsic character to fulfil its difficult and
necessary mission on the Continent. While its achieve-
ments have already been great in spiritual transforma-
tions and community welfare, and its indigenization goes
on apace, those who guide the movement will have to
keep before them increasingly certain indispensable
conditions of success if they are to make a truly creative
contribution to the spiritual life of the Continent at this
very critical hour.

One thinks first of the missionaries from abroad.
These must identify themselves absolutely with their
community. Their identification must cover not only
working hours, but social hours as well. They must
find their very recreation in achieving more intimate
and sympathetic contacts with the people they have
come to serve. Let them not forget that human tides
from all parts of the world reach these shores, and
become incorporated into the national life. There are
countries in South America in which second generation
Britishers and Americans are enthusiastic nationals.
There is nothing more shameful and depressing than
to find now and again throughout these lands missionary coteries suffering from a subtle superiority
complex, who have founded a " little Britain " or a
" little America " in the heart of their adopted country.
Not patronage but sympathy in the full etymological
and Christian sense of that term must be the watchword. The word from abroad must become indigenous flesh, or it will fail to obtain a hearing for the
eternal Word it presumes to echo.

It is equally necessary that the spirit of unity and co-
operation should become increasingly real and concrete
among a race which has been schooled in the imposing

unity of Catholicism, which is by nature ecumenical in its sympathy and outlook, and which will never take kindly to any religious system which is unable to demonstrate the essential unity and inner cohesion of its parts. We joyfully admit that there are a number of missionary organizations working in South America which have not seen their way to belong to the general co-operative movement, and which, at the same time, are carrying on an admirable and creative Christian work in certain areas. It would be an incalculable step forward, however, in the spiritual history of Latin America were the project of a Federation of Evangelical Churches, which is to be discussed this year at Rio de Janeiro, to become an effective reality. No organic merger of religious bodies would be advisable nor should be attempted. But the demonstration of the fundamental unity and solidarity of the evangelical forces would make a profound impression in the Latin-American world.

It is no less imperative that the typical worship service in Protestant churches in Latin America be conducted in an atmosphere of the greatest reverence. This desideratum refers in part to the type of church building needed and in part to the type of service carried on. Let it not be forgotten that if æstheticism has been the bane of Spanish Catholicism, there is a certain chaste æsthetic harmony which must be offered to the ear and to the eye in order that it may be made easy for Latin-Americans to engage in meditation and worship, for these people have a much more sensitive æsthetic sense than Anglo-Saxons are gifted with. The architecture of some of the new evangelical churches in Brazil has been able to create in a marvellous way that chaste beauty which should mark the community centre of evangelical worship.

Above all, there must be the greatest reverence in the conduct of the service and in pulpit utterance. In recent years there has appeared in some quarters a

tendency to introduce into the pulpit something of
the atmosphere of a Rotarian luncheon. Preaching
and worship have fallen on evil days when religious
thought has to be spiced by the banal prelude of a joke.
A mode of presenting religious truth which might pass
muster in some parts of the Anglo-Saxon world could
easily damn the effectiveness of pulpit utterance if employed in addressing a Latin-American audience. The
Latin spirit, when in a religious atmosphere and mood,
is much more serious than the Anglo-Saxon, and the
slightest attempt at banality in the pulpit produces a
fatal reaction in superior spirits, while engendering a
shallow tinsel religiosity in the inferior souls who are
willing to accept it. The following sentiment of a
distinguished Cuban minister to which he gave utterance at an Evangelical Convention held at Habana in
1929, should be laid to heart by those interested in
Latin-American evangelism. This gentleman said:
" The chief danger which threatens Protestantism is
triviality. A great part of the blame of this belongs
to jesting and frivolity in the pulpit."

A further pressing need in Protestant circles in Latin
America is the adoption of a new type of pioneer evangelism. An equivalent must be found for the Master's
mode of speech on the Galilean hillsides and for
Paul's discussions in the school of Tyrannus. Neither
Jesus nor Paul appear to have accompanied their words
by any ritual act on such occasions. " Christ lives in
the fields," said the great Fray Luis. Two things are
needed by Christian evangelists in Latin America to-
day : they must bridge the gulf between religion and
conduct by the high quality of their lives ; they must
bridge the gulf between religious thought and other
thought by taking religious ideas out into the open
air, and there proving that they are worth while being
considered for their own sake, and not merely as part
of a ceremonial act. For that reason there is a supreme
place for what has come to be known as the *Con-*

ferencia sin Culto. It has been proved in recent years that no subject so attracts a Latin-American audience as that of religion when it is dealt with outside the precincts of holy places by a person regarded by his audience as conversant with the problems which perplex modern men and women. The moment the official representatives of Protestant Christianity in Latin America step out into the open, and become interested in presenting the faith that is in them in such a way as to challenge the man in the street, a new day will have dawned in the spiritual history of the Continent. When people have become interested in Christ and the Christian message, it will be time enough to initiate them into the significance and privilege of worship and of church fellowship. But so long as they get the impression that the chief interest of Protestants is to set one type of religious organization and ritual over against another, which, whether they believe in it or not, happens to form part of their religious inheritance, so long will the progress of true Christianity be delayed.

The time has also come in the history of Protestantism in Latin America when the wealth of Christian literature which is being produced in other than English-speaking countries should be made available for readers whose intellectual life is nourished to a very slight degree from Anglo-Saxon sources, but is steeped in translations of French, German and Italian authors. At the present moment the most potent cultural influence playing upon the cultured mind of Latin-Americans has its source in Germany. The most influential review in the Spanish-speaking world is *La Revista de Occidente*, a magazine edited by a group of Spanish intellectuals, all of whom have been educated in Germany. Through its pages the latest pulsations of German thought are transmitted to all the leading centres of the Spanish world. Scarcely is an important work in science and philosophy produced in Germany when it is translated into Spanish and given the widest publicity. Important German works generally appear in Spanish garb before they appear in an English one. Spengler's *Decadence of the West* was already exercising its influence in South American universities when it was scarcely heard of in Anglo-Saxondom. When one considers that the most vital and creative thought on the modern religious situation is being done in Germany, and that the most potent Protestant movement of modern times has its source in the same country, it is time for those interested in Christianity in Latin-America to begin to take advantage of the new intellectual climate which is settling down on these lands. At the same time, the vigorous Protestant movement in France, with its increasing high-grade literature, should also be allowed to speak directly to Latin America.

Reformed Christianity in the Southern Continent has too long been nurtured on the translation of second-rate religious books produced in North America and Great Britain. Unfortunately the best and most representative religious works published in these countries have only infrequently found their way into Spanish. The first step towards the creation of a true indigenous literature lies in the provision of strong enough ferments and pure enough models from the literatures of other countries. This has always been the sequence followed in the history of literary influence. Let the writing of original books in Spanish and Portuguese by those capable of producing them be encouraged to the utmost limit, but let not the evangelical movement fail to produce the equivalent of that veritable flood of translations from foreign literatures which is at present inundating the Latin-American book market.

Not as a rival and antagonistic system, but as a depository of certain basic truths and of a certain religious spirit which the Latin-American world needs, Protestant Christianity is in a position and has a mandate to proclaim and incarnate the eternal things lying at the heart of it. Surrounded by passionate forces it must become passionate too. Fearlessly proclaiming that it is not adequately represented by any of the *isms* of current controversy, it must give itself with utter abandon to creative thought and action. It must above all else echo and bear testimony to the Word of the living God who is our contemporary, and is on the march, wending His redemptive way through the din and welter of the present.

If it is true, as Troeltsch says, that the highest artistic expression of Protestant genius has not been in painting or sculpture or architecture, but in music, the present spiritual discord offers an unprecedented opportunity for the creation of new harmonies. But these must be incarnate harmonies. The Protestant movement in Latin America dare not try to rival the older religious movement, incarnating itself in artistic monuments which, however appealing to the eye, are predestined to decay and fail to catch the quintessence of the common Christian faith. Let its speciality be music, but the music of life and human relations. Let it, like the great South American poetess, seek to enshrine in each convert its " most enduring melody," keeping ever before it the vision of Fray Luis de León that Christ is " Health," the inner principle of harmony for men and nations. This music of the soul is the necessary prelude to that higher music of endless agony, symbolized by the Other Spanish Christ in the painting of Velázquez, a music whose rugged road melody only heaven and future generations can understand.

(c) *As regards Religious Ecumenism*

Ricardo Rojas in a passage already quoted suggested the possibility of an expression of Christianity emerging in South America which should transcend all

foreign cults. Will the two youth associations discussed in the last chapter with their attitude of religious
ecumenism give rise to such an expression ? Is such
an expression possible ? If it is, can it be deliberately
engineered ?

Let us consider the Young Men's Christian Association in relation to this problem. Its institutional form
closely resembling that which distinguishes Associations in North America, together with the ecumenical
position it has adopted in religion, create a serious
problem at the present time. Many activities which
the Association introduced into South America for the
first time have since been copied and adopted by other
organizations. In certain directions it has not been
able to retain its leadership, in others it can no longer
be a pioneer. It is perfectly true, of course, that in no
organization on the Continent which has attempted to
reproduce aspects of the work and spirit of the Young
Men's Christian Association does there exist, or can
there exist, the same spiritual atmosphere and the same
attitude towards life, because the Association is grounded
upon a Christian foundation and possesses ideals which
its imitators lack. At the same time the maintenance
of the institutional machinery, which must be kept in
motion if the Association is to discharge its traditional
service to youth, has grown increasingly difficult.
The demands of administrative activity within the
organization and the need of raising money outside it
in order that the machine may be able to function,
absorb the time and attention of many a secretary who
longs to be able to give himself with abandon to the
work of intimate personal contact with men and boys.

In Protestant countries, at least a very large proportion of Y.M.C.A. members have some connection
with the Christian Church, while its supporters are
enthusiastic Christian men. In South American
countries a very small percentage of the membership
come under church influence, while the majority of

those who support the movement financially are not Christian men, being interested exclusively in the general social influence which the Association is able to exert among youth in their community. This involves a double problem of evangelization. The membership must be evangelized if the Association is to become a Christian organization, and not simply an organization which carries on Christian activities. Its supporters must be evangelized if the Christian character of the movement and its permanence in the community are to be guaranteed. In a word, tasks have to be assumed which in other countries are assumed by the Church. The problem, therefore, arises whether the Association, looking into the future, should continue to specialize in altruistic service for youth, doing what it can at the same time to turn the thoughts of youth towards Christian principles, or transform itself into something different to meet the demands of the present hour.

A distinguished Association leader, Mr C. J. Ewald, has taken the view that the general character of the movement in South America cannot and should not be altered. While youth is youth there must be provided for it the kind of home which the Association offers, and it will need to be guided in the kind of activities which the Association carries on. Mr Ewald, however, has taken the view that the Association is unable by its very character and position in the community to give that adequate and vocal expression to the basic Christian message which the present situation demands. His view is that a parallel movement to the Y.M.C.A. should be organized to devote itself exclusively to spiritual and cultural interests. This would involve the formation throughout the Continent of groups of men and women, related or unrelated to any given church, who, adopting an ecumenical position, would devote their energies entirely to promote the interests of the spirit. The idea is not new of course in the modern world, in which men are less disposed than formerly to accept the idea of Cyprian that in order to be a good Christian it is necessary to be an enthusiastic churchman. Such an idea also symbolizes a widespread conviction among Christian leaders in South America that Christianity on the Continent must rid itself of many conventional trappings which constitute a stumbling-block to spiritual progress, and get down to the rock foundation of Christ.

What, however, would constitute the cohesive link between the individual members of each group and between the individual groups themselves? Would they be groups of seekers, of people interested in a general way in the life of the spirit and gathered together for the study of religion, or would they be groups of finders? If only the former, would they possess that driving-power based upon personal experience and conviction without which no creative impression whatever can be made in the modern world? If the latter, would it be possible to avoid that theosophists and members of similar groups with clean-cut principles should form the chief nucleus, as actually occurred in Buenos Aires when the attempt was made to form such an ecumenical fellowship? If, on the other hand, the group adopted a definite religious position, could it avoid becoming a sect, albeit the sect of the "ecumenicals"? Would not the same thing take place as, according to Keyserling, has taken place with Theosophy, which has been obliged to take on a particular form in order to be able to live and propagate itself? Is it not inevitable after all that every creative movement should have to bear the stigma of sectarianism in relation to the current ideals of the time in which it appears? A movement founded on vague aspirations, or on the least common denominator discoverable among the very different types of people who compose it, may conceivably grow into a religious movement, but it will much more probably

S

develop into a philosophical club. If it becomes the latter, it will discharge a most admirable and necessary function, but the creative spiritual work must be done by crusaders.

But supposing an ecumenical movement were launched, the members of which were not " Christians " but " Christophiles," lovers and admirers of Christ. What then ? Christ must certainly be the starting-point and foundation of any religious ecumenical movement. But what Christ ? The moral leader and the religious genius, or God manifest in the flesh —or both ? One thing is certain, there is no evidence that the simple lovers and admirers of the historical figure of Jesus—of which there is happily an increasing number in South America—possess a sufficiently dynamic spiritual life to constitute a crusading movement. On the other hand, there is an increasing number of cases, both in South America and elsewhere, where the figure and demands of the so-called historical Jesus are driving his lovers and admirers to despair. They recognize his sublime claims, but are utterly unable to fulfil them. Their lives are marked by an intolerable tension. They have not discovered the significance of Christian faith, nor enjoyed the relief, the strength and the buoyancy which it confers. They feel towards Jesus as the hero of one of Schiller's poems felt towards virtue. Challenging virtue to give him achieving power along with its inexorable mandate, he shouts at length in utter anguish and despair : " O virtue, take back thy crown and let me sin."

The religious movement which has a future in South America must learn to discern the significance of Jesus as " Christ " and of Christ as " Jesus " in relation to life and thought in their wholeness. It must be founded upon a myth which is more than a myth, the historic reality of God's approach to man in Jesus Christ, not only in the form of truth for the illumination of the human ideal and the meaning of the universe, but in the form of grace for the redemption and equipment of men and women to fulfil the divine plan of the ages.

The future is with those who militate in the name and under the leadership of the "Other Spanish Christ," who proclaim and incarnate the full-orbed meaning of the "Health" for men and nations which He signifies. Loyal response to his "Follow me" will disturb the peace of the sepulchre and bring out the living creative quality of Christian peace. It will throw a bridge across the traditional chasm between religion and life. It will lead to the formation of groups of crusaders inside and outside the present religious organizations. The supreme preoccupation of the crusaders will not be what institutional form is most suited to religious life in South America, or what will be the ultimate institutional expression which will predominate on the Continent. They will be concerned to keep on the Road, to listen attentively to the Divine voice that guides them, to challenge in Christ's name everyone and everything that meets them on the way, to recruit others for the great employ. Aware of the new Spring time that breathes across the Continent they will sow seeds in the furrows as they pass onward. They will rejoice also when their own turn comes to be sown in some wayside furrow to fecundate the soil and hasten the harvest.

INDEX